Life

a soul journey to a Greek olive grove

"He saw the cities of many men, and knew their mind."

– Homer. Odyssey, i. 3

This book of the ride is dedicated to the many helpers encountered along the way, to Alex for putting up with me and Susannah for her many roles including part-way companion, editor, emergency contact and, of course, being there at the end.

James Brennan, Ronnie Brown and Rob Campbell all kindly commented on earlier drafts .

Nick Clancy generously and expertly designed the cover and route map.

This paperback edition first published 2020

Contents

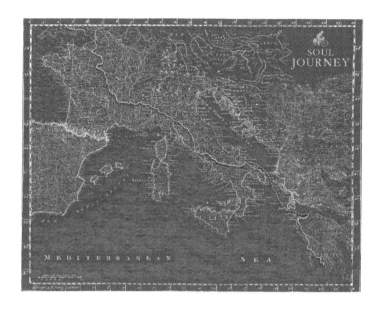

Chapter 1. Departure

As the bike swooped down the snaking descent to Newhaven Harbour on a perfect July morning I kept one eye on the ship gliding across the calm, glistening sea towards the mouth of the River Ouse below. My soul journey was headed across the English Channel on that ferry. Of the several versions of me crowded onto this bike along for the ride it was my starry eyed 15-year-old self, full of the promise of adventures ahead, who whispered honeyed words into my ear. 'Once a traveller, always a traveller' the 60 year old version of myself heard as we all set out for an olive grove in southern Greece. With my other eye on the road my mind was a jumble of lived memories, some neatly (too neatly?) stored away, others lurking in the recesses waiting to pounce at unsuspected times and some, like this year's loss of my brother, still raw sat on the top of the 'in tray'. Then there was the whole 'who am I/what does it mean' existential stuff back up for grabs on this, the cusp of the Third Age. And just to stir the whole witches' brew 20 kms into the day's ride I was still dealing with the jingle jangle after effects of a Brighton beach disaster on this new morning when I spotted my first cyclists of the day. We'll get back to Dylan later but for now I had to give my full attention to trailing the fully kitted out young roadsters ahead of me down the remaining switchbacks. As we pulled through the harbour gates to the booking office I was rather relieved to see a middle-aged bloke in functional unbranded clothing locking up a touring bike. My first helper of the quest?

Paul and I were just introducing ourselves outside the terminus building as a Tiggerish figure bounded over to us from the car queue. "Going far?" he inquired. Paul and I eyed each other before he offered "just a loop though Northern France" and taking my cue I tried to echo his understated vibe with "a run down to Greece". Tigger then took over to explain his bike was in the car and he was on what sounded like an annual French camping trip to ride and watch the Tour. My ears pricked up – cycle guru Andy had told me that as my route lay across France in July I should keep my eye out for the Tour de France itinerary and detour to enjoy the spectacle if at all possible. "Where are you planning to catch it?" I enquired casually of Tigger not mentioning the Guru's suggestion. "Oh a little campsite I know near Rouen from where I'll cycle over to the Tour route-they'll be swinging through middle of next week but you'll be long gone by then". I made a mental note to check out the route and timetable in detail as I suspected (correctly) that Tigger had a rather different idea than I about what 'a day's cycling' might entail. This was after all meant to be my summer of slow travel.

As the five of us cyclists on the ferry that morning already illustrate the modern world of cycling is 'a broad church' which accommodates all sorts from the easy-going to the driven. My previous cycling experience had included daily commuting around Bristol, group jaunts around National Cycling Network (NCN) routes, a little road cycling to Triathlon event level (limited to one annual race per year since commencing at 55 years of age) and one cycle endurance experience (the Vätternrundan) at 57 years of age, 300km around Lake Vättern in Sweden to keep a Swedish sister-in-law and her Ironman husband company (never again). So I had a pretty clear idea of what I wanted of the cycle route to Greece but other than my Swedish 'jaunt' (12 hours of caffeine fuelled discomfort) I had no overseas cycling experience to draw on.

My winter route planning had proceeded logically but ended up being somewhat compressed by events. I had decided early on that I wanted to ride the Loire across France and cross the Alps and didn't feel the need to cycle the length of the Adriatic and through the Balkans...I went that way in 1977 en route to India and back and it remains a long haul in my memory. The dads' cycling group of which I am a founder member did the coast to coast across Devon to Plymouth in 2016 and whilst this remains one of my favourite routes I couldn't really justify to myself using this to connect with the long detour down the western French seaboard to Nantes and the mouth of the Loire. Therefore I had settled on the increasingly popular Paris route which takes the Newhaven-Dieppe ferry across the Channel. It looked pretty manageable to cut south from Paris to the Loire. Italy was a long way and time off and preliminary research had indicated a pilgrimage route (the Via Francigena) might solve the northern half to Rome and the rest I optimistically decided would sort itself out in due course. Which left the little matter of the Alps. The crossing that appealed on geographical and historical lines was Mont Cenis (arguably in the elephantine steps of Hannibal) which pointed me firmly towards Torino which came recommended by an Italophile friend. Armed with a downloaded gazetteer for the London Paris Avenue Verte (ie car-free Route), a GPS device and mobile phone I was feeling (over!) confident that the run down to Paris would be a relatively straightforward navigation.

'Have you used Open Street Map much?" Paul enquired over breakfast on the ferry – full English for him I noted as I chewed on a not so fresh croissant – a first day error I would put right in the days ahead. 'Not really' I admitted as an alarmingly technical discussion of digital navigational aids ensued. Suffice to say there were clearly a lot of options which could be made as technically challenging as one wanted! I had come armed with a Garmin Edge Tourer GPS device which came with European Open Street Maps preloaded 'for the casual cyclist'– what could possibly go wrong? Over bounded Tigger to our table with further nuggets of advice – notably that a copy of a French roadmap was a good backup and that provincial French roads bypassed many towns which can catch an unsuspecting dry mouthed cyclist out if he is banking on refreshment at the next roadside settlement.

Back out on deck I watched the receding white cliffs with a tingling feeling on the back of the neck as I distinctly felt an adolescent hitch-hiker's thrill to the same spectacle across the 45 years span which separated us. At last this year's rite of passage had begun in earnest. The whole rationale for the trip related to my 60th birthday some 5 days previous when I had metaphorically downed my stethoscope and gone cycle-about after 30 years of doctoring. Was I embarking on some sort of quest? Quests, we are told, commence with a 'Call to a far-away Goal'. My goal was an olive grove which on Google Map lay an estimated

2500 kms away which felt far away to me. But what had been the Call? The journey was obviously marking a transition. I had been feeling jaded by the day job for some time and was happy to be cycling away but it was also partly in commemoration and recollection of 'temps perdu' relating to more youthful journeying and partly to mull over recent life events notably the aforementioned loss of my one remaining brother. To put it bluntly I felt a deep Call to wave two fingers at the Grim Reaper and celebrate Life.

There was also to be a cultural dimension to the journey which in a rather grand summary was to be a re-exploration of my European roots. I grew up in Liverpool surrounded by the neoclassical civic architecture of the great Northern Victorian cities. I was educated in an overtly Christian based system and had been encouraged to add the optional Ancient Greek 'O' level to the obligatory Latin. My father, the only other member of the household educated in ancient Greek language enjoyed testing me on my Greek vocab. I had learned to appreciate ancient history and especially archaeological site visits with him and had pursued those interests by studying Archaeology and Anthropology at Cambridge, travelling across Asia as a young man and later living and working in Nepal. But it was only latterly that I had rediscovered Greece.

Four years prior to my 60th birthday in a chain of circumstances triggered by reading the obituary of a travel writer called Patrick Leigh Fermor I had bought 100 olive trees standing on an acre of stony terraced hillside 300 metres above the Bay of Messenia in Southern Greece. It had been the locally based Fermor's 'Mani' book which had served as our travel companion in the area 30 years previously. This ride was conceived sometime between that purchase and the previous autumn as both a practical way of getting a touring bike down there but also a self powered link to another world whose classical past had patently contributed to my own formative years. A quest requires a destination which is not only attainable with especial difficulty but which must hold a deep inner meaning for the quester. How deep was that Classical Greek contribution, how had it not only reached Northern Europe but thrived there for centuries and what lessons towards a more sustainable future did a Greek olive grove hold were some of the barely articulated sub currents in my mind as I conceived the journey. But events (dear boy) had also played into all this as our land purchase coincided with the threat of Grexit and our subsequent plans had been blown awry by Brexit. So a further imperative of the journey had appeared - a tiny statement of protest to celebrate via two wheels all things European! Indeed there appeared to be as many dimensions to this ride as there were versions of myself crowded onto this bike taking it in turns to steer. If all diversions were pursued this journey would indeed be an exercise in slow travel!

Saturday 7th July, on which my birthday auspiciously fell, saw a handful of friends (the quest companions) and I cycle out of Bristol on a beautiful summer's day, weaving through early Saturday traffic building up around St Paul's where Carnival set up was well under way. It was a very Bristol scene as the speaker towers were being assembled from white vans by laid back dreads in the morning sunshine. My youngest daughter had declined an invite to 'dad's campsite 60th' in favour of St Paul's Carnival with her mates – can't understand why! As the early dub beats gently receded I reflected that I was leaving Bristol for the summer but not running away for good from this likeable, easygoing and attractive city where I had pursued a career and raised a family. We headed onto the iconic Bristol Bath railway path and were soon spinning along, happily chatting two abreast when a roadie swept by at pace and Cycle Guru, who was up the front chatting with Bev, our lone woman cyclist that morning, suddenly took off in hot pursuit. Knowing Andy he was 'covering the break' and would be back once he'd made his point. Sure enough Andy was back in our micro peloton well before we reached the banks of the Avon midway between Bristol and Bath.

There is an interesting subtext in cycling relating to speed - the mildest mannered non-competitive cyclist will still sometimes feel the need to dig very deep indeed to 'cover' a faster climber who overtakes on a hill. I have observed the same phenomenon at ParkRun, that excellent volunteer led Saturday 5km run around local parks which has swept across the UK and is now being exported further afield. There seems a deep felt need to 'keep up' at the very least which is no doubt conducive to survival in less forgiving circumstances. The extent to which this is driven by an innate need to win is, of course, contested. I'm pleased to say amongst my mature cycling buddies, the 'dads with daughters' group which came together as our girls hit secondary school, this is muted. We all seem, by and large, happy to spin along within our capabilities enjoying the banter.

So it was a convivial morning ride that swelteringly hot July day, alongside the Avon, to a relaxed early pub lunch in a surprisingly quiet riverside setting – the calm before the storm as the England World Cup quarter final was happening later that afternoon. We were on a schedule to a rendezvous in a Bradford-on-Avon pub for kick off, carefully selected as 'showing Sport and welcoming a diverse clientele' in a hasty rearrangement a couple of evenings earlier. This urban rendezvous hadn't been part of my original riverine camping birthday party plan as, let's face it, no one expected the England football team to get this far. But given that several of the guests were old Liverpool mates with whom I'd travelled on European football campaigns (red, not blue nor national white) as I explained to my wife, provision of Match viewing, even in deepest Wiltshire, was non-optional.

Our route left the Avon temporarily to cut through the rolling ridges to the south of Bath by way of the Somerset and Bath Railway which used to bring coal to the city. After a long campaign and appropriate bat conservation measures two magnificent tunnels have been reopened to cycle traffic complete with a musical installation in the deepest section. On a hot summer's day to plunge into the cool of a long tunnel is bliss indeed. But these tunnels are not just disused coal train routes adapted to a modern transport system but have another story to tell. William 'Strata' Smith between 1791 and 1799 worked on the Somerset coal field and lived for a period on land falling between the tunnels. The cutting of the neighbouring canal had revealed very clear strata which can also be admired by the modern cyclist in the railway cuttings on either side of the tunnels. Smith who travelled extensively in his coal and canal survey work systematically noted the fossils he collected from different strata leading to his great insight that allowed him to produce a stratigraphic map of Britain relying on fossils to provide the 'time stamps' associated with each strata. Thus this son of a prematurely deceased Oxfordshire blacksmith became the father of geology and after a life of toil earned a royal pension and recognition from the emergent scientific establishment. As with several other branches of scientific knowledge this had been prefigured by the great Leonardo da Vinci, basing his observation like Smith on aquatic fossils in the banks of a cutting in his case near the Arne which I was to discover between Siena and Florence. But that all lay far off in the future (and the past) as I returned to the 'Now' of the dark cool tunnel soothed by deep cello strokes reverberating along the long narrow passage.

Emerging back into the light our route swung round to Bradford where we soon located the Three Horseshoes, our suitably whacky pub rendezvous. Old friends bounded out and greeted the cycling party warmly and we were swept in just as the match kicked off (which we won thankfully) and my 60th birthday party 'kicked off' properly half an hour later at the campsite. The river Frome glides lazily past the site and a long-established swimming club, the Farleigh and District, allows weekend membership to campers. So idyllically we all swam, on what turned out to be, the hottest weekend of the year in the UK, both before and after the festivities. The main event was a BBQ for which all had been forewarned to prepare a short musical performance of some sort to accompany the food. Most of us managed some sort of rendition. I had devoted energy in the time since my brother's funeral in March to work up a version of the Bob Dylan classic 'Mr Tambourine Man'. Listening and watching multiple versions I was mesmerised by a very young looking Bob performing at the rather primly dated 1964 Newport Folk Festival. It hadn't made the final selection for Geoff's funeral playlist, rejected as too long, giving way to 'Blowing in the Wind'. Nevertheless I was determined to have a go at it in loving memory of Geoff and our last gig together – appropriately Dylan at the London Palladium whom we had both, independently, seen only one time previously at Blackbushe Aerodrome exactly 40 years before. I was pleased to give an acceptably amateur performance around the campfire ably accompanied by my friend Rob an occasional guitar playing journalist. The evening slipped past enjoyably around the campfire with memorable performances including a Devon cider song and a Scouse punk ballad commemorating both my much loved SouthWest adoptive home and my Liverpool roots about which I am prevented from getting too nostalgic by my dear Devonian wife ('If it's so good up there what are you all doing down here?').

The party brought together representatives of the several identities I have acquired through my life. Young children are comfortable with this concept of multiple, non-exclusive identities as they describe their home by street through town, country, continent, planet, universe etc. But our apparent need to identify with a group often defined in opposition to another group appears to be a widespread human phenomenon. I'm Red not Blue on Merseyside, but I'm English not German in the pub watching the World Cup. Ethnicity is a fascinating branch of anthropology which I studied as a young man, marvelling at the extravagant tribal markings used to signify group membership in settings as widely scattered as the Amazon jungle, West London Afro-Caribbean culture and the punk club scene in Liverpool. The point is amidst all this ethnic group definition we all come together at a higher level of group categorisation even when apparently divided by separate interests at a lower level. We forget this at our peril on the continent of Europe. The ride ahead was dedicated to celebrating our commonality whilst enjoying our diversity across the continent.

Sunday dawned just as idyllically as the preceding days. After a glorious morning swim shared with my cousin Clare, with whom I had last swum on family skinny dips enjoyed during Lakeland hikes in childhood, I gradually pulled together our disparate camping party for the obligatory Sunday walk and pub lunch. When hosting a social event to which one has invited friends and family from near and far it is sensible not to leave too much to chance. My wife, Susannah, and I had reconnoitred the site a fortnight previous and found a good pub within striking distance. But we had run out of time preventing exploration of the whole walking route so it was with some anticipation that I set off at the head of a sprawling party downstream along the Frome. Under a blazing sun we made our way through riverside meadows which had once comprised the deer park of Farleigh Hungerford castle whose medieval walls we passed beneath. The Norman de Hungerford family added their name to a much older Anglo Saxon locality term meaning 'ferny pasture' manor which was listed in the Domesday book. The de Hungerfords were well connected to the House of Lancaster rising over two generations of successful feudal support for first Henry IVth and then Henry V[th]. By the 1420's Walter

Hungerford was as close to the ultimate source of feudal patronage as it was possible to be and reaped the rewards after fighting at Agincourt to be accoladed a Knight of the Garter and the first recorded speaker of Parliament. The castle was hugely expanded with the aid of ransoms paid for French noble prisoners during that seemingly unending period of hostility referred to as the '100 years' war (1337-1453). This rural backwater of Wiltshire had once been at the heart of European power politics. Successfully swapping sides during the Wars of the Roses the family steered their fortunes through the changing times upto Henry VIIIth when they unwisely fell in with Thomas Cromwell who took the then Baron, once again Walter, down with him on charges of both treason and in Walter's case buggery – they were beheaded on the same day and placed on neighbouring spikes. Pick your patrons wisely!

The sun glinted no longer on knights in armour hereabouts but on the languid flowing river whilst the stately parkland trees provided much needed shade as we strolled down the Frome towards Iford Manor, an impossibly beautiful honey coloured manor house tucked away here in Wiltshire. We paused on the medieval stone bridge above the river to which the Edwardian garden designer Harold Peto had added a figure of Britannia which lends it a rather surreal air – echoes of Damien Hurst's towering and characteristically brash Ilfracombe harbourside figure of Verity which had entertained our Dads' group on the previous year's cycle. As we idled in the sunshine a man supervising his paddling child below was more than happy to share his identification knowledge for the swooping insects criss-crossing the river's surface. 'Damsel flies not dragon flies' mainly on account of their 'very different wing pattern' we learnt and subsequently confirmed by close inspection that damsel flies rest with the wings closed vertically above the body as opposed to dragonfly wings which remain open at rest. I have subsequently been taught by a retired colleague how to recognise numerous members of the Order Odonata and can claim a Blue Emperor resident at my favourite Greek swimming cove. Beyond lay the ubiquitous tearoom with the genteel chink of cups on saucers and hum of the happy middle aged enjoying a day out. Whilst members of our party went for ice-cream I couldn't take my eyes off the house. A perfect grade 1 listed Georgian mansion yet as I learnt a façade added to a medieval core and artfully created formal gardens complete with scattered classical statues which were rather more integrated to the whole than Brittania on her bridge. Here, already, was a fine example of the way in which classical ideas had come to permeate a seeming 'English' landscape. Of course the Edwardian Peto was a late contributor to this trend which dates back to the work of Palladio (1508-80), a Venetian architect of the Renaissance who reintroduced Europe to the Roman building virtues described by Vitruvius back in the age of Julius Caesar and Augustus as 'stability, utility and beauty'. The early classical architecture of Britain follows this Palladian style with key exponents such as Inigo Jones (1573-

1652) and Wren (1632-1723). However I was delighted on a visit to Split on the Croatian coast to discover that Robert Adam (1728-92) had made an extensive study of Diocletian's Palace before returning from the Grand Tour with a complete sampler book of classical designs on which to base his own spectacular contribution to domestic neoclassical architecture in England. With a fine example of Adam's work in the form of Pulteney Bridge, over in Bath scarcely 10 miles away there are plenty of examples of neoclassical architecture in the immediate vicinity as there are throughout Britain. Here was very tangible evidence for that flow of ideas which I was keen to pursue to its source. But that July Sunday we wandered on up the lane past one last classical allusion in the form of a statuesque nude female lolling across the top of a gateway before we wound up to the village and a welcoming pub where a lunch table had been readied for us. Sat surrounded by friends enjoying Gloucestershire Old Spot pork and warm ale it was hard to believe that an exotic adventure was beginning and such familiarity would soon start slipping away.

The remainder of that sunny Sunday slipped by with more river swimming and some leisurely campsite lolling as those attendees who needed to ready themselves for work on Monday started getting themselves organised. Meanwhile jolly parties headed home from the swimming club trailing happy but exhausted children past our encampment all seeming impossibly English in a sort of pre-war way – which war I wasn't even sure of – such was the wistful sense of midsummer timelessness. Perhaps thoughts of foreign fields were playing on my psyche as I luxuriated in the current company surrounded as I was by my wife, her brother and Caroline my sister-in-law who never fails to make get-togethers go with a swing. Despite her best efforts we got into our sleeping bags before midnight and I was up to greet the dawn on the day of departure, just as impossibly sunny as the weekend that had preceded it.

Four of us readied for the 'grand depart' – two friends Tim and Rob who work out of Bristol and had taken the Monday off to ride through into Hampshire with brother-in-law Alex and me. Having been waved off by Susannah(due to rejoin me later on the Loire) our route lay south on the National Cycleway Network (NCN) route 254. After commencing the journey with a vertiginous ascent past the castle mound of Farleigh Hungerford (no historical diversions this morning) we spent a very pleasant morning wending our way through the South Wiltshire Downs. This was rolling agricultural country sparsely inhabited with mixed arable and pastoral farming. I was raised very much as a city boy who took a childish delight in my model farm as a young child. Some exposure to rural matters was gained over the annual Lakeland Easter holiday but this of course was mainly to upland sheep farming and so my experience of cattle farming has been minimal. We were cycling beside a high hedge alongside a lane from beyond which came the unmistakeable sound of a herd of cattle on the move. At the same time a low voiced call could be heard coming from the top of the field. As we rounded a bend towards the top of the lane two young farmers were standing beside their pickup calling down to the cows. When I enquired I was assured this was nothing special and common practice amongst local cattle farmers. It felt good to have discovered this relatively empty zone of the crowded South of England where rural life continues to beat to a different rhythm.

Our route led across Longleat which I was determined to cross from north to south having previously traversed on another Sustrans route west to east with a particularly toilsome ascent from the stately home up into the woods above Warminster which I rightly assumed the party would be happy to avoid. So we were all new to this route which took a bit of finding in the increasingly deserted South Wiltshire lanes weaving between the modern trunk roads that punctuate the rural calm. A tiny lane led past thatched cottages confirmed by a bored adolescent on a bike to be the way to the 'back entrance' and sure enough suddenly an intimidating gateway indicated the start of the Marquess of Bath's pleasure park. What was rather wonderful was that this northern entrance was closed to all non-staff except cyclists – I would have loved to have been a fly on the wall when John Grimshaw, founder of Sustrans and chief designer of the National Cycle Network negotiated the route with the Marquess. It leads directly past the safari park experience meaning the first mammalian sighting of my trans-european ride was a giraffe! This driveway leads down towards the huge Elizabethan mansion house which of course was the site of an obligatory group photo shot before we headed for a morning snack at a pub just the far side of the Park. This was the setting for a minor disaster as a sandal made a successful bid for freedom from my cycle pannier. Of course I remained mercifully ignorant of this fact for a further five hours until I went to slip it on my overheated foot at end of day. Argh, how could I have been so stupid! Not the last time on the trip I would gnash my teeth at my own carelessness.

However this lay ahead as we rolled across Wiltshire and into Hampshire on the NCN24 following the valley of the River Dun which joins the Test heading for Southampton Water. This is trout fishing heaven and Rob, once a keen fisherman, would surely have been tempted if we had let the pace slacken. But I had 'bigger fish to fry' and after a spectacular tea stop in the Close of Salisbury Cathedral the final push of the day took us along the banks of the crystal clear chalk River Dun as the evening insects were disturbing the surface tempting the lurking trout in the late afternoon sun. We arrived at the Mill Arms just as the last rays shone on the riverside terrace of our pub destination in Dunbridge ready for beer and food and jokes about hopping to Greece on one sandaled foot! My lack of footwear didn't prevent me from seeing Rob off on his train from the neighbouring Mottisfont and Dunbridge Station, according to official statistics the second least frequented station in Hampshire – the first must have tumbleweed - where I fell into conversation with an elderly gentleman and his wife. 'Where are you going" he asked in a soft northern accent in between watering the flower bedecked planters dotted along the platform....emboldened by my first beer 'Greece' I replied. 'Oh' he said in a somewhat downbeat way 'you'll be wanting a dog whistle then' before going on to explain that the elderly lady helping him water the platform flowers and he had cycled all over Europe but had found groups of semi wild dogs irksome in northern Greece! After thanking him for his advice and turning down his kind offer of going to hunt out the dog whistle I learned from his wife that the poor chap was just embarking on an uncertain course of treatment for prostate cancer. This cancer had seen off my father some 15 years previously so it is an affliction for which I have a very healthy degree of respect. He brushed my condolences aside and wished me well before returning to his watering. I hardly need add that I found the exchange quietly moving and think of him whenever packs of Greek dogs threaten as they occasionally do but thankfully less often, apparently, in the south than the northern mainland.

After waving Tim off the following morning to get his train to work (poor chap) it was a reduced party of two that pushed across from the Test to the Itchen and a rather fine stretch of riverside path leading down Southampton Quay. Brother-in-law and I were due to part company on reaching the coast – he was returning home westwards whilst I turned eastwards. Knowing that we had set a rendezvous for Patras on the north coast of the Peloponnese in Greece some 12 weeks hence left us both mildly amused over a final cup of coffee on the quayside – was I really going to be cycling for the remaining months of the summer whilst he did a family trip, worked, holidayed, worked some more – well that was the plan! We took our farewells in a characteristically stoical British manner and that was that, as I cycled away from the quay in search of NCN 2 heading east along the Solent....I was on my own...for now.

I was forewarned by my research that the south coast flagship NCN route 2 was still under development. Indeed having driven this way as a spotty youth in a girlfriend's mini from Reading to Dorset I recalled it had been a disappointing road trip until Bournemouth with infrequent vistas onto the coast proper. I was therefore unsurprised when NCN 2 after recrossing the Itchen promptly dumped me in the suburban centre of Woolston. Signage was either non existent or certainly very missable and after heading to the local train station which is usually a good place to pick up the trail and still not seeing signs I enquired of a postman whether there was a cycle trail anywhere amidst the massive redevelopment at the confluence of the Itchen with Southampton Water. Amazingly he had no idea, amazing as when I pushed on barely 500 metres I swung round the corner onto a beautiful 3 metre wide brand new cycle route along the Solent.

There is no feeling quite like cracking a route problem with a functionally and aesthetically satisfying solution. The sun was shining on the Solent and the view was spectacular across to the Isle of Wight. The new route along the foreshore led through a country park created on the site of the previously grim (now demolished) Royal Victoria Hospital, a military hospital where many of the First World War wounded were sent. I 'did' the First World War poets in English at school and it was sobering to read that Wilfred Owen, a one time resident of Birkenhead immortalised by the 'old lie.....Dulce et Decorum Est', was just one of 100,000 military casualties processed at this industrial scale facility, before getting sent north with shell shock to a specialist hospital in Edinburgh where he was to be inspired by Sassoon and other wounded officers. Incidentally, the Latin quote is from Horace – the Augustinian poster boy of Latin poetry. In what will turn out to be a recurrent theme Horace looked to the Greeks for inspiration. He, in turn, influenced the Romantics, especially Byron, who directly references him in Childe Harold. Latin poetry and especially Horace came to be hard wired into the English public school education system via innumerable school songs. Owen was well versed in Romantic Poetry but would have also studied Horace in Latin as very much part of the school curriculum, a practice which continued well into the 20th Century. Thus the cultural strata are laid down, each referential to those preceding.

Whilst classical Rome became the model for empire the extension of that Empire along the silk road to the East meant South Asian influences grew in importance. Queen Victoria was after all Empress of India. The young Wilfred Owen was (unusually) quoting Tagore to his mother as he departed for the front whilst many more would come to quote the imperial poet Kipling.

Even as late as 1977 when as a long haired, lanky youth I first crossed the Khyber Pass to reach the sub continent it was possible to take tea with turbaned tribesmen up the Swat Valley who recalled fondly appearing in a London Jubilee. They would have been too young for Queen Victoria's Diamond Jubilee of 1897 and I suspect were recalling King George V's Silver Jubilee of 1935, a rather more plausible forty two years earlier. I was vaguely following what remained of the hippy trail in the footsteps of George Harrison and the rest. Indeed my first awareness of imperial goings on was at the annual Police Ground openday in Allerton, Liverpool where mounted police would race across the recreation ground gripping lances held out in front ready to dip at the last moment in an attempt to hook a hooped 'tentpeg' hammered into the ground. I share this memory with one Paul McCartney according to his biography whose parent's house (before he lost his mum) backed onto the self-same police grounds.

Cycling as a flow activity is a perfect pursuit to enable the ebb and flow of memory here triggered by a memorialised war hospital taking the mind from the First World War poets via tent-pegging Merseyside policemen to that summer in Rishi Kesh when George Harrison's love affair with Hinduism began. Indeed as I frequently remind my global health students the charity concert was re-established in the modern era not by Bob Geldof and Live Aid in support of the Ethiopian famine but rather by said George and Ravi Shankar in support of the, then East Pakistani survivors of civil war and famine in the Concert for Bangladesh. Incidentally the associated cholera epidemic triggered the invention of oral rehydration therapy, one of the great therapeutic advances of the 20th Century. Ah there I go again ...word association football as my late brother used to say about such discursive thinking. But with age comes greater appreciation of the layering which underpins culture.

Heading east for me has always triggered this great tsunami of associations which can be brought together under the heading "Silk Road'(Frankopan 2015). The road from this island down to Italy then onward to the east Mediterranean is the first or rather last part of that Road. When Alexander the Great emerged from Northern Greece and turned east towards what is now Afghanistan I'm sure he never questioned his direction – to the west lay the periphery – the centre of the world lay to the East. And thus it would remain until the New World changed the order of things, shifting at a stroke the centre of the world westwards and young men started heading West. This of course was to be the making of Liverpool and much else besides but that's another story.

The long shadows of imperial warfare, of Alexander, Hector and Lysander, wounded British Grenadiers (and the mellower echoes of Hare Krishna and all that came after) gradually receded as I pressed on and approached my first ferry crossing on the river Hamble. Now a quaint riverside recreational centre this was once a bigger port than nearby Portsmouth and site of a major medieval ship building industry. The wreck of a Henry V warship lying in the mud a little way upstream emphasises its one-time importance as a port of embarkation for the French wars I had encountered in deepest Wiltshire. Over a late quayside pub lunch I savoured my traverse of the Solent listening to the cries of gulls and the tapping of halyards on masts as I watched the tiny Hamble ferry pick its diagonal course back across the estuary towards me.

There is something so right about pushing a cycle down a jetty to board a ferry for what was the first passage of the journey. The elderly but sprightly ferryman indicated where he wanted my bike and we settled down for the 10 minute crossing snuggled back against his tiny cabin sheltered from the surprisingly brisk river breeze watching the river slide by. All too quickly on the lowish tide we were across and I was gingerly pushing up a seaweed covered causeway to the easterly bank. Once safely back on the dry the path cut inland a

little before regaining the coast proper on a windy
stretch leading into Gosport. After a largely rural
afternoon it was invigorating to join the adolescent
cycle race from the local school back towards the town
hardly pausing for breath before pulling up at the Ferry
across Portsmouth Harbour. Now this was what on
Merseyside we would call a proper ferry – a ship with
wide gangways designed to cope with rush hour crowds
– though this afternoon's passengers were a desultory
lot with scattered urban commuting cyclists and
occasional French tourists amongst their ranks. The
view over to the historic dockyard exercised me
throughout the all too brief crossing – the Victory
looking a mite less impressive at this distance than
when I last saw her up close during a family weekend
visit. I had hoped for a night with jack tars (or at least
my nephew and his mates) but university was out for
the summer and there was no justification in lingering
along the foreshore as I retraced a route enjoyed the
previous year in search of my wife's family Southsea
roots. I was bound for the exotic sounding Hayling
Island which according to my research would get me
back into open country and an opportunity to test out
my new, one-man tent. The ferry onto the island (third
and last of the day) did not disappoint. The turquoise
water with boys swimming by the ferry landing stage
gave the scene a positively Mediterranean feel. The
'islanders' commuting from Portsmouth were a far
more friendly bunch than the urban Portsmouth lot
and there was plenty of idling time for my enquiries as
to camping and drinking options on the island and

their enquiries as to where I was going. Oh yes I was proudly informed their ferry had previously carried a transcontinental cyclist from North America no less – headed to an address somewhere nearby which took in cycle tourists . 'Warm Showers' I offered – 'aye that's the one' the ferryman's mate responded as I explained that I had also enrolled on this altruistic cycle accommodation site. Before we could explore this topic further a youngish chap who had just got on interjected with "is that a Thorn?". It turned out the basis for his well informed enquiry was the fact that his partner was also the proud owner of a Thorn. Thorn I should explain are a small Bridgewater based company celebrated amongst the long distance cycle touring fraternity (and yes it is largely male!) as fitters of quite simply the best British Touring Bicycles designed for ultra-long distance reliability and comfort. I had been introduced to Thorn by cycle guru Andy but my new shipmate's story was more complicated. It emerged that his partner's previous bloke had purchased two Thorn touring bikes (his and hers) prior to departure on a long distance cycle ride which had presumably had its roots in an attempt to save a deteriorating relationship which hadn't got as far as the starting line. Her Thorn had never left on tour and now commuted daily to Portsmouth. I didn't like to enquire of my shipmate at what point he had appeared on the scene suffice to say he had nothing but praise for island life and cycle-ferry commuting whatever the bike! I believe I saw Hayling Island Ferry as few have previously seen it that day – more of an Aegean island hopper than a channel cutter.

My night on the island was memorable for a lovely evening ride on the western shore in the golden light of the setting sun along the' Puffing Billy' disused railway path, my first camp in a rather tame English campsite, a long hike to the pub recommended by the ferryman's mate and an ultimately disappointing exit from the World Cup by Belgium at the hands of Croatia. I have Belgian niece and nephews and we were hoping to enjoy the rivalry of a semi-final match later that week. But it was not to be and I passed a beery couple of hours with a Nottinghamshire miner turned electrician who also enjoyed his football, unlike an otherwise seemingly rather introverted and quiet Hayling Island population. My ferry companions had been misleadingly unrepresentative!

My first night under canvas (or rather extremely lightweight parachute material) was reasonable though I did question the 300g saved by voids in my inflatable sleeping mat. Rather than a mat (with voids) it might be more accurate to describe this as an inflatable skeleton as it outlined the human frame providing cushioning under all the bony prominences. If one lies perfectly still on one's back all night that is! If, like me, one rolls this way and that with periods on one side or another then the cushioning rarely coincides with one's bony prominences.

Be this as it may I got myself up and organised in the grey morning light even remembering to turn the bike upside down on its handlebars to check for the source of a strange juddering the previous afternoon. Low and behold the front wheel nut was working loose and the problem solved with a turn of an Allen key. Given my lack of mechanical expertise I was well chuffed with this rapid diagnostic and treatment plan. Time to get going and find a café. The route led me off the island and into Emsworth where my wife's eccentric now American aunt habitually holidays on her biennial Hampshire pilgrimage. I headed into the village centre my head filled with fond memories of exotically West Coast Barbara harking back to her unlikely Southsea roots. This is perhaps how I came to park a fully laden bike in such a way that whilst I was basking in the snug café enjoying my 'full English' breakfast it crashed onto its side.

When I emerged the front wheel was jammed facing the wrong way by brake arms that had been forced 'inside' the frame. Oh dear - I realised my early morning mechanical achievement had been only a foretaste of challenges ahead. Undaunted I took out my now trusty multi tool and set about de-jamming the front wheel by dismantling the front V brakes. This proved straightforward until I attempted to reassemble them. Hmm how to get some tension in the setup? Check out the rear set up and copy. No joy - disc brakes on the rear so no help there. What's this spring doing hanging loose – reengaged and suddenly I'm back in business except what had previously been a pleasantly responsive brake lever was now a mushy pull with the bite only coming at the end of the tug. Good enough on the flat but an accident waiting to happen on the downhill. Hmm...what to do? 'There's a good bike shop in Emsworth!' offered a middle aged gent sat on the neighbouring bench whiling away the post breakfast hour watching my efforts. I looked up in frustration and realised I was being offered a solution that I would be foolish to ignore. Receiving a 'God Bless' in response to my muttered thanks I righted the bike and swung onto the saddle and took off in the suggested direction. Ten minutes later I found myself in a short queue thanking my lucky stars for helpful Christian gentlemen awaiting the attention of a single handed lad who was politely advising a mother on a suitable purchase for her daughter. When my turn came around with an equally polite manner containing no trace of condescension I got a crash lesson in V brake adjustment. I think he was pleasantly surprised by the fiver I thrust upon him 10 minutes later but in my scheme of things his input had been priceless.

Off again I found myself underwhelmed by the morning stretch skirting Chichester harbour on a purpose-built cycle track sadly alongside a rather busy A road. As cyclists learn to do I 'cracked on' to get these miles done and behind me. Once I'd reached the Chichester turn-off I traversed the city until I reached a rather impressive canal basin which led me out of the built up area via the Chichester Canal built to reconnect the city with the sea. It was by now the heat of the day and as I paused at a bridge I sensed the stillness in the warm air with a heat haze shimmering above the canal and out across the water meadows. Dragon flies (definitely not damsel flies) dancing on the canal surface provided the only movement visible looking up and down the banks. My eye was drawn to the cathedral spire of Chichester at the exact vanishing point of what felt like a Constable. Had he ever painted here? I later googled and learnt that a Lord Egremont at the nearby mansion of Petworth hosted both Constable and JMW Turner and it was the latter that produced a classic view across the meadows reminiscent of my vista that glorious summer's day.

Pushing on I re-emerged on the south coast proper at Bognor Regis – first visit for me to a southern byword for resorts to vie with Blackpool up t'north. Well it was a truly British scene at Bognor that sunny early afternoon with all ages promenading in shades and tattoos, ice creams and fags galore – just like a scene from Martin Parr's early New Brighton photographic work. I parked up at a convenient kiosk café and took myself down to the RNLI station to dump my things before taking a plunge. As the day before, the sea remained a calm turquoise perfect for a swim on another bakingly hot day. As I got out, I checked in with the lifeguards to ask about that night's World Cup football. They had heard it was being broadcast on Brighton beach which confirmed my thoughts of heading over to Brighton for that evening's apres-ride entertainment. Pushing on via Littlehampton to Worthing NCN 2 deviated a little inland again but I knew thereafter I had seafront cycling ahead all the way to Newhaven.

As I dropped back down to the coast at Worthing I was intrigued to check out the town as it came highly recommended by my dear, deceased brother. There had been a woman in Worthing, indeed one who'd been brought to Bristol, and much fond talk of bohemian goings on around the family residence at the head of the pier. So it was to the pier that I headed with my sun addled mind half expecting to find the bird man competition in full swing with supporters thronging the neighbouring pubs. However the early afternoon sun beat down on less colourful proceedings as the early summer crowds thronged the pavements, cafés and pubs in another take on the great British seaside resort. Just beyond the pier I found the Crab Shack which offered the perfect seafood and chilled cider late lunch. I had ordered beer but cider had arrived providing a minor Montaignesque moment of contemplation – as the great Montaigne teaches us that the best things in life happen when you don't get what you think you want (Bakewell 2011). In retrospect I think I was still trying to reconnect with my brother looking at the neighbouring seafront houses wondering which he had visited before the realisation sunk in that he'd gone and I was wasting my time. Allowing the uncharacteristically brilliant sun to banish such bleak thoughts I remembered I needed accommodation in

Brighton which would be busy on a summer's World Cup night and turned to Booking.com for the first of many times on this trip.

It was our friends Paul and Lucy who had sung the praises of Booking.com for last minute rooms whilst cycle touring during their impressive Eurovelo forays down both the Rhine and Danube and my first trial was successful to the extent that 10 minutes later I was holding a reservation in a cheap hostel in central Brighton 2 minutes from the Pavilion. So taking a final delightful swig of golden cider in the sunshine I unlocked the laden bike from the promenade bike stand and wended my way through the crowds around the coast via impressive docks at Shoreham to the very familiar Brighton Seafront.

I knew Brighton from a three year stint as external examiner to the Medical School's Elective Programme. This is that period in medical student studies when the student is free to identify a medical placement which will provide experiential learning in an area of practice of their choice. As many choose to experience medical realities of life in low and middle income countries my developing country experience recommended me for this honorary post. It had been very enjoyable and not particularly onerous to quality check the medical faculty's assessment process for students' elective presentations each year and had entailed an overnight in a midrange seafront room. Arrival at my rather shabby inland hostel reminded me those 'professional' days were over. "No" said the reception girl to my request for cycle parking "you'll have to bring it in" which given the steep flight of external stairs just to get to the front door didn't feel particularly helpful. So chaining up outside I ascended the steps less than impressed. However once across the threshold the charming Spanish girl running the desk saw my dilemma and agreed I could put the bike on a rear fire escape landing which had been extended to provide a smoking area. That way it wouldn't impede the gangway. Moreover the fire escape led down into a rear courtyard accessible from a back street enabling the cycle parking process to proceed with minimal disruption to either of us. "Claro....perfecto" I muttered inappropriately getting into the Englishman abroad communication style (add 'o' to half remembered Latin word root for Spanish) and escaped up to a shabby attic bedroom, for a shower and shave in preparation for my World Cup outing.

An hour later I was headed to the beachfront with a definite buzz in the air. Large numbers of youthful punters were drifting in the same general direction and once down by the pier the unmistakable twang of inebriated young men singing "Its coming home" could be heard on the air swirling around the pier like the murmuration of starlings I had admired on previous more wintery visits. And then suddenly darting across the road at the heart of the singing I caught a glimpse of the focus for all this excitement – a Gary Southgate, England Football Manager, lookalike! It must be remembered that during that week as the Tory Cabinet had starting its inevitable implosion amidst the emerging reality check of Great Britain's de facto status in the world outside Europe that Mr Southgate had emerged as the unity candidate and could have swept to power if there had been a general election that Wednesday, July 11th. Tracking the 'great man' took me to another Brighton institution the Volks Club where plenty of young men were warming up and I was directed to the neighbouring beachfront openair cinema arena for the Match.

This ticketed venue didn't come cheap but provided an appropriate sense of occasion for the 'Most Important England Football Match' since the last one! What was great fun was the multinational reality of a modern British crowd...I found myself swapping jokes with young French and Spanish folks at least until the game began and it all started to get serious. I was in the bar queue reassuring less experienced and excitable young men that they wouldn't miss anything as nothing much happens in the first minutes of these big games seeing how each side tests out the opposing formation. So, of course, we missed the early English Goal and really the entire match went downhill from there. As I picked my way through the detroitus of a big disappointed crowd heading for my hostel a couple of hours later there was an overwhelming sense that the party was over and it was time to leave the country!

Early the next morning under a cloudless dawn sky I let myself out carrying my stuff back down the fire escape and rode out past the site of the previous day's denouement towards the beginning proper of the great adventure. The air was fresh with a light southerly blowing up and over the emerging chalk cliffs as my route took me high above the English Channel. After a bracing hour the route descended dramatically into Newhaven and the waiting ferry.

"Housing" Paul was saying over breakfast across the ferry café table – "with Sheffield Council". I had asked the "what do you do when you're not on your bike" question in response to his explanation that he had always been a keen cycle commuter. He turned out weirdly to be the second bloke I had met that week who had started out life down a pit in Nottinghamshire and then had been forced to explore other careers following the Strike. In Paul's case that had included teaching geography and latterly "telling people they can't have a council house because there are none"....."there are only so many ways of saying that" Paul added which perhaps explained why he was passing his Summer vacation on a solo bike ride. Indeed Paul was a very likeable contrarian. As he himself said, "It's weird how I'm often out of synch....when I was doing a long commute on a bike in Lycra shorts years back everybody looked at me as if I was weird and now that I don't really bother with Lycra the Mamils (middle aged men in Lycra) all look at me as if I'm weird".

As the voyage progressed and France hove into view we headed out onto the sundeck continuing our life stories in that marvellous way one does when you encounter a sympathetic fellow traveller. Cast free of our moorings we seem better able to see our lives in the round and open-up to others similarly unshackled. Paul it turned out had crossed the picket lines to work during the Strike for heartfelt reasons derived from his perception of a lack of democratic process in the build-up, a position he now regretted. A true contrarian who was ignoring my southward voie verte to track the 'bumpy' northern French coastline to the west. We rode up the ramp from the ferry port together and bade farewell at the first roundabout where my route was signposted off to the left, with an encouraging green sign. I was off on a foreign shore about to ride my first Voie Vert!

Chapter 2. Losing Myself in Northern France

The two young lycra clad roadies bound for Paris were last seen disappearing into Dieppe town – a strategy I disdained preferring to 'crack on' along the voie verte inland from the coast. The green car free lane arrived at the next roundabout on the outskirts of Dieppe with no further cycling signage to be seen. Unfazed I approached a young lad messing around on his BMX on a concrete path leading off the roundabout and brushing off my schoolboy French enquired for the voie verte to be answered casually, in what I took to be the affirmative, so off I set. Mistake number one – voie verte is a generic term for car-free routes not specific to the Avenue Vert between London and Paris. 5 kms later as the route I had taken merged into a dual carriageway heading up a shallow valley away to the South-West from the coast it was clear to me that I had blundered. However I was not (yet) ready to retrace my route back to Dieppe – pride would not permit such an early loss of time (and face)! At the first village I loaded up with bread and cheese and sought a correctional route across to the correct valley heading more to the south east.

Out came the Garmin Edge Tourer and the words of my military brother-in-law came to mind – 'you need to input waypoints rather than your final destination'....hmm now what was the next place south of Dieppe described on the Avenue Verte ....'d'Arques la Bataille with 'the ruins of its medieval chateau dominating the valley'. Now this is when a critical lack of practice with GPS devices led me astray. As logic would dictate the first 'waypoint' to enter is 'current location'. Less intuitively 'current location' is remembered by the machine to be the last time you hit that button. So after I had entered my next waypoint it cleverly gave me a route assuming I was still in Dieppe. I recognised the suggested route to be heading in the wrong geographical direction but couldn't, at that point, work out why. I figured out where I was going wrong a couple of days (and several lengthy detours) later. Fortunately on this occasion a rather flushed portly local bar-tabac proprietor smelling strongly of pastis took pride in his local geography and after establishing my desired objective, painstakingly if a little tremulously drew out a correctional route on a napkin which he handed me with a Gallic flourish "et Voila...Bonne route"! Waving my thanks I remounted and with a sense of relief half an hour later saw a sign for the Avenue Verte.

Within minutes I was in my element spinning along a dedicated cycle path on a fine gravel surface tracing the route of a disused railway south across the Pays de Dieppe. No sign of the medieval chateau which I'd missed on my detour but progress sufficient within an hour or so to pull up at a welcoming shaded bench looking out across a stream to a meadow and enjoy my bread and cheese. A father walking out with two young children on trainer bikes went by and as they receded into the distance I found myself enfolded in the calm of the rural French countryside. The dappled light of the warm afternoon sun beneath the ribbon of woodland contrasted with the glaring brightness of the pastureland beyond, where a herd of red and white speckled Normande cows, the local dairy breed, were grazing. I found myself relaxing into the adventure as the fretfulness of missing the route receded from my mind. This was what I had left home for and the long summer had truly begun.

As I packed up my lunch remains a guy with a red sweatband came by on a laden bike. He was younger than me, swarthy looking with a beard and a jumble of bags suspended in a slightly haphazard way from his cycle frame. We exchanged nods and after securing my own two rear panniers (tidily!) I mounted up and soon found myself riding alongside. 'Bonjour je m'appelle Matt' I called over. After a halting exchange in French we rapidly established that our best medium of communication was English as Lorenzo had been working in London the last couple of years and was now headed home to Rome. He had already had his fair share of (mis)adventures. Having taken the ferry a few days before me, he had lost his bank card somewhere along the way. Taken in by a kindly Normandy farming family I learnt the card reissuing process had taken a week and felt somewhat better about my lost hour or so. Undaunted he expressed his determination to achieve his dream of riding home from his work abroad. I wished him well and pressed on idly wondering if our paths would cross again. A couple of hours later as I paused to check the route he sailed by joking that I needed to 'keep going Matt' if I, like him, was going to cross the continent. Our paths never crossed again – the first of many such encounters with fellow travellers. I wonder how he got on in the spirit of the fellowship of the road. Fellow travelling for a shared hour or few miles is always a pleasure but few independent travellers wish to tie ourselves to another for much longer. Independent travel is just that – the freedom to stop or go wherever and whenever one pleases. A freedom which is to be cherished all the more on the road, perhaps, because for me it distinguishes travel from the settled life left behind.

As the afternoon shadows lengthened the surrounding countryside fell away on either side of a thickly wooded viaduct which led as the evening drew in to the substantial settlement of Forges les Eaux. The name encapsulates its raison d'etre first as a mining town where iron was manufactured and later as a spa. Judging from the hotels visible from the old station up on the viaduct it had known better times and I headed to the edge of town for the signposted campsite as the preferred option. The pleasant lady at the reception cabin pointed down an aisle with hedge delimited plots on either side and I settled on the first without neighbours. Having slung my tent up (a 5 minute marvel) I was returning from the shower when I realised the neighbours had arrived.

There is something very suburban which happens at campsites especially if you have the misfortune of understanding the neighbours. For, of course, barely two hours drive south of Dieppe they were English with mewing infant and sullen four year old being jollied along on what looked to be the first night. Lots of opening and closing the family car as suddenly remembered bits of essential kit or distractions for the four year old were fished out by one parent or another. As I got into my civvies ie non cycling set of clothes leaving my newly washed cycle wear to dry beside my coffin like free standing tent I reflected on my comparative minimalism and congratulated myself for shedding stuff. Whatever this journey was about it certainly included a flight from 'stuff'. That said I was to learn that everything is relative and I was to meet folk far more minimalist than myself.

So I did have a Kindle as well as a cheap phone to take to the picnic table outside the 'snac' where I ordered beer, sausage and chips from the campsite proprietress, a charming woman who was highly informative on the key question – "Ou allez la Tour?". Yes it would be coming through the area in a couple of days...indeed through the next town south Gournay-en-Bray the day after tomorrow....I would find the detailed itinerary online and here was their Wi-Fi code. Thus a pattern was set for this leg of the journey of checking in on the Tour each day whilst also thinking of the next day's ride. I worked out that with a full day's ride I should be able to reach Givenchy in the afternoon and spend a couple of hours there amongst Monet's lilies and memories of times past before getting to Vernon where the Tour was due early in the following day's race itinerary. Perfect! I headed back to my tent excited by the next day's prospect if not by the coming night's repose and my second attempt at lying supine on the skeleton mat. This time I did remember to insert it into the sleeping bag prior to passing out which at least reduced the proportion of the night I spent physically separated from the mat if not exactly solving the problem of keeping the mat between the ground and the body when turning unconsciously in the night.

The only other early riser leaving at 05:00 am the following day was an intriguing fellow camper on a battered small wheeled bike with what appeared his earthly possessions hanging from every inch of the tube frame in a way that made Lorenzo look tidy. He had a lit Gaulloise in his mouth as he cycled nonchalantly past me heading for the gate and the open road beyond – yes I really had woken up in la France where things are still, thank god, done a little differently than in little England! Following him out of the gate I was disappointed not to have the opportunity of a chat 'en velo' as he had disappeared back to the open road!

Today I was resolved to get some kilometers under my belt towards my planned Tour intercept. This section of the Paris Avenue Verte wound through rural lanes and I decided given I had a 100 kms to ride to stick to the 'D' road for the opening shift. It was a good call as one of those classic Normandy main roads led straight as an arrow up and down gradual inclines with a generous 1.5m wide surfaced area flanking the marked car lane. As I got my head down and bashed out the 25 km pre breakfast leg both cars and lorries pulled wide respectfully and I even got the occasional honk of encouragement. The Tour de France was en route and much of France seemed to be wishing 'bon courage' aux veloistes!

On arrival at Gournay the town was en fete with a market just getting under way. Having walked the high street and noted what was on offer I stood in line at the Neuchatel cheese stall and learnt from an interchange before me as the gentleman tested three before finalising his selection 'pour demain' (tomorrow). I asked the stall holder to select me one 'pour aujourd'hui' (today). The heart shaped rind covered cheese was duly wrapped in waxed paper to which I added a punnet of nectarines and headed for my breakfast selection – the poulet roti stand serving chicken with lightly curried potatoes. Never has it tasted so good straight from the bag sat on the kerb whilst admiring a proper French market filling up with locals. This, I thought, was what cycle touring on the continent was all about. Avoiding the temptation to spin it out I slipped away having spotted cycle signs which led out of town down quiet lanes across rolling Normandy farmland gradually climbing onto a high plateau with scattered farmsteads and wide open panoramas. An exhilarating couple of hours across this high country led me back down to the historic town of Gisors on the River Epte.

There, on a perfect Norman motte stands a 12th century castle of historic importance, forming the Norman frontline against the Isle de France, bastion of the French crown in Paris to the south-east. From the local information board I learnt that in 911 Rollo signed a pact with the French King assigning the land west of the Epte to that branch of Vikings who later came to be known as the Normans. Of course this has particular resonance for the British as Norman attention would later turn back across the Channel with fateful and long lasting effects on British land ownership. It had only been a few days before when traversing Wiltshire and Hampshire with the lads that we had been commenting on the remarkable persistence of land ownership since the Norman conquest. There was lasting evidence of the feudal Norman power structure in my own family – my mother was a Myerscough which is sufficiently uncommon (compared to the ubiquitous Ellis's in Wales anyway) to be traceable back to the land of William de Myerscough north of Preston, one of the aforementioned Norman feudal lords my uncle Frank always asserted. Serfs like us took the place name with them when we migrated to the cities centuries later. Somehow, we were still under the Norman yoke! Chewing on this fact I looked in vain for a suitable lunch spot failing which I set out again down a small lane which stopped me in my tracks!

For the lane's name sign read Rue Jean-Paul Sartre which resonated as my journey had already been dubbed my Ride to Freedom. As I cycled down the bramble choked lane in the early afternoon sun I was magically transported back to the black and white TV version of Sartre's Chemins de la Liberte watched with my family in 1960's Britain in which Mathieu (more resonance) and seemingly everybody he encounters wears grey macs or uniforms, smokes Galloises and suffers to the backdrop of Nazi invasion. No wonder existentialism won the heart of so many angst ridden adolescents in post war Britain. I can't say I was amongst them. But the main thing I picked up from those ernest images as Mathieu takes cover with his rifle awaiting the arrival of the Panzers (atop the village church tower?) was that life should be lived authentically, its twists and turns the consequences of prior decisions which therefore should not be made lightly

Around the same time in adolescence I happened upon the I Ching on an elder brother's bookshelf. If Jean-Paul Sartre was demanding authenticity in decision making – here lay another approach to teenage dilemmas – a throw of the dice. But I soon learnt the subtlety of the Ching ; before you get to throw the die you first had to frame a question and it's the framing of the question that helps to clarify the dilemma. Whilst many of the dilemmas were of a romantic nature there was the constant background defining issue of what was one to do with this life? Intrigued by youthful travels and in search of something seemingly more exotic than the North-West of England I set my sights on the study of Archaeology and Anthropology. Having frankly struggled with the challenging Oxbridge papers (the Maths paper was a long list of questions which only a genius could attempt in the allotted time - mere mortals were invited to attempt what one could!). I got through so narrowly as to be offered a deferred place giving me eighteen months of freedom! So I worked for a year in a knickers and tights factory in Liverpool before heading East in search of the past, the 'other' and myself. Much later I learnt of the world of phenomenology, the study of philosophical meaning in our relationships with the everyday, which Sartre had taken forward to suggest the self could only achieve unity though taking full responsibility for one's life, choices and actions on the road to freedom. Having spent half a lifetime claiming Maggie Thatcher had derailed my anthropology career and that my return to Liverpool - to study medicine (or to 'get a trade' as I preferred it) - had been forced on me, only now, do I realise that I have been deluding myself about those external forces. My medical career had been of my choosing and I had never fully embraced that fact. That afternoon's ride down the Rue Jean Paul Sartre and along the bank of the lovely Epte provided the opportunity to make this connection on my road to freedom.

But there was to be another step back into my adolescence that day as I pulled up at Monet's

Givenchy. Dim memories of a trip here 50 years before with parents and brother now filled my consciousness. I thought I could see the famous lilies from that trip or was that the multiple versions spotted in the great galleries that were playing tricks in my mind. Certainly it must have been rather different from the heavily commercialised hamlet with massive car park into which I was now directed. Having chained up and changed out of my cycle cleats I found myself thankfully at the tail end of the day's visitors exchanging jokes about concessionary charges for young and old with an American family in front of me in the queue. Once inside I made a beeline for the gardens and wasn't disappointed. The domestic garden was as splendidly kept as I remembered it with broad flower beds separated by walkways which act now to dilute the press of humanity. Once at the back of this garden a tunnel under the road leads to the riverside ponds where the famous lilies are to be found.

Drawn into the magic of the place I found a quiet spot to contemplate, remember fondly my mother's love for this place and the painting it inspired and observe the pleasure others took from contemplating the beauty of this special place. The water flow is arrested by the ponds so creating an atmosphere of stillness punctuated by the lilies surrounded by the carefully planted shrubs on the banks. The elegantly arching iconic bridge lends the whole ensemble an oriental air. The only place like it, tellingly, that I have visited are the temple gardens around Kyoto in Japan where water, light and plants are brought together with a similarly quiet but spectacular beauty. An outgoing American Mom whilst photographing her daughter was heard in response to a throw away comment of mine committing to painting a version of the photo on her return. Why did I want her to?

I think at some level she stood for my absent, long dead and unfulfilled mother, Mabel, who came of age in an era of wartime frugality when opportunities were limited, followed a career in radiography but invested her ambition in her three boys, painted and drank. She taught me to aspire in all things, to be mindful of my responsibilities to others and to appreciate the power of art and music to express emotion. She disappeared round the corner of the path as I broke out of my reverie.... I wonder if that maternal portrait ever did get painted? Maybe it doesn't matter, it was the thought that counted, but part of me hopes she kept to her contract made that day with the funny guy in cycling gear.

On a spin around the house I had no memory of Monet's own personal collection amongst which Cezanne was the standout – as he had been for my mother. Indeed I now realise why Giverny is such a shrine given Monet's father like figure to the impressionists and Cezanne's linkage to what would succeed it. In the late afternoon sun I lingered beside banks of red geraniums surrounding the back of the house providing splurges of colour which conveyed an impression that remains in the mind's eye as I write this some months later.

Onward the path less travelled took me out along a back lane above the valley of the Epte as it ran the few kilometres from Giverny to the Seine at Vernon. I picked my way through a veritable commune of artists' residences from back in the day now largely given over to rather ritzy holiday homes. Once gaining the banks of the Seine the atmosphere abruptly changed with a buzz of activity around the bridge spanning the river. A large stage had been erected in a fenced off area where a soundcheck appeared to be underway. I engaged a gent on a nearby bench in conversation to work out my options. "Oui", he confirmed, "the bridge would be closed tonight in readiness for the Tour which would cross the bridge from Vernon on the far bank before turning north towards Rennes". "Oui, there would be a fete this evening as tout le monde arrived for the big event."

The evening was almost upon me as I crossed the bridge admiring the forceful River Seine below me and I went in search of a place to lay my tent. I figured the river bank was my best bet but was a little taken aback to realise there was another fan park under construction on the far bank. Whilst somewhat smaller than the area back across the bridge (which looked like a full festival) this more family friendly space still included a DJ stage, bar and fair. Clearly there were going to be a lot of punters milling around later and if

I was going to successfully bivouac on the riverbank I would need to find a quieter stretch. Following the left bank's riverside walk upstream it soon appeared more promising. The town vibe by the bridge morphed into a more suburban feel as a stretch of quite ritzy house boats came into view. Beside them was a wide strip of park dotted with trees. Perfect for my planned midnight pitch so all I needed now was a secure place to lock up the bike. The houseboats were accessed by a series of sturdy steel gangways which looked promising. One, in particular, was sufficiently overgrown that I figured my laden bike once chained up to the gangway would be invisible from a casual passerby. There was a doorbell beside the gangtry which I rang with no response. Looking over at the houseboat moored below it was notably less tended than the smart residences I had been passing. Indeed it appeared dilapidated to such an extent that I found myself wondering if anybody lived on it. No matter I decided and locked the bike to the gangtry using the hinged heavy steel bar lock which had been one of my wife's parting gifts. I added a small cable lock to secure the panniers and slipped surreptitiously away with my handlebar box containing my valuables slung by a strap over my shoulder in search of welcome refreshments.

The town was beginning to fill up as I took an outdoor café seat beside a trio playing Gallic versions of Rolling Stones classics. The ageing rockers weren't actually too shabby as they belted out a passable version of Brown Sugar to the relaxed and amicable early evening crowd.

At the end of the set I went in search of dinner and rapidly learnt that the town centre bistros were all fully booked out on what was clearly the big night of the summer in Vernon. Having briefly admired the timber framed 16th century houses at the heart of the old town I selected the most promising of the several Turkish take aways which had plastic café tables tucked in off the street in a pedestrianised area where one could enjoy the generous portions of flatbread and kebab. They even sold beer and so after a filling dinner I was ready to check out the DJ stage. There was a fairground atmosphere back down by the river, young and old enjoying the balmy evening on the river bank.

By 11 o'clock it was slowing down and I reckoned I could safely slip up the riverbank and retrieve bike and belongings from their discrete parking place. Having retraced my steps as far as the houseboats I strolled along the riverbank grateful for my torch as it was all a bit disorientating in the dark. All was quiet apart from the occasional couple. I found myself watching the inflatable police boat lights as they processed up and down patrolling the river in what was basically now a locked-down town awaiting the arrival of tomorrow's Tour. The river meanwhile flowed with a quiet strength back down toward the light and hubbub of the town centre. There was no moon yet but I started becoming more aware of the stars as the town lights gave way to a scrubby woodland and suddenly a large riverside mill. Hang on, I hadn't seen this before! I had definitely come further upstream than I had intended.

Registering this fact my relaxed musings on the evenings events suddenly jerked back into a more immediate and chilling thought....where then was my bike?

With a mounting sense of unease bordering on panic I retraced my steps until I was back at the houseboats. There without a shadow of a doubt in my rapidly sobering mind was the gangway leading down to the dilapidated boat where I had locked my bike. Nothing. I carefully checked the neighbouring houseboats downstream. Yes they were the smart riverside residences I had seen early that day and ruled out as being too exposed to be able to leave all my stuff outside. But here where the overhanging willows created a natural barrier I had felt sufficiently confident of privacy as to secure the bike. Without pausing for further thought I rang the bell again, and this time, eerily there was a disembodied response from the speakerphone beside the bell attached to the riverbank anchor post of the gantry. "Oui?" - I responded without hesitation " Bonsoir je suis un veloist Anglais et j'ai quittai mon velo ici – ou est ca? " The madwoman of Vernon responded in equally vehement terms that as far as I could understand her I had no right to lock my bike against her railings leading to her boat. That this was private property and she had removed my bike. If I wanted it back I would find it leaning against the wall further back from the riverbank. Without pausing to respond I darted up the bank and in the light of a nearby lamppost saw my trusty stead AND panniers leaning there unlocked and unloved awaiting collection by anyone so minded as to give them a home. Having reclaimed my worldly belongings back I went to the bell push to continue this discourse with the devil. "You had no right.....I am just beginning a summer long journey....this could have been the end of it.....why? How?". The how was easy 'anglegrinder' the devil woman told me 'easy as butter' she took satisfaction in telling me down the wire - the why never got beyond her appeal to private property. I had always learnt that the Englishman's home was his castle....well I had learnt the French can be just as bourgeois if not more so!

In high dudgeon I walked along the bank calming after 200 metres and threw up the tent. As I was settling down in the tent a late dog walker leaned over and said kindly 'comme c'est merveilleux' – how marvellous that I should be camping and if I needed for anything to just knock on his door at one of the houses fronting onto the quayside park. As I had learnt in my northern youth 'there's n'out so strange as folk' but we come in all shapes and sizes and the point is, as always, to try and get along with all ...but the mad woman of Vernon had proved to be one step too far I reflected sleepily as I drifted off.

The following morning I woke surprisingly refreshed. Doubting my memory of the previous night's events I inspected the bike in the morning light. There resting on the luggage rack was the hinged steel bars of the lock still closed as I had left it but crucially with one steel bar cut neatly in two. And there on the gunmetal bike frame were the telltale scratches where the angle grinder had gone through the steel bar and nicked the bike frame. At least the mad devil women of Vernon had a relatively steady hand. Determined to pay her back if only symbolically I strode back up the riverbank and threw my now useless steel lock under her boat mouthing a quiet curse as I did so. "One less thing to carry I guess" was a consoling thought as I set myself back towards Breakfast and the Tour.

My strategy was to head for the bridge which I knew lay on the route and then work backwards for a bend which would slow the peloton a fraction to improve my chance of getting a glimpse of the riders. As anybody who has ever attended a professional cycling road race will confirm the speed works against it as a spectacle. I learnt my lesson at my only previous spectating experience when the Tour of Britain came through Bristol. I joined my work colleagues to see them flash past our clinical base in Southmead before I went up to my office, closed down my computer, picked up my things and cycled 2 kms to the Downs to see them return from a long loop out to the Severn, back along the river Avon, up a steep climb of the Avon Gorge and round the Downs to the finish. It was all over and the guys were all cooling down on their exercise bikes beside the team trailers when I got there!

So having committed to the Tour detour I wasn't going to miss it! I found what I was looking for right at the start of the bridge, a sharp right hander where the main road joined an old lane and swung round in a gentle climb onto the wide modern bridge. Having enjoyed a mock sprint up the road to cries of 'allez allez' I spotted a likely looking café 100 metres up the lane, just off the route, where I was met with nods and smiles. I settled in for my coffee and croissant keeping an eye on my laden bike now secured only with my light cable lock. I needn't have worried – I was well away from the hag's lair and amongst friends for I had lucked upon the café rendezvous of the Vernon Cycling Club whose representative members that morning were of a similar demographic to myself. Rose wine was already flowing with nods and winks and once my route had been learnt I was welcomed into the merry band. Where I had been going wrong the white bearded gentleman to my left assured me was not drinking enough rosé wine. One of his comrades lent across with a conspiratorial air gesturing to his wine with the words 'doping traditionelle' and the cycling club of Vernon fell about in peels of laughter. The banter ran through some previous epic runs before my own effort was toasted amidst much bonhomie. The cycling fraternity I reflected (not for the last time) really does continue a fine tradition of inclusive comradeship which cuts against the introversion of those more mean spirited which I perhaps unfairly associate with being locked away from one's fellow citizens behind the wheel of a boxlike automobile.

Our cycling reveries were rudely interrupted as the vanguard of the Tour circus swept into Vernon heralded by a flight of helicopters, the blaring noise of pop music and outriders in bizarrely branded vehicles throwing merchandise at the crowds by now lining the approach to the bridge. This went on for well over an hour during which the crowd and the local gendarmerie fought a subtle battle, the former continuously seeking vantage points the latter dedicated to keeping the roadway clear. In what seemed a reasonable compromise the end result was a bank of spectators 3 to 4 deep forming an arc around the outside of our bend and I positioned myself on a curb at the back which allowed me to catch my first sight of the peloton a couple of hundred metres down the road before they swept round and away over the bridge. With the clatter of the camera carrying choppers overhead resembling a Vietnam movie soundtrack the peloton raced through in a huddle of speed and intensity, fleeting glimpses of individual riders (was that Geraint?) amidst the multicoloured horde. They were only 43kms into a relatively straightforward 181km day. For us spectators the peloton shoots past, with an unusually rapid deflation even by sporting event standards after the prolonged hype. The bridge lay open ahead of me and after a final "Bonne Route" from my new friends I was off into the noon day heat before I got further stuck into the rosé wine! The bridge was open to cycles but not cars and we cyclists all enjoyed another mock sprint across before I swung south east planning to pick up my Avenue Verte route further down the Seine. The main road on the North bank of the Seine had been reopened to traffic by now and I enjoyed trailing a portly elderly gentleman in full cycling kit who clearly knew what he was doing as we swept down the outside of a long queue of traffic to take traffic lights at the perfect moment as they were just changing and I slipstreamed in behind him ahead of the traffic.

The cycling thereafter seemed to go awry. Was it the heat, my continuing unfamiliarity with the Garmin GPS, the morning wine or the geography? I suspect a combination of it all but what had seemed a relatively straightforward navigation task of following the Seine got complicated by its meandering route and I found myself climbing up and down the steep right bank three times completely unnecessarily. At least I was earning views in the glaring midday sun across the fields of stubble high up on either bank. Down below a ribbon of human occupation clearly dating back a thousand years backed onto limestone crags dotted with chateaus reminding of the approach towards Paris. This was all Bourbon country as the scale of historic houses emphasised. Seriously overheated and out of water I was grateful to find a patisserie at the gates of an enormous elegant chateau at La Roche Guyon. The need for refreshment out won curiosity and I gorged on cake, ice cream and chilled fizzy lemon in the air conditioned salon. In extremis it's the refreshment stops that light up in one's mind! As I cooled down and rehydrated I started to take in my fellow refreshment guests. A gaggle of girl guides filled the quiet salon with their giggling energy before settling down to consume their ice cream. A well heeled young cyclist in all the gear quietly ignored me at the next table – this was another world to Normandy and felt like I was entering the Parisienne bubble of self-sufficiency. Back at the chateau gate this long contested approach to Paris was evidenced by the death of one owner at Agincourt, a long period of English occupation during the Hundred Years War and more recently Rommel's bunker as the allies fought their way across Normandy. A rather chilling reminder in this Brexit year of all years of the uncomfortably recent past of western European warfare.

Back out in the heat and climbing the right bank a fourth and final time I finally rejoined the Avenue Vert on some high country lanes amidst woodland. I started to enjoy a faster late afternoon session crossing the rolling limestone plateau of the Vexin above the Seine making sufficient progress that my thoughts were beginning to turn to where I might be able to pitch a tent before the regional parkland I was crossing dropped into the urban banlieues of Paris. Suddenly I swept down a hill into a pretty stone village. The main street opened up to form a narrow square outside a welcoming looking auberge where enough trestle tables had been set up to feed a small army. As I took all this in I realised the fifty people sat at the trestle tables were all in cycling gear and were cheering me in!

Surreal after a long day in the heat alone on a bike. Well I couldn't very well ride past so I dismounted and acknowledged the welcome. The English group, as I might have guessed from the quaffing of beer all round me, were the first I had encountered on the Avenue Vert, riding London to Paris for charity and I found myself sat on the end chatting to the organisers, a very pleasant pair of outdoor type couples who were suitably envious of my trip. They were an offshoot of Virgin's corporate responsibility department which kind of fitted –jolly fun filled capers packaged as charity built around a challenge – nothing too extreme and therefore accessible to all. As a keen park runner and sometime participant in charity rides and 10 km runs I try not to be cynical. It's very much on the positive side of life but I am sure I am not alone in that nagging feeling of corporate unease that somehow we are all being manipulated to put a good face on stuff that is less altruistic at heart. I guess my younger Marxian purity led me to the conclusion that the internal logic of capitalism was unfailingly self-interested and amoral, a system internally driven by the profit motive and all else was window dressing!

However as the sun lowered and the attractive party members enveloped me in warm beery good humour there really was very little to take offence with! Indeed I couldn't have planned it better – today was July 14th, Bastille Day, when freedom and unity is celebrated across France and I had lucked into this fete in just about the last village before the urban sprawl of Paris.

It would be mad to push on. Whilst buying a beer from the friendly patron I established the two crucial pieces of information for an itinerant cycle tourer....yes there would be food available that evening as it was the village fete, hence the trestle tables, and no there wasn't a campsite in the village but the patron would have a word with the mayor who would be coming for the fete. Well I must say I had no idea what the mayor might consider his responsibility towards this itinerant cyclist but I maintained an outward show of insouciance when asked where I was going to stay by my new mates. "Oh I'm told the mayor's going to sort me out" I found myself blustering breezily as all fifty Brits remounted and set off for their corporately booked accommodation in the nearby Paris dormitory town of Cergy. Whatever lay ahead I knew my evening would take me closer to La Vraie France.

Back at the bar I was being served by a very camp somewhat younger man who checked whether I would be happy to eat coq au vin with the band. I was very pleased to confirm this and settled down to write that day's blog entry. Before long the mayor announced his arrival by quietly but formally greeting me with 'You are I believe the Englishman on a bicycle with a tent'. I looked up to note a mild-mannered bespectacled accountant type who clearly took his office seriously and was immediately both welcoming and gracious. With a shrug he told me he was sure I would be able to put up my tent in the garden of his house round the corner but this would only be possible after his official duties which would last some time. Having only left the Tour de France that morning I was attuned to French sensitivities and aware of the upset caused by the Sky Cycling team's director belittling of French mayors earlier that week. Dave Brailsford, said director, in the war of words over Chris Froom's alleged doping had launched a stinging attack on the recently elected French president of world cycling's governing body accusing him of having a "French mayor" mentality. This had caused great offence across the French cycling world and beyond for as I had learnt that very day at Vernon the Tour is indeed a showcase for localism which is symbolised by the mayor in France. So here I was, an English cyclist, deep into the approach across the Isle de France towards Paris, dependent on the hospitality of the local mayor in the very week when certain aspects of the win at all costs English mentality had wounded the national psyche.

This Monsieur le Maire however rose above such diplomatic spats. As the trestle tables filled and a rather disjointed amateur orchestra struck up a programme of light Bastille Day music the camp barman whom I now took to be the Patron's partner handed out song sheets and soon had us participating in community singing complete with gestures which entailed mass humiliation. I must say I was pleasantly surprised to find the French just as capable as the English of taking the piss out of themselves in the right circumstances. Once the musical interlude came to a ragged climax I was served the same coque au vin et frites as the band followed by cheese and wine brought over from the head table of dignitaries by the mayor himself with a short speech welcoming me to the village of Sagy. Rising bucolically to my newly allotted role as honoured village guest I returned the speech in my best schoolboy French weaving in a reference to this reaffirmation of 'the entente cordiale'! Judging by the applause from top table this exchange seemed to have been in tune with the mood of the gathering and the wine flowed as the good people of Sagy continued their relaxed Bastille Day celebration under an increasingly starlit sky. Soon the tables were cleared and we all set off in a slightly inebriated winding procession through the village and out into the fields in the gathering darkness. I had no idea what was going on but this was clearly Sagy en fete and the anthropologist in me was keen to observe the attendant ritual. This element turned out to be a rather underwhelming firework display on the village recreation ground but things took a more interesting turn as we processed back to the village centre.

There the crowd gathered around the town hall and sang folk songs until a white haired rather wild looking gentleman pulled up a stepladder, ascended and took a barely noticed long dead fir tree out of its stand. This he ceremonially burnt before replacing it with a fresh tree in what appeared to me to be an unusually timed rite of passage. Asking the locals appeared to confirm that we were celebrating the end of the year and the beginning of a new cycle of things. Given that I had been watching combine harvesters hard at work until late into the evening bringing in the harvest in this part of Northern France there was possibly a sense of the passing of the seasons but I must say given the continuing glorious weather it still felt like midsummer to me. I note that in medieval days the feast of St John on the 24th June was associated with bonfires and wonder whether several rituals got bundled into the present secular 14 July celebrations. As the festivities drew to a close Monsieur le Maire took me aside and suggested we retired to his neighbouring farmhouse. There in the barn he proudly showed off the two vintage military jeeps which he drove to displays around Europe including England. I was then shown to his spare room where I slept dreaming of singing crowds storming stone ramparts led by a camp Bonaparte eating coq au vin in a tricolour hat.

I came to the following day keen to get going as the big holiday weekend in France proceeded onto the World Cup final later that day – France versus Croatia – and I wanted to be in Central Paris for that experience. After a disappointingly supermarket breakfast from the mayor's cupboard (beggars can't be choosers!) I got going after a friendly send off both from my new friend the Mayor but also the gay patrons of the auberge who had just emerged to start the clear up! With "Bonne Route" ringing in my ears I made rapid progress to Cergy where the Vexin limestone plateau tumbles down towards the Seine. There on the southern slopes a huge formal park allows vistas south over Paris with the relatively modest grouping of skyscrapers of the `Defense' financial district clearly visible above what is otherwise the unusually uniform seven storey high profile of central Paris. With a rising sense of excitement at my approach to a major foreign city on a bicycle I set off on what was rapidly becoming an urban cycle trail winding its way cunningly via disused railway lines back down to the right banks of the Seine. There I found industrial scale river barges moored to massive quais carrying the fruits of globalisation in the form of Chinese containers no doubt crammed with stuff. As if to reinforce this sense of approach to a global hub I fell in with an Irish financier on his Saturday morning leisure ride with whom I exchanged European viewpoints. He confirmed the impression already formed that Paris was well placed to take financial business from London. As I was to confirm further on in Rome the modern world is returning to an era of metropolitan urban hubs where power and wealth are concentrated and pull against their host nation states in many important ways. For the rest of the morning I meandered along the banks of the Seine through what seemed like an entire gallery full of impressionist painting backdrops complete with elegant stretches of tree lined river bank and colourful elegant riverside residences. The prostitutes of the demi monde, the draw for those impressionist artists at the turn of the century, have long abandoned the river-banks in pursuit of business along the continent's trunk roads. I can attest to this phenomenon having encountered several such tawdry trysting lay-bys along my route in each and every country through which I cycled. Whilst plenty of goods still make their way into Paris by boat very few people do. And judging by the quiet cycle ways not so many cyclists. Suddenly there was a sign right off the river bank to St Denis which I had been watching out for and in an incredibly sudden transition the cycleway led straight into the station plaza of St Denis where what seemed like a hundred kebab vendors were hawking their smoky offerings from open charcoal grills to the backdrop of Senegalese sounds as this part of global Paris appeared solely given over to francophone West African rhythms. Having been wholly absorbed for four days in rural Normandy this sudden emergence was all the more exciting. I rode round the plaza on my bike and just took in all the sounds, smells and people swirling around the kebab vendors who managed an air of cool and menace in equal share. A cycle is a privileged position to observe urban scenes with an ever present option of escape if it all gets too much.

On this occasion the deadline was external and related to the reason for the party atmosphere. All work had stopped for the day as the entire French nation held its breath readying themselves for the big game. I set off into town and at the first traffic lights joined a young man on a very cool battery powered e-trike with an impossibly elegant bohemian young girlfriend on a more traditional basketed French urban bike. I enquired whether they were going to the centre which they affirmed with a friendly "follow us". As we weaved our way along the boulevards sometimes on traffic free cycle lanes sometimes sharing the tram lanes I became aware of a city poised, awaiting something. At every junction stationary traffic set off a cacophony of car horns as if the city was giving voice to the rising excitement. At the next junction I thought of checking with my guides their destination..."le Beaubourg" ....man was this my lucky day. I knew enough of Paris to guess this would be a good place, in this arty largely pedestrianised quarter, to catch the match. As we pulled into the district I bid my young guides my thanks and pulled off onto a promising street lined by heaving café bars each open onto the street with both indoor and outdoor screens. Of course I had the challenge of not only finding a perch amidst all this madness but also of securing my fully laden bike nearby without a decent lock thanks to the mad woman of Vernon! Thankfully I found a space on a cycle hoop outside a couple of promising bistro bars where on my second attempt I squeezed onto a stool sandwiched between a table of three middle aged women and a table hosting a man of my age, a pretty young woman half his age and her dog done up for the occasion in a French football shirt. By craning to the right I could just glimpse my green panniers amidst the jumble of bikes parked up on the cycle racks outside the cafés. Having made my introductions, I caught the attention of the busy maitre d' sporting a red white and blue wig for the occasion and started a tab. The match kicked off to a roar which reverberated around the packed neighbourhood and over the opening exchanges I got to know my new friends. Helen to my left turned out to have been born and raised a Chelsea fan now resident in Australia over on her annual European visit with Dutch and German born Aussie girlfriends. My stool was awaiting the arrival of their Paris based friend who they described as a Grande Dame of travel writing – I was intrigued. The beer had only just arrived when a guttural roar outside announced the first French goal. In a common quirk of the modern world our TV cable content was marginally delayed compared to the signal reaching surrounding cafés. Weirdly our 'live' TV football experience was prefigured by the really live crowd packing the Beaubourg neighbourhood that sunny Saturday afternoon in July.

Helen and I conversed knowledgeably around the ebbs and flows of the game as Croatia came back with an equaliser which quietened the crowds and made a game of it for the duration of the first half. Meanwhile I had the 'pleasure' of making friends with the pug done up in the national strip who was integrated into goal celebrations by being smothered in kisses by his pretty young owner. Over half time I got into discussion with her papa-gateau who was a likeable guy of exactly my age who had spent time in London as a young man. Life had brought him back to Paris and yes, it was complicated, gesturing fatalistically across the table to his young companion absorbed with her pug dog as the second half got under way. Amidst ever wilder jubilation the French pulled away capping their victory with a fine goal by Mbappe the nineteen year old discovery of the tournament. My steak frites had arrived and the vin rouge was flowing when the grande dame arrived. As we all squeezed up amidst the introductions I found myself next to her and seizing the opportunity asked her advice as to how to take forward my writing ambitions for the third age. Helen had introduced me as the crazy guy riding to Greece and she told me without hesitation in that marvellously direct American way "You've got your story....go write it"! I made my farewells as the celebrations got under way outside ("its coming home" I was reminded more than once by celebrating passers by making the point that this was France's second triumph to leave the English crying into our beer over what might have been - ouch!). I retreated to the nearby Seine where I needed to pay homage at the Pont Neuf to my younger, more intrepid self. At age 15 I had arrived in Paris on my first hitch hiking trip with Dick a school friend and we had slept at my insistence under the Pont Neuf 'avec les clochards' as described in Orwell's 'Down and Out in London and Paris'. Leaning my bike against the fine stone balustrade of the bridge I peered down into the dark subterranean depths and mused on the lines my brother's old poet school friend Peter Robinson had written which we had read out at the funeral memorialising his trip with Geoff to this place around the same time

CREPUSCULES i.m. Geoff Ellis

There's something about the light this morning
I wouldn't have wanted you to miss –
as when twin towers' and stained-glass windows'
ashen stone was tinted rose
briefly by a dusk at Paris,

or the storm-light around a pavement café awning
tormented by late squalls in the Marais ...
No, I wouldn't have wanted you to miss

today's dawn, like a shepherd's warning;
it sweeps low clouds of purple-grey
across those higher white ones
tinted pink too by the sun's
emergence behind scratched winter boughs
with turquoise patches and some blues ...
No, I wouldn't have wanted you to miss this.

A young lad was sat nearby drinking from a bottle of
wine. Sensing my reflective mood in this island of calm
surrounded by a maelstrom of car horns and shrieking
celebrants he offered the bottle in a gesture of shared
humanity and I drank gratefully. 'Do not ask for whom
the bell tolls, it tolls for thee' came to mind from the
same period of early reading of classics from
Hemingway's masterpiece quoting John Donne in my
layered melancholic rumination on death loss and

shared humanity. Time to head for my bed not under the Pont Neuf on this occasion thanks to the wonders of plastic cards and Booking.com.

I awoke in the night feeling rough with the shits. Ah, Paris, Paris. My last minute booking had placed me in a garret room with a classic Parisan rooftop view out of the dormer window onto neighbouring roofs, drying washing, TV aerials and chimney pots which matched the mood. By mid -morning I was over the worst of it and to cheer myself up I brought the blog up to date and took some time to check my stats – 566kms to date compared to the Tour de France's 1568kms covered in the same time frame. Pas mal! I had a couple of chores to get on with, not least (remembering those unnecessary climbs a couple of days back) the purchase of a road atlas of France and the replacement of a pair of reading glasses sat on in the big match excitement. Back out on the Rue Rivoli round the corner from the Louvre there were empty bottles in the gutters and a palpable sense of the morning after the night before. I found a rather smart opticians selling spectacles and asked the equally smart young assistant whether she had any 'supermarket style reading glasses'. She smiled knowingly, enquired as to the required magnification and reaching into a drawer pulled out a pair for 10 euros. "Mes felicitations pour hier" I commented as she bagged the specs – looking at me over her glasses the mask of Parisian formality fell away and she said, smiling the whole while somewhat condescendingly, "You're English aren't you.....it's our turn now!" As I walked back to the hotel via les Halles I reflected on the mood in the city and thought she had hit the nail on the head. The last time I had been in a city with this morning after atmosphere was back in 1997 returning across London from an election night party at a friend's in Leyton, East London. There were echoes of that sense of Cool Britannia under Tony and being in 'the place to be' that day in Paris with the World Cup 'after' party planned for that afternoon. It was time for an Englishman to hit the road!

Having repacked, I checked out and set off warily amidst the Paris traffic tracking the Seine eastwards. At the second set of lights where the Quai Hotel de Ville becomes the Quai Henri IV I pulled alongside a fully kitted out Parisian road cyclist complete with supercool wraparound glasses. As I glided to a halt distracted by trying to second guess the traffic lights I put my unclipped left leg out only to realise the now stationary bike was irreversibly committed to a lean to the right due to my sloppy repacking of the panniers and the resultant change in weight distribution. As I desperately tried and failed to unclip my right cycle shoe I gracelessly gathered momentum in my stationary fall to the right where I ended up lying in the gutter with a laden bike on top of me. I looked up to note simultaneously the disdain of the Parisian cyclist glancing down at me, the change of the lights to green and the accelerating traffic including said cyclist pulling away. It was going to be a long day!

As the chic banks of the Seine in central Paris gave way to the working quais where building materials were stored I headed up the River Marne mistaking the tributary for the main stream fortunately coming across a pleasant riverside café almost immediately where I took lunch and re-established my location. Correcting my error the route then followed the river fairly clearly for a further 20kms to Villeneuve St Georges where I doffed my cap to the 60 early pioneers of the Tour de France who started the first stage (Paris-Lyons) here in 1903. Maurice Garin completed that 467km stage in 17 hours and 45 minutes (26kms/hour) on a machine I suspect far inferior to my own. I was to reach Lyons a fortnight later!

My modest target for the day was the Forest of Fontainebleau which I had identified as an off road route option leading on from Paris to a possible wildcamping opportunity. Weaving my way through the south eastern suburbs I managed to find local cycle routes out to Melun where I remet the Seine one last time before crossing to the south bank and heading towards the forest which I entered from the charming (and well heeled) village of Barbizon. Seeking the advice of the two gentlemen at the bus stop as to the best route across the forest by bike the elder white man clearly thought the whole thing was a bad idea whilst a more friendly black man was non-specifically encouraging. Leaving them to ponder their widely divergent advice I headed on taking a well surfaced broad track into forest that was immediately striking in the maturity of its trees and the extent of the heather. Indeed the 'forest of heather' as it was known in French has always been treasured as an accessible magical wilderness by all who venture here from royals to artists. In the mid-19th century French artists including Millet and Corot painted here forming what has become known as the Barbazon school. Influenced by the English landscape painting of Constable exhibited at the taste-setting Paris Salon in 1824 these painters studied the trees, rocks and ferns of Fontainebleu developed a realism which provided a bridge from the romantic period to the impressionism exemplified by two young painters who visited Barbazon to study under these realists – Monet and Renoir. So here were seeds sown that would later give fruit at Givenchy.

I had stopped at a roadside pizzeria and having invested in pizza and beer was hopeful of finding a suitable camping spot as I headed deeper into the woods in the gloaming. An owl hooted as I pushed the bike up a steep sandstone incline to a rocky knoll - a perfect site for my encampment. It had an out of time quality with its heather filled breaks and rocky outcrops amidst the oak, scots pine and beech unlike any forest I have previously encountered. From the westerly slope I had a view of deepening purple hues through the Scots pines as the light faded, giving way to evening's empire as the undulating forest drew me deeper into its kingdom. There was no question of a campfire in my mind - all rather too dry to risk being the cause of a forest fire so I reclined against a fallen tree trunk enjoying the gloaming and quietly munched my pizza swilled down with beer. I realised I was all in, settled down in my little tent pitched flyless on yet another cloudless evening and rapidly passed out beneath familiar stars.

I jerked awake in the middle of the night in pitch darkness to the sound of movement behind my head out in the forest floor coming my way. I raised myself as quietly as I could and then leaned back on my elbows (still in my sleeping bag) and then froze listening intently to the approaching sound of movement. I was terrified as I tried to work out what was going on. There was a definite snuffling quality amidst a brushing sound of disturbed woodland floor. This had to be a wild boar! I racked my brains for any nuggets of wisdom addressing what to do when this situation arises. I had famously learnt 'what to do when a bear approaches your tent' from a ranger in the Adirondacks on a hiking trip in N America in years gone by (bang pans together to scare off said bear) and I did know boar can be dangerous but what I did not know was how wild boar respond to scare tactics. I did have a mental image of what a wild boar's tusks were like and weighing up my head position relative to the ground suddenly sat bolt upright as I decided I had been leaning back at tusk height. The sounds were now directly behind the tent coming straight for me. It was too late for flight and fight wasn't realistic so I adopted the time-honoured approach of freezing and hoping I wouldn't be noticed! As he came beside the tent the boar hesitated, snuffled some more, then apparently satisfied went on his way. Never has a camper been more relieved to lay his weary head down and I am rather proud of the fact that I dropped straight back off to sleep, threat seemingly over.

I must say there was an element of relief on waking to find my clearing free of all evidence of wild animals the following morning. A lovely ride took me across the awakening woodland past more dramatic rock outcrops to emerge on a surprisingly suburban cycle route with mature student commuters headed for the nearby INSEAD, a top end graduate business school which clearly offered a highly desirable learning environment. A little further on I emerged in front of the extensive Renaissance Royal Palace fronted with formal gardens and a sweeping horseshoe stairway. It had been built by Francois Ist who was a patron of the arts at a time when Italy was at the peak of its creative curve and France was becoming a world power. It is said that Francois 'brought the Renaissance to France'. He certainly knew a master when he met one inviting Leonardo da Vinci to live out his later years in France and hanging his painting the Mona Lisa here above his bath tub in his newly built palace. Another staging post in my journey as I backtracked the route by which ideas of the classical past had reached the Liverpool of my childhood. Later Fontainebleau was where the then all powerful Louis XIV, the sun king, spent his early autumn hunting season - presumably with plenty of wild boar on the menu. Having satisfied my curiosity the morning essentials were rapidly sourced at the neighbouring café occupied by a trio of elderly gentlemen discussing the news over their coffee and croissants. A cross country route to Orleans? Yes, one of them assisted as I poured over the map confirming what looked like the most direct quiet route. I had been toying with the idea of following the Canal du Loing due south which met the Canal d'Orleans at Montargis along which I could ride west to reach Orleans where I was due to rendezvous with my wife the following evening. But studying the map it was clear that the canalside route whilst attractive would trace two sides of a triangle on a slow surface. The minor road option via D36 and D9 would be both more direct and as I had learned on my morning push to catch the Tour de France a few days earlier far faster as was confirmed by my café informant.

The way south of the forest lay through gently rolling agricultural land with occasional hamlets centred around medieval churches occupying local prominences. In the Eglise Saint-Martin at Fromont the square church tower in undressed grey stone reared above a barn like nave entered from one end through a huge arched doorway enclosed by ancient wooden shuttered gates. Through the gates in the medieval gloom could be glimpsed figures painted on the wall. These dated from the 1400's when this area was experiencing the anarchy of what became known as the Hundred Years War at the height of what we recall as feudal chivalry. This was essentially a power struggle between war lord families (the Plantagenets rulers of England and the House of Valois rulers of the Ile de France) for control of the emerging predominant western European state of France. It was complicated by a dynastic civil war raging within France that led Burgundy to an alliance with the English against the Dauphin. In a pincer movement east by the Burgundy forces and south west by the English army the two forces came together to take on the siege of Orleans, unintentionally triggering the turning point of the war. The siege would be famously lifted and the English, led by their Plantagenet lords, repulsed with the divine assistance of Joan of Arc, the Maid of Orleans. Contemporaneously the wall painting I was admiring portrayed three well-dressed young men, one clad in the finery of a knight, one in the finery of a high minister of the church and one in the finery of a merchant. Confronting them are three corpses. Known in medieval art as the 'Dit des trois morts et des trois vifs' this not uncommon image tells the story of the three kings or young noblemen who in one version are enjoying a hunt when they become separated from their retainers in mist to be confronted by the three corpses. Each has their own response ranging from a desire to flee to one of confrontation. The corpses in their turn remind them that they were once equally materialistic and pleasure loving but are there to remind them of the transience of life. I was reminded that my own cycle ride escaping from the Grim Reaper would bring only a relatively brief respite and I ventured back into the sunshine of the present keen to press on. After a hot hour's ride through the midday sun I stopped at the next hamlet by a grassy verge to drain my water bottle in the shade of a farm building. Surveying the scene all was quiet in the midday heat with not a person to be seen nor an engine to be heard. Where was everybody?

Coming through the deserted streets of the next slightly larger place (Puisseaux) I came round the corner of a much bigger 13th century church to enter a square where I discovered the locals....having lunch of course. The local restaurant was busy inside and out where the tables filled one corner of the pretty square surrounded by period stone built houses. When in France...I found myself a peripheral table which suited me just fine and I was soon tucking into the 8 Euro plat du jour, a fine chicken casserole. Looking around me there was a smattering of itinerant tourists but the vast majority of the lunch service was taken by local men sat in threes and fours presumably reflecting different occupational teams as they came and went in vans with ladders. The waitress was charming, the sun was shining and once again I found myself congratulating myself on the journey. Transient though the pleasures of the flesh might be they were to be savoured all the more in that certain knowledge of the end that awaits.

The afternoon session speeded up again as the hamlets came and went along the quiet but straight backroad I was following through the Val du Loire countryside. Was it Beaune la Roland where I stopped at a restaurant bar to refill my water bottles and the patron was just finishing service in a rather dingy street corner establishment on a crossroads of grey stone houses that somehow sent a chill down ones back. Unlike the busy square of Puisseaux there was something dead in the air here. Monsieur le patron was knocking back the pastis in a doomed attempt to chase the demons away whilst what I took to be his learning impaired son attended to the needs of the one remaining table of lunch customers. Periodically the patron disappeared through the swing kitchen door, through which could be glimpsed grimey undone washing up, to do what remained unclear. On his return from his second such visit he caught me preparing to self serve water from his equally grimey bar tap into my water bottle and made quite a show of washing my bottles as if I was unclean. I guess grime is relative and I had shared my night with a wild boar so perhaps I was looking the part but I was happy enough to make my escape from this place and very grateful for having grabbed lunch when I had. In retrospect I wasn't surprised to learn this place had been the site of a holding camp for Jews during the French chapter of the holocaust.

My road south east led into my next forest, the forest of Orleans, and I noted a camp site at Etang de la Vallee. It struck me after my wild camping encounter a campsite might be somewhat tamer in the best sense of the word. The final straight stretch shaded from the lowering sun had me breaking 40 kms/hr on my now trusty Garmin as I zeroed in on the promised lake side camping. Just as I veered off the D9 I came across the Chateau de Combreux, an enormous moated neogothic pile all shuttered up amidst what appeared a caravan and camping site. Stopping to review the map as it seemed a bit too soon to be my camping I realised I was headed 5 kms away and this wasn't an official site. Looking more closely it was obvious that this was an unofficial traveller site and I idly wondered what sort of evening would unfold if I cycled on and pitched amidst the caravans. But the pull of promised lakeside camping was stronger than my curiosity and 10 minutes later I was approaching a wide expanse of lake with the unmistakeable sound of children happily at play in the water. I checked in, took up a minute part of the now familiar hedged plot assigned to me and wearily trudged across the field to the lake and a life restoring swim off the sandy shore. Out past the water lilly clogged shallows I admired the shoreline of surrounding broad leaf woodland cloaking the far bank. Floating on my back far beyond the shrieks and chatter of holidaying children I reviewed the day's 80 kms ride and felt like I was beginning to 'hit my stride'. Neither too long nor too rushed this had felt like a nicely paced day.

The couple running the campsite were juggling a young family with the business and provided an outdoor shaded snack bar area with large screen TV now showing highlights of that day's Tour de France. As I relaxed over a beer enjoying the Tour update awaiting more pizza I surveyed the run in to Orleans now a mere

30 odd kilometre distant. It looked like being a leisurely morning ride across the forest to the Canal d'Orleans which I planned to follow to its meeting point on the North bank with the Loire on the outskirts of Orleans. Over a last beer with the campsite couple I established this had previously been a lakeside restaurant site linked to the chateau in earlier days. The young woman's family had lived and worked here in her childhood but had been driven into the city to earn their living where she had reached adulthood. It was her boyfriend who had sought out a fresh adventure away from the rat race and had first identified this opportunity which had earned her support when she realised he had rediscovered the lake of her childhood! Now she found herself negotiating with the absentee landlords of the long abandoned chateau over the lease to their campsite. Having wished them well in what seemed to me an entirely well conceived venture I retired and slept a sound, boar-free, sleep.

The next morning I enjoyed my first morning swim of the ride on a now beautifully peaceful lake better able to appreciate the water fowl grazing its banks and shorelines. My eye was drawn to a wood-slatted pier perfectly reflected in the still water which looked to be an ideal Tai Chi platform. With the sun beginning to climb and give out some real warmth I clambered out and took up my stance, feet shoulder width apart, hips and shoulders aligned with the feet head carefully balanced such that I could feel all my feet in contact with the wooden platform. Then imagining a string pulling the crown of my head up to the sky I relaxed my hips allowing my weight to sink through my lower back and down through my hips, knees, ankles and feet down the wooden piles of the pier into the earth. Raising my arms until they reached the horizontal and relaxing at both shoulders and wrists my hands fell into a soft open posture facing back towards my chest. Closing my eyes I consciously calmed the mind reviewing thoughts briefly as they appeared in an effort to let them go gently. Was that a moorhen? Don't know and it doesn't matter if it is or it isn't...it's a bird and I'm fortunate to be here and now amongst water birds. I'll be with Susannah tonight.....good, looking forward to it, enjoy this moment of solo calm all the more now. Will there be a good route from the campsite through the forest or will I get lost.....don't know but no doubt I'll survive and enjoy whatever turns out.....and so on. In class with Mark the Teacher's calming example we quite happily manage 20 minutes of this *Zhan Zhuang* 'standing like a tree' Qi Qong meditation.

Alone and relaxed on the pier in Etang de la Vallee that day I don't know how long I absorbed the suns rays enjoying the fusion of ying and yang but on reopening my eyes and going into my Chen style form to glide up and down the pier in a flowing harmonious series of balanced postures was to be content in the now. I shy away from intellectualising what's going on during Tai Chi Qi Qong but suffice to say having dabbled with quite a few different practices over the last 30 years I settled on this practice 10 years ago and I continue to be thoroughly absorbed by it. When at the end of a winding journey down from the Tibetan plateau into India some years back I found myself in a yoga retreat I commented to the teacher on the similarity of the mental space reached through yoga and buddhist meditation he Indian head rolled, smiled knowingly and commented on the "many routes to the one". I know of no better summary statement of the South Asian genius developed over thousands of years for inner exploration.

I settled the modest nights' bill and set off down a promising woodland trail which wove through the pleasant mixed deciduous forest without the breaks and drama of the rocky outcrops encountered in Fontainbleu but more shaded which as the sun rose was a blessing. Leaving the forest at Fay-aux-Loges the lane I was cycling on tracked a wide somewhat overgrown canal which soon allowed access onto a grassy towpath with a single narrow stoney rut. This was perfectly negotiable at a more stately but acceptable pace than the road – perhaps 15km/hour – and I was treated to the sight of a magnificent white horse and rider charging along the opposite bank. After a while I reached the magnificent confluence with the Loire where for approximately 800 metres the canal runs beside the river separated only by a graceful stone embankment. I had made it to the end of stage 3 where I was due to meet Susannah and pickup Eurovelo 6 turning eastwards up the mighty river Loire. Within a couple of kilometres I was on an urban quayside with riverside cafés and the hum of city life. Our prebooked hotel and rendezvous was upmarket compared with previous accomodation in a urban hotel chain whose Orleans branch was advertised to be right on the river convenient both for urban delights and the cyclepath. And so it proved – a modern not inelegant two storey complex facing the river across a tree lined quayside avenue just downstream from one of the principal bridges.

I checked in, parked my bike in the old vaulted outbuilding being used as a bike store (noting a decent looking cycle tourer already parked there) before heading to the comfy double bed in our room. I exchanged messages with Sus as she got on her train in Paris to confirm her arrival time a couple of hours later that afternoon. We decided it might save time if I checked over her rental bike at the same time as giving mine a routine maintenance once over. Heading back down to reception I was pleased to see the same helpful young lady was at the desk who had checked me in and enquired as to whether Sus's bike had arrived. After characteristically thorough research of her options Susannah had decided against manoeuvring her bike through two capital city inter-station transfers (Paddington-St Pancras, Gare du Nord-Gare de Austerlitz) and opted for a sophisticated bike rental service which delivered to and collected from hotels pre-specified by the customer. "Un velo pour Madame Gibb, non je ne sais rien" the receptionist informed me. "But maybe my colleague took delivery – she will be in later". A call to Montpelier where the bike company was based confirmed their end of the arrangements. Where on earth could the bike have been misaddressed to. Mumbling away to myself in irritation like a grumpy Tony Hancock at the way the 'best laid plans' go astray I headed back to the bike store to at least check my own bike over. Then I spotted the label on the parked bike which had been sat there the whole time. 'Madame Gibb' read the label and my cloud of irritation vanished. Back in the now I wiped and oiled, went to clean up and catch the closing stage of that day's Tour on the room TV when, with a knock on the room door, domestic bliss was regained. "How was the journey?" "Smooth enough", I learned, and "how is the bike" – "looking good", I opined. "And the helmet?" "What helmet?". Oh dear, back we went to the Montpelier based bloke who once again confirmed it had been delivered with the bike. Back down to the helpful receptionist who was just going off duty. She would enquire of her colleague as to the whereabouts of a helmet but in the meantime was able to book tonight's dinner at a suitably well heeled restaurant to mark our reunion.

Orleans was buzzing and the restaurant not too stuffy and serving really interesting food (I had to date eaten every night at my camp site since arriving in France save for my Vernon Turkish takeaway and my matchday Paris bistro after which I'd suffered the shits). So, yes, I was starting from a low base when judging what fine French cuisine had to offer. Relaxed, reunited and happily well fed we retired to our heavy curtain, lined hotel bedroom, passed out and came to at 10am! No problem it was the start of our 10 days of cycling together, we had pre-booked the accommodation for the first couple of nights and been modest in our distance planning so I was very relaxed about a late start. Then Sus reminded me of the helmet problem. Having remembered that everything closes for lunch still in France (how civilised) we immediately set about resolving the helmet issue. When Sus interrogated the 'other' receptionist she had no memory of taking receipt of her bike and helmet from the courier company but digging around came up with three random cycle helmets from the hotel reception store room, none of which fitted and certainly did not match the carefully copied specification of the bike rental company. After a couple of phone calls we raced off to the main bike hire operation in downtown Orleans where we bizarrely encountered a young man from Bristol in his second week on the job, who couldn't have been more helpful but seemed doubtful that his boss would allow him to loan us a helmet on the 'say so' of another company based in faraway Montpelier who weren't part of their Loire cycle hire consortium. Sensing a lost lunch 'hour' which In France is two hours minimum on our opening day I was despatched to purchase a helmet at the local store coordinating by phone with Sus as she pursued the extended hire negotiating process. This was by far the most complicated situation I had been involved in since leaving Wiltshire and it was with huge relief that I learned over the phone that Sus had sweet talked our new best mate from Bristol into letting her take one of their well fitted modern cycle helmets. If you ever read this Andy I owe you a beer down one of our Bristol brewery taprooms! So from the fangs of frustration we snatched a pre-lunch start (sort of) setting off up the Loire day one of our joint journey just after 1.00pm.

Chapter 3. Conjugal Cycling on Eurovelo 6 to Burgundy

Cycling with my wife proceeds most enjoyably provided certain rules are followed:

> Rule 1: The stronger rider brings up the rear.
> Rule 2: The front rider determines the pace and the stops.
> Rule 3: Should the rear rider pause for a distraction (eg wayside information board) then the front rider will press on regardless and require the rear rider to catch up.

Mindful of the above we were soon rolling smoothly eastwards along the Loire towpath on the left (southern) bank admiring once again the extensive stone embankment protecting the junction of the Canal d'Orleans with the Loire. The Loire remains navigable up to Orleans and the canal construction dates from 1672 designed to complete a navigable link from the Atlantic coast all the way to Paris via the River Loing and ultimately the Seine. This enabled barges filled with salt water tanks to transport live fish to the markets of the growing city. This historical curiosity played into my reverence for French gastronomy reinforced by the previous evening's dinner. All boded well for this section of the journey which I hoped to be relaxed and somewhat luxurious.

However, having lost a morning and with accommodation booked that night upriver at Sully Sur Loire there was no time for a lazy lunch. Having enjoyed our first stretch of the river, impressively wide with wooded islets, we found a sunny café table at Jargeau, home of the Joan of Arc sausage (the French don't down-play the Maid of Orleans around these parts), but didn't linger. Having regained the north bank via the bridge at Chateauneuf-sur-Loire our next target was the oldest church in France, just upriver at Germigny-des-Pres.

The church lay a couple of kilometres off our riverside path but time had been regained, the cycling delightful and the Byzantine style cupola beckoned us across the fields. Built by Theodulf of Orleans in 806, just 6 years after Charles the Great (Charlemagne) had been crowned Emperor by the Pope in Rome in contested circumstances, it was designed as a private chapel. It is all that survives of a palace complex destroyed by the Vikings before Rollo had been appeased with Normandy. The coronation in 800 is now seen as an historical turning point, heralding the beginning of the Carolingian (Charles becomes Carol in some languages) Renaissance, which scholars use to define the beginning of the medieval period. For my journey back into the classical past this represents a key staging point in the journey of ideas from Ancient Rome (and by association Greece) into Medieval Europe. Charlemagne emerged from a whole series of Romanised Germanic dynasties, collectively referred to as the Franks, holding sway between the Loire and the Rhine after the fall of Rome. Charlemagne was an archetypal soldier-scholar who fostered an epoch marked by the exchange and development of ideas across Europe. Central to these of course were theological issues for which Charlemagne had an official advisor. For many years this was Alcuin, an Anglo-Saxon scholar originally based at York Cathedral, the acknowledged star pupil of the generation succeeding the monastic Bede. A student of grammar, a poet and inveterate correspondent Alcuin was invited to join Charlemagne as a trusted advisor and is credited with returning Latin to a mutually intelligible lingua franca across Europe and popularising a version of the Latin script which with the later advent of printing would become 'Times Roman'. By the end of his life he was the Abbot of Tours, a telling example of Anglo-Saxon influence at the heart of Europe! Theodulf, the builder of Germigny-des-Pres was his successor as theological advisor to Charlemagne. The centrality of religion in this emergent Western European State has been well captured by the term 'credo-state' in distinction to the nation states of the modern era....in other words a state built around a commonality of belief rather than ethnicity.

That belief was, of course, in general terms in Christ but not just any form of Christianity. The foundational belief had been laid out in the Nicene Creed ...which takes us back to Rome itself and the incomparable

Constantine, who first adopted Christianity as a state sanctioned religion. In 325 C.E. he convened at Nicea, just to the South of the site for his new city of Constantinopole which he was busy planning, the first state sponsored attempt to reach a consensus agreement on what it was to be a Christian ...previously plurality of belief had been the status quo in Rome. In this sense he can be seen as the originator of the credo state and it this foundation myth - of a Christian Roman Emperor - which was spectacularly being co-opted in 800 as Charlemagne was crowned "Emperor of the Romans" by Pope Leo III (whose papacy he had saved) on Christmas Day at Rome's Old St. Peter's Basilica.

But if the credo-state is defined by a shared belief the interpretation of those beliefs becomes a critical aspect with far reaching policy implications. The Creed had been an attempt to standardise a core set of agreed beliefs that the Christian Church East and West could coalesce around. It emphasises three core beliefs....'We believe in one God, the Father..... We believe in one Lord, Jesus Christ.......We believe in the Holy Spirit'......within a more complex statement in which the seed of schism lay. The Eastern Church and Western church drifted apart, the former inevitably focussed around Constantine's Eastern capital whilst the West remained centred on Rome. The theological arguments driving division are somewhat opaque to the modern mind but suffice to say that whilst everybody seems happy to accept God the Father's role in the genesis of the Holy

Spirit Jesus's role is seen to be more problematic. Theodulf defended the 'Filioque' clause to the Nicene Creed in effect arguing that the Holy Spirit also came from the Son. Whilst his efforts at resolution (and those of many others over many centuries) were to ultimately prove unsuccessful the fact that he was deputed to represent the West in this debate gives some sense of his importance.

On a more material plane the chapel which he left for us to admire was exquisite. There were very clear echoes of Charlemagne's own Palatine Chapel at Aachen built contemporaneously, one of the great sights of Europe which I happened upon on one of my earliest hitchhiking explorations of Europe in adolescence. Like at Aachen the focal point for the oratory lay under a central dome. Acknowledged to be the masterpiece at Germigny the dome was brilliantly lined with tiny pieces of coloured mosaic. The overall impression was very different from the later medieval churches....more oriental with a sense of reaching back to a different age in Western Europe. These edifices trigger the question when did the eastern and western church architectural styles bifurcate, the western church becoming ever more elongated in the nave and rectangular in the apse (the so-called Latin cross) whilst the eastern retains a more symmetrical pattern (cruciform Greek cross) with, as in this example, a magnificent hemispherical dome above the altar. This Carolingian architectural style with its conscious use of Byzantine elements which were themselves modelled on Roman precursors is a survival of classical ideas of structure and form shared by east and west. Thereafter the west would go its own way and develop a new gothic tradition seeding the great medieval cathedrals which follow. I lingered in the graveyard taking in the beauty of the cruciform chapel's form, the tranquility of a rural French summer's day and the sense of reaching across the ages to what some historians have dubbed the foundation of modern Europe.

Returning to our route along the banks of the Loire we moved forward in time just under a thousand years to be greeted by the massive turrets of the Chateau of Sully sur Loire. Its impressive form appears the epitome of a Chateau of the Loire built in the 18th century in this case as a true castle to guard an important crossing point on the river. After a fine riverside meal near our chambres d'hotes that evening I looked up its history to learn that the writer Voltaire had been a guest on two lengthy occasions. His enlightened views had upset the powers that be to such an extent that he had been forced to leave Paris and take refuge here. Candide, his satirical masterpiece has been on my reading list ever since it was recommended by my linguist buddy Ian back in Cambridge days to counter my youthful optimism (which I must admit to having largely retained). For the record I, like Steven Pinker and Hans Rosling, am persuaded by objective empirical evidence of improvement in the wellbeing of my fellow human beings over time. I, unlike Professor PanGloss, do not base this on an a priori belief in a benevolent god! I find it to flow from human endeavour and therefore concur with Candide when, after his shocking travels, he retires to cultivate his garden, the work keeping him and his companions "free of three great evils: boredom, vice, and poverty". As a manifesto for buying a small olive grove this ain't half bad – though I wouldn't bet on it solely as a defence against poverty!

Leaving Sully and the chateaux of the Loire behind we headed east into the heart of the French inland waterway system connecting the three great navigations of the Loire, the Seine and the Rhône. As we cycled in the welcome shade offered by poplar trees lining the river I found myself speculating on why there are so many such linear plantings in France as to make this a notable landscape feature. On the advice of a friend I was maintaining a blog and posted this obsevation. Within 24 hours I had a response from an old family friend who happens to be a forester pointing out they are the result of a deliberate Napoleonic planting policy to create shaded routes to facilitate troop movements....black poplar being favoured for its quick growing characteristics. The instant feedback from followers is one of the delights of a travel blog – and can, as here, enrich the journey. I did find it a struggle to keep up to date at times but especially during the solo legs the write up provided a focus whilst sheltering from midday sun over lunch or in a restaurant bar over the evening meal.

We were now approaching Briare on the massive aqueduct carrying the Canal Lateral across the Loire at this point. This canal was a late addition to the impressive network constructed in 1822 to complete the connection of the Loire with the Rhône basin, hence connecting central and southern France. As the French canal traffic grew exponentially in the nineteenth century the unreliability of Loire navigability this far up-river necessitated the building of an aquaduct to allow canal traffic to change sides of the Loire at Briare to access the Canal Lateral. As a result Briare is a town dedicated to canals with canal basins, hoop like bridges and the aforementioned aqueduct.

Checking into our chambres d'hotes for the night we absorbed the pleasant quayside atmosphere before finding a low key restaurant where the waitress recommended the local white wine, the Cour Cheverny made with the Romorantin grape. We had done some very amateurish wine research over the course of a pretrip 'fine' birthday dinner when a very informative sommelier gave us the basic overview of the division of the Loire into three sections. The lower Loire that leads to the Atlantic mouth of the river goes through the Muscadet region which is dominated by wines of the Melon de Bourgogne grape. The middle Loire is dominated by Chenin blanc and Cabernet franc wines found in the regions around Touraine, Saumur, Chinon and Vouvray. As we were now on the Middle Loire we added this grape type which I had never heard of previously to the list. I won't embarrass myself by trying to describe the wine other than stating its flinty dry excellence! We were heading up-river now towards Sancerre home, par excellence, of the Sauvignon grape characteristic of the upper Loire our destination for the following day.

The French summer sun continued to shine down on us as we made steady progress on greenways following old towpaths alternately along the banks of the wild Loire and the Canal Lateral du Loire. The locks along the latter were charming reminders of the extensive canal traffic of past centuries with a sturdily built lock keeper's cottage beside each flight. More modern transport trappings were the regular cycle service points equipped with large foot driven air-pumps and tools on chains – 'a public good' in the best sense of the words. By now Susannah and I had developed an easy-going rhythm punctuated with refreshment stops when facilities attracted. In a nice example of how the Eurovelo 6 route along Europe's great rivers (the Danube, briefly the Rhine and the Loire) brings new economic life to these once busy routeways we found a canal side seasonal café for lunch that day where we chatted with Dutch holidaymakers on their bikes and marooned English boaters whose rivercruiser was moored up beside us. Apparently there was a problem with a lock up ahead and all canal traffic had been stopped pending its repair which explained why we had seen no pleasure craft moving the last day or two. Cycling on we quietly celebrated the freedom of being in control of our own progress. The afternoon shadows were lengthening as the hill on which Sancerre is perched came into view. It was the weekend and mindful that Sancerre might be busy we had booked ahead a little hotel beside the river at the bottom of the hill. We were a little put out to find an absence of any sign of life at the hotel. Indeed it all felt a little desolate sandwiched in between the canal and the arches of a massive aqueduct but eventually we got a response to our telephone calls and were allowed into a perfectly pleasant traditional little French hotel. Keen to walk up the hill we didn't linger and ascended via a path through woods towards Sancerre proper. The 312m chalky hill on which the village is perched really does tower over the surrounding countryside with spectacular views. The final approach carried a gradient warning addressed to cyclists which vindicated Susannah's decision to take a room at the bottom. As the old town centre came into view music could be heard and the whole place felt en fete in a low key sort of way. We joined an extended family of locals outside one of many café-bars and were delighted to see a blackboard listing local producers of different Sancerre whites allowing us to climb the hill metaphorically in a wine 'flight' of ascending vineyards. Our delightful neighbours were full of chat whilst keeping an eye on children and grandchildren respectively insisting we shared their local nibbles – hams and cheeses to die for! It took us a while to tear ourselves away to go all of 50 metres to an adjourning restaurant to continue in similar vein. After a late summer evening stroll we were admiring the view from the terrace of the chateau at the top when I found myself wondering why wine making parts of the world are so often very attractive and whether this was connected with the ecology of grape production requirements, the prosperity that wine production generally is associated with or perhaps the effects of the product on the beholder. But whatever the reason some of the most beautiful places I have visited have been amidst vineyards and the hill of Sancerre with its panoramic views over the pastoral Loire valley below in the crepuscular light was certainly up there. We wandered back down enjoying the scented late evening air to find our desolate little hotel had been transformed by the act of food preparation led by Madame in a very traditional way which rendered it more of an auberge with a discerning clientele. After a comfortable night the sumptuous breakfast served the following morning had some of the best home made jams of the trip. A glass of Sancerre in the future will always bring back happy memories of the fete on the hill of chalk above the Loire.

Our route followed the flood dyke on the bank of the Loire with open views of the approaching abbey church tower of La Charity sur Loire on the opposite bank. A fine medieval bridge carried us across into a buzzing market day scene in this well visited attractive old town. The medieval abbey church remains impressively massive despite being reduced to a surviving transept and chancel by severe fire damage nearly 500 years ago. The location for this medieval abbey is no coincidence – the bridge at Charitie was an important crossing point of the Loire carrying one of the four main pilgrimage routes towards Santiago de Compostela in the Middle Ages. This route was used by pilgrims coming from the north (Scandinavians) and east (Poles and Germans) and ran from the important abbey of Vezelay which allegedly held the relics of Mary Magdalene to the north east before passing south west to Limoges. This was one of three major routes running South West converging by the Spanish border whilst the most east-west route via Arles crossed through the Pyrenees to join up with the other routes near Pamplona in northern Spain. Given my plan to travel through Italy following the Via Francigena pilgrimage route I was intrigued by this (brief) connection with the celebrated Camino de Santiago.

When it comes to pilgrimage my received image from childhood was largely based on Chaucer's Canterbury Tales. Later, based in Nepal, I acquired some first-hand insight into the nature of traditional pilgrimage whilst walking the Annapurna Circuit. We had crossed the Thorong La, the 5416m high point of the route before descending to Muktinath, a sacred Hindu site dedicated to the God Vishnu, considered to be one of his eight most sacred shrines. This, as is so often the case in the Himalayas, is also a Buddhist power place where Guru Rimpoche is said to have meditated en route to Tibet where he is credited with introducing the Buddhist dharma. As we made our way down the trail designed for caravans of yaks crossing in two single files several thousand pilgrims were making their way up, walking in family and village groups which filled the trail. So much so that where the trail crossed the river Gandaki by way of a typical Nepali pedestrian suspension bridge it would be sometimes necessary to wait half an hour for a gap to permit safe crossing. On a later Himalayan pilgrim trek to the great August full moon gathering on the banks of the high altitude lake of Gosaikund I bedded down for the night with fellow pilgrims on the floor of a Buddhist temple. I'll never forget the transformation to the temple as all formality gave way to the bivouac spirit of families in transit enjoying the break in life's routines that pilgrimage brings to those for whom paid holidays are unimaginable.

Such traditional pilgrimage is a far cry from romantic hiking trips. The wonderfully titled and conceived first book by Robert Macfarlane "Mountains of the Mind' (Macfarlane 2009) explains how the culture of romantic walking in the mountains developed in part as a side trip in the Alps from the Grand Tour. As children we walked in the Lake District every Easter in a tradition which in the case of my father and uncle could be traced back to the Liverpool Institute School Camp at Troutal in the Duddon Valley founded by HH Symonds, then their headmaster but who would go on to become a founding figure in the Lake District National Park. 'There's not a trouble that can't be walked off by a good day in the Lakes' was a family byword. My father's dying words to me after commenting on our seeing Everest together expressed simply a mild regret not to have spent more time in the Lakes. So a modern yet still romantic notion of mountain walking was drummed into me from an early age. I therefore feel able to state with some confidence that the contrast could not be greater between the bustle of a traditional pilgrimage and the sublime calm of a mountain hike. I had no idea whether the Via Francigena would resemble the former but it felt like something to sample.

All this was still some way off as the extraordinary architectural ensemble of La Charité came into focus. The nave had all but disappeared save for one wall shored up with domestic houses built from the stone remains. The streets around were filled with local visitors enjoying market day in the summer sun. This was the first physical evidence of Cluny we had encountered on the trip, the power base of the Benedictine order which dominated monastic Christianity in medieval Europe between 910 and 1130. This 'daughter church' was second only to Cluny, which had been the biggest church in Christendom at this time and lay on my route south. Charitie was officially inaugurated in 1106 by Pope Paschal 2nd, who was negotiating with the Byzantines some 300 years after Theodulf of Germigny-de-Pre, still trying to resolve the great Schism! A surviving original stone relief sculpture designed as a Tympanum above the door depicts the three Magi worshipping the Christ Child.

There was a quality to this medieval stone sculpture which spoke of another age. The faces of the three Magi came to life when inspected with an Old Testament quality which was uncanny. Staring at them I realised it was their eyes which lent them life in a way I had not previously seen in medieval figures. I have subsequently learnt that some medieval sculptures have traces of soft metal in their eye sockets which would have housed glass eyes so I suspect this life-like quality of medieval sculpture was once more widespread. Be that as it may my visit to la Charitie was one of those fleeting glimpses into another era when one occasionally escapes the tyranny of time.

Life back out in the sunshine was more mundane but no less enjoyable as we lunched next to a mounted stuffed wild boar head which allowed me to illustrate my blog with a faux image of my encounter in the forests of Fontainebleau. We eventually tore ourselves away, returning across the Loire to head South to its confluence with the River Allier. The Loire along this stretch was magnificently wild but sadly plans to stay by the confluence in a Bed and Breakfast hosted by a man who offered naturalist trips by canoe came to nought as he cancelled our Booking.com reservation at the last minute due to a rival commitment. This gave us something of an accommodation problem with no obvious riverside settlement to head for. Booking.com having taken away now gave back as I identified a moored river boat offering accomodation at just the right place. The enterprising owner 'Jerome' of the

'Petit Bayou' in the spirit of his namesake's book 'Three Men in a Boat' had given his a lick of paint and posted it as a romantic getaway for two! The spartan on board facilities (a cold tap in the galley and a chemical bucket toilet) were supplemented by the fantastic wetroom shower facility maintained presumably at council expense in the neighbouring 'snac' bar-tabac serving a mooring for 10-20 boats. There the lovely proprietor (previously married to an Englishman outside Derby) was able to serve us beer for post ride refreshment and excelled by providing a bottle of white wine. This permitted a deck-top sundowner on which I had insisted in recognition of the unique solution to tonight's accommodation conundrum. As the twilight enfolded us here by the confluence it felt like we had reached la France Profonde! Dinner required a short exploration of the riverbank offerings but once we had settled to the idea that there was no middle choice between a pizza and a three course meal we took the latter and ate well! I'm not sure our rather leisurely day on this stretch of the Loire had fully earned it but I recall lying down in a rather cramped cabin beside my beloved and passing out feeling replete!

Waking on board was novel and encouraged us to get going with yet another memorable cycle aqueduct experience (across the impressive River Allier far below) as we set our sights on Nevers and thence Decize where, continuing the nautical theme, we were booked into a new marina hotel. The day began well with a breakfast stop at a boulangerie with outdoor seating clearly aimed at the itinerant cycling market. Over coffee we were joined by a delightful couple, she on a clearly vintage Peugeot bicycle. It turned out they were from Brittany and her bicycle had been a parental gift for her 12th birthday some 40 odd years previous. Her yellow vest (this was actually one year before the 'gilets jaunes' grass roots protest movement took off) sported on the back an arrow pointing out to her offside when riding with the reminder written in bold below '1.5 metres' – the distance in law a French driver must leave by way of a gap when overtaking a cyclist. The British Highway Code reads 'leave plenty of room' which, if being interpreted by an irate Somerset commuter on a narrow lane with cyclists in his way, may mean as little as a hairsbreadth. I like the 1.5 metre rule – everybody knows where they stand (or fall)! I enjoyed the exchange of journey info so much that I was a couple of kilometres up the cycle path when I realised that I'd forgotten to pay. The race back and subsequent catch up of Susannah reminded me I had something in reserve for the challenges ahead after our relaxed passage a deux came to an end.

This day's section took us into a rare centre of nineteenth century industrialisation in France. The key ingredients for early industrialisation are coal, iron ore and access to the sea. France is actually rather poorly served in terms of coal reserves relative to many of its Western European competitors amongst which Britain was pre-eminent. This helps to explain how the British flourished in the nineteenth century and early twentieth century age of empire compared with the French. It also helps to explain French reliance on nuclear power and the industry leading expertise of EDF now contracted to the British nuclear site nearest to our Bristol home in Somerset. We had already cycled past two nuclear reactors, Dampierre and Belleville, of the four on the Loire alone. Each had well designed visitor centres and the cycle route had clearly benefited from EDF sponsorship at each site. The investment in hearts and minds was presumably designed to keep the French public on board with nuclear in a way long abandoned in the UK where nuclear power stations in my experience nowadays feel secretive and nuclear has become a 'dirty word'. Personally I was persuaded long ago that the scientific wonders of the nuclear age should be harnessed for peaceful energy generation despite the longlived nature of the radioactive waste so produced. However sustainable sources are growing exponentially and it may be soon possible for them to supply all our needs at the end of the carbon age but as yet this is far from certain hence the need, in my view, for some continuing nuclear capacity in responsible hands.

An opportunity arose to deviate to an eleventh century chapel, dedicated to St Etienne, a couple of kilometres off our trail which I was keen to take up. From the approach down a muddy lane the chapel initially appeared to be an outhouse of a local farm. However on entering I learnt that this mistaken impression was lent by the fact that it had been pressed into service as a barn after the French Revolution. However it had now been recognised as a national monument. Inside a simple single nave design with lime washed walls gave this isolated little chapel a wonderful sense of cool calm. I was not alone finding the place affecting....the simple stone altar bore sundry messages from passing travellers some simply commemorating their journey others commending themselves in the manner of pilgrims to a higher power. As I emerged back out into the brilliant midday sun there was a lingering sense of leaving sanctuary, a powerful metaphysical feeling in my experience. A little reminder of the olive grove at journey's end - part refuge, part sanctuary in my mind.

However that all lay a long way ahead as I rejoined Susannah for a hot afternoon spinning along the canal towpath towards Decize. The Loire at this point widened out enormously allowing for a marina and much besides. We found our rather boxy modern hotel as advertised on the marina and set out to walk into Decize situated on an island in the river. The pleasant riverside walk led to what had once been a prosperous town which had now fallen on harder times. Frequency of restaurants in a town indicates both the strength of the tourist dollar and the extent of expendable income available for eating out locally. Given the high prioritisation for gastronomic activities amongst the French the lack of restaurants in Decize seemed to me a key indicator of its hard times. Returning to the modern Marina we realised we had started from the best option around, ate a typically good meal and turned in for a rather hot and stuffy night.

After a couple of days following canal banks we would now be climbing above the Loire to Bourbon-Lancy, a medieval hilltop town set above a 19th century spa town below. After several days on canal riverbanks we were unused to climbing and coming as it did towards the end of day we were definitely puffing by the time we pulled into Bourbon. This turned out to be a very pretty town where we had booked into an old spa hotel. Since the Tour de France was now hotting up (figuratively and literally) I was keeping my eye out at afternoon refreshment stops for screens. Generally it would be on in the background and that afternoon as we sought directions to our hotel at a bar-tabac I noted it looked like being a particularly exciting run in. The hotel turned out to ooze faded grandeur with an impressive staircase which led us into a sepulchre like reception area. After checking in we were just entering the lift laden with panniers when we encountered the first of many aged fellow residents complete with Zimmer frame and a faintly severe faded elegance which was not unimpressive. Exchanging polite bonnes apres-midi's madame feigned to ignore our sweaty cycle gear as we slipped out of the lift gratefully into our suite. Presumably the declining popularity of the spa (which was clad in scaffolding suggesting it was undergoing a long deferred renovation) had reduced demand to the point that a vacant suite could only be filled at the modest rates we were paying on Booking.com. So it was that I was sat butt naked cooling down after our exertions in a grand suite enjoying the closing stages of that day's Tour de France live on the wall mounted screen feeling rather pleased with myself. The image of me so seated (taken from behind thankfully) posted on the family What's App group by my wife lives on in the memory of brothers-in-law in particular!

Our evening exploration took us back up into the medieval town which was a stronghold of the Bourbons as the name suggests. The House of Bourbon are one of those European royal houses who crop up time and again in the annals. The first fiefdom of the family recorded in the 900's centred on the nearby Allier, a tributary of the Loire. Masters of the strategic marriage they subsequently crop up all over southern Europe in different periods ruling Spain, Naples, Sicily amongst others and still can be found in some anachronistic survivals - the current Grand Duke of Luxembourg is in part a Bourbon. Of course to a modern the term conjures up a chocolate sandwich biscuit. It turns out that this is the result of a marketing ploy by Peek Freans. Mr Peek had been a ships' biscuit maker in Devon but in one of those 19th century business success stories from the era I now refer to as globalisation mark 1 with his partner Mr Frean the company rapidly expanded to become THE biscuitmakers of the empire. They had enjoyed great success with 'the Garibaldi' but less so with their new chocolate sandwich biscuit in 1910 going under the frankly racist name of the 'Creola' ie the mixed race biscuit! So it got the royal whitewash treatment with its rebranding as a Bourbon and the rest, as they say, is history. Indeed it remains in the top five favourite British biscuits outdoing its illustrious predecessor the Garibaldi which has slipped down the rankings in modern times. Meanwhile in Bourbon-Lancy that evening the medieval walls and surviving timber framed houses provided a romantic backdrop for an al fresco biscuit-free hilltop supper.

The following morning back down at the spa breakfast we re-entered our French version of 'Waiting for Godot' as various elderly clients were assisted to their places, mostly alone but for an occasional genteel female pair. One old gentleman was serving himself (to a morning aperitif) but most were served at their table by the long suffering female maitre d' (apparently there is no female form for the term!). It was just too darned complicated for most to serve themselves with their favourite selection from the buffet whilst juggling sticks, zimmers and breakfast trays. Abandoned by my wife this dystopian vison led me to a brief cogitation on my newly semi-retired status and the distance in time or headspace between my breakfast companions and myself. Unresolved and mildly downcast by the prospect I was pleased to be chivvied on by Susannah who had reappeared kitted up and ready for the off as we had a biggish day ahead of us.

Today was to be our last on the Loire, the last great 'sauvage' river in Europe, by which the French mean 'wild' in the sense of undammed. Certainly on a particularly deserted meander this morning as we sat sheltering from the midday sun in the shade of the well forested bank looking out across mudflats on the far bank one wouldn't have been surprised to see a croc or two basking in the sun or a family of elephants taking the waters! On reaching Digoin we headed across the river on our last aqueduct carrying the Canal du Centre towards the Saone and Rhône navigations and thence to the Mediterranean...a reminder that we were skirting the Massif Central to our south through which passes the European watershed between the Atlantic/Baltic and Mediterranean basins. I bade farewell to the Loire with a shallow swim off the riverside walk below Digoin where we ate a packed lunch. An exhibition of nature photography emphasised the wild nature of the river and the excellent birding to be had along its banks. We'd seen our fair share of herons, geese and the occasional kite. I certainly intend to be back to complete the Orleans - Nantes western leg of the Loire a velo.

Heading to the east of the Loire along the Canal du Centre we pushed on towards Parai le Monial. According to Booking.com accommodation was in short supply and we had been pushed somewhat upmarket into a very tasteful chambres d'hotes place right in the heart of old town with a price to match. No matter as our conjugal cycling was drawing towards a parting of the ways so we were happy to treat ourselves. That afternoon the obligatory Tour de France catch up, which had become part of the daily ritual, was enjoyed in a café at our destination before commencing the search for our rooms. Geraint Thomas, our new Welsh cycling hero was having another excellent day and comments about the young French challenger Julian Alaphillipe were rather muted. Incidentally I hadn't encountered a shred of anti-English hostility - speaking reasonable French I generally find this to be the case. It's undoubtedly a generalisation but one that holds in most situations – the more people think you, the foreigner, are trying to make the effort to experience their culture the more welcoming people become. The worst I would accuse the French of is limited to the bourgeoise who (having been the inspiration for the term) are particularly snobbish. Otherwise I rather enjoy the French sang-froid and the accompanying dry sense of humour.

The pressure on the accommodation in Parai was understandable once we realised the large numbers of youngish families wandering around with name badges were all attending the same evangelical conference (of 4000 souls!). The traditional church was huge and notable for a series of time boards carefully and meaningfully presented in the main side aisle. They presented 20 millennia of human history in a parallel series of timelines variously describing changing philosophical, political and artistic movements with at the very heart of the exercise the timeline describing the names and reigns of successive Popes in an unmistakable statement of power and continuity! It was a stark reminder (as intended) of the longevity and influence of the Catholic Church.

Whilst Parai had enjoyed a quietish few centuries as an outlying religious centre associated directly with Cluny, all that changed in 1920 when a nun met Jesus here, in the flesh, so to speak. Now the Chapel of the Visitation our next port of call was thronged with conference attendees bringing a palpable sense of religious tension to the space. I hadn't experienced anything quite like this since Lhasa! We retreated from the spiritual to the gluttonous at a Michelin Bib restaurant which lived upto expectations that night. We noted our Brittany cycling friends at the next table – as my father used to say 'always a good sign to be eating where the French go'!

As we cycled out early the next morning we passed the prayer festival site where unlike the sort of festivals I find myself at there was plenty of early morning life with spontaneous standing prayer circles rather strikingly in evidence. It turns out that the revolutionary plans for the demise of the Catholic Church in France in 1789 were unsuccessful and it appears to be staging yet another comeback.

As we headed toward the mining region of Montchanin between the Loire and the Saone basins that day cutting across increasingly rolling country which felt fresh and green despite the hot weather I found myself reflecting on the resilience of religion in Western

Europe. I think my father fully expected it to die in his lifetime having been a fully paid up member of the largely left leaning interwar generation many of whom atheistic, like him, rejected the religion of their parents to pursue progressive ideas which resulted in the UK in the postwar Atlee-led Labour government and the creation of that great British institution the NHS. Cycling through France that day I wished my parents were still alive to hear of our journey in their tracks – both had enjoyed cycle holidays on the continent back in the late 1930s the previous peak in popularity for cycling. Indeed my choice of tertiary educational subjects was largely down to parental influence...my father's early introduction of us three boys to the interesting experiences to be had travelling, enjoying different cultures and visiting archaeological sites clearly fed into my first choice of degree archaeology and anthropology whilst my mother's radiography career in the NHS sowed the seed of my graduate application to medical school. My subsequent career has in retrospect been an attempt to resolve both, the yin of 'global health' research and the yang of 'community child health'. It has been my experience that my parents have never really left me – even when I have actively pushed them away – they drift back into your head in unsought ways! Having observed the last minutes of many people's lives as a doctor I have always been struck by how commonly people seem to sense a return to their beloved mother and/or father in the moments preceding death. A steep unexpected climb now we had entered hilly mining territory put paid to these ruminations.

As the afternoon progressed our route became progressively more and more squeezed between the canal, a main train line, the N70, a major trunk road headed to the south of France and our Eurovelo 6 cycle route. The only wildlife we saw in this transport corridor that afternoon was in the canal but was no less spectacular for that - the prolific catfish population which had presumably just bred producing swirling black balls of baby catfish with a pronounced swarming behaviour. The transport congestion gave us a navigational challenge as we hit our first major roundabout in the last couple of kilometres before arriving at our accomodation for the night - a typically well-appointed French service station hotel complete with swimming pool shared with many motorists but at least two other cycling couples with whom of course we bonded. We were leaving the Eurovelo route the following day so our route didn't coincide with either couple – rather satisfyingly the three couples were each heading off in a different direction. For us this was a decisive turn right southwards onto a greenway leading down through southern Burgundy following an old train line complete with viaduct to ease our route into the basin of the Saone via its right tributary, la Grosne.

After a week cycling the central French canal system the rolling hills, the drama provided by some increasingly rocky outcrops and the exhilaration of crossing the impressively long viaduct over a wooded valley to emerge into some sort of promised land covered in vineyards stretching across the rolling landscape in the afternoon light all felt rather revelatory. To place this in context back in the Bristol planning stages, once I had Susannah's sign up for the Loire, I had set about identifying a Chateau to stay in for a night as necessarily swanky trophy accommodation on the Loire! Sus did casually let slip that she had been put up at a 'classic Chateau of the Loire' where I was led to believe she had been wined and dined in some style by the previous but one man (he of the Harley Davidson....with whom I certainly wasn't competing....but nevertheless one remains mindful of previous offers!). Now I had slowly come to realise that the vast majority of the 'classic Chateaux' are actually between Orleans and Nantes on the lower Loire and when I had searched on Chateaux I couldn't find much within striking distance of our route...until one got well down into southern Burgundy where a privately owned Chateau stood out with an owner occupier host offering Bed and Breakfast (and his own estate Burgundy wine) who, by all reviewers' accounts, was a character. So, largely because of this, we were turning south before hitting the Saone taking a chance on this lesser travelled route which explains my excitement on encountering such wonderful country. The route was idyllic, following a disused railway line between stone built villages oozing with charm in the afternoon sun. Across the vineyard clad valley the rather more substantial village of Saint Boll slowly approached with a church tower and a rather fine looking French Second Empire style 19th century detached house complete with baroque balustrades and 'mansard' roof (that typical French look with four sloping sides, each of which becomes steeper halfway down). This turned out gratifyingly to be our accommodation for the night. I joined Monsieur le Patron in the bar restaurant across the road where we companionably caught the end of the day's cycle racing together over a biere presse before rejoining Sus by the elegant swimming pool at the bottom of the lawn. This was the life. We had got our daily washing chores off pat by now and the elegantly painted blue shutters provided the perfect drying rack for our sweat encrusted cycle gear rinsed and resplendent again drying in the still warm southern French sun. Dinner was superb as we were now in Burgundy one of the great centres of French cuisine. A perfect day knowing we had 'cracked it'.

So much so that the next day we lingered for a morning swim after a breakfast to die for (homemade jams to go with elegant pastries which could only be possibly justified by cyclists such as ourselves!). The old railway ran between two lines of trees and for the first time since leaving Bristol three weeks earlier a few raindrops fell as we dawdled across the Burgundy countryside admiring the massive white Charolais cattle characteristic of the area. Apparently there are 1.5 million head of these cattle in France. That's a lot of beef and a lot of methane. Somehow I can't see

Burgundy amongst the early adopters of the plant based diet which we must move towards to mitigate climate change.

We left our cycle path at Cormatin, winding our way along a quiet D road through another idyllic village at Chapaize then into a densely forested area before a gentle climb led us round the corner to be confronted by the giant turrets of Chateau des Nobles. As we cycled up the drive to Susannah's final destination we passed a battered old Renault parked haphazardly across the driveway opposite a series of outbuildings which were clearly in use as a working estate before rounding the corner turret to find the main entrance bedecked with flowers, a lawn stretching ahead towards an elegant seating area, a rustic shelter housing a bbq area and towering over the whole ensemble those fairytale turreted towers one at each corner of Chateau de Nobles. We had arrived!

Monsieur Bertrand was sat up a short flight of stone stairs just outside the main door set in the curtain wall in the shade of one of the massive towers sporting a large floppy hat against the bright Burgundy sun. I was delighted to finally meet him having corresponded via email during the trip planning. The issue which had led to some dialogue was the all important one of le diner! At Susannah's insistence I had enquired as to the restaurant options locally and been informed that the recommended restaurant was 5 kilometres away. Now my wife is adamant that she will not get back on a bike after a vinous evening meal. I think this relates to an unfortunate incident early in our relationship when at my insistence we had lingered for one too many glasses of white wine on a summer's evening at a charming dockside bistro in Bristol. The cycle route home that evening required the negotiation of some train lines set into the quay with the predictable result that Sus's cycle wheel got wrenched from her control by the rails throwing her to the ground. The subsequent ride home was an exercise in gritted teeth fury for her and recriminations for me. It turned out the next day she had fractured her collar bone! The incident left two enduring legacies – a newfound respect for my wife's tenacity especially when angered and a no cycling rule once evening relaxation has set in! In Bertrand's response to my enquiry he let it be known that the nearer restaurant at 2 kilometres whilst walkable would be 'far inferior' and that he could 'give me a car' to go to the better restaurant at 5 kilometres! I kept reading and rereading the phrase he employed in French, even going so far as to check it in the dictionary (and with Google translate!) but I kept coming up with the same meaning – he would give me, not a lift in the car, but the car itself.

Anyway here we were 'in the flesh' so to speak and Bertrand was proving to be as charming and urbane as he was in his written communication. Casually indicating the old Renault and remembering our correspondence he explained that ' we have three cars, one for me, one for madame and one for le chien

....mais le chien est mort' so we were welcome to use it to go to the restaurant (at 5 kilometres naturellement).

It was then explained that due to a rodent infestation in the roof of the converted outbuilding where he usually housed his paying guests we were to be accommodated in the family guest accommodation in the tower. We were shown up to our room through the gateway into a massive stone hallway with glimpses of an elegant salon beyond as we turned up a winding stone staircase which led to the first floor where we entered the tower via the medieval roof space. Large enough to house a tennis court this was an intricate lacework of wooden beams which we were informed provided a home to his other valued visitors - a roost of bats. The solution to the modern bathroom problem (presumably the original owners used a garderobe type arrangement ie a hole in the floor of a small projecting room) was a sauna like cabin constructed in this roof space. Bertrand then threw open the door to the upper tower bedroom a beautiful circular stone chamber occupying the whole cross section of the tower. It was flooded in light from two large windows with a fireplace of baronial proportions over which was a striking oil painting of an ancestor in full armour. Bertrand proceded to issue us with careful instructions as to prevent disturbance of the roosting bats...the only rules seemingly in operation in what was otherwise a haven of relaxed tolerance. The tour included the winery where Bertrand produced his own rustic white Bourgogne (hard to compete in terms of reliable quality with modern winemaking technology he confided) before we were left to our own devices exploring the grounds.

I of course was delighted that the Chateau was proving as colourful as I had hoped. Susannah was still coming to terms with sharing her quarters with bats. I decided against sharing my bat story from my days as a young anthropology student with the Ashaninka Amerindians in the Peruvian Amazon. Falling asleep in the village plaza (a clearing created in the forest where temporary wooden huts were situated) after a long shamanic ayahuasca session I was awoken in the night by my friend Mike (already thinning up top) disturbing a vampire bat attempting to feed on his scalp. The following morning I discovered two clean incisions in my big toe where the bat had inserted its razor-sharp incisors to feed on my blood. I had forgotten to enquire as to the species from Bertrand but despite France's proud claim to provide a home for 34 species of bat I thought that Vampires were unlikely to be amongst them. However as the afternoon shadows lengthened and a chilled glass of extremely local Bourgogne had been enjoyed Madame relaxed into the adventure permitting herself to be driven (carefully) in the dog car back to Chapaize for a suitably gastronomic Burgundian dinner!

Sunday morning we went back down to Chapaize on our bikes for the morning market (suitably artisanal if somewhat overrun by the arrival of a tourist coach).

The church was surprisingly substantial for such a modest hamlet with a striking high tower which confusingly looked Italianate. All became clear on reading this had been a Benedictine priory church built by masons from Lombardy. Inside the three naved space in pale stone had a pleasantly sparse cool feel. We explored the forest and a couple of neighbouring villages on our way back but the Chateau remained the star of the show. What a backdrop for Sunday afternoon Tai Chi on the lawn in front of the massive towers and cycle maintenance in the barn outbuilding where I also found the box pre-delivered for packing Susannah's rented bike. After the slight confusion with the cycle delivery to our hotel in Lyon the pick-up was much smoother. All we had to do was place the bike in the box and the courier company did the rest (with Bertrand's kind cooperation). We enjoyed our last night in a medieval Burgundian tower (no bat incidents) and breakfast in the salon with Bertrand and Françoise before suddenly it was time to part. Bertrand in a final act of kindness was driving Susannah to Macon for the TGV Trainline to Paris and thence via London to Bristol whilst I was pedalling south to the heart of medieval monasticism at Cluny. Over breakfast Bertrand had sketched out his take on medieval monastic politics, focussing on the Cistercian breakaway from the Benedictine order which had occurred locally. Like most such movements this was an attempt to go back to basics, returning to the simple rural working life once advocated by Benedict, which appeared to resonate with Bertrand having grown up on an olive farm in Morocco and pursued a presumably successful career as an art dealer before returning to the land in the family chateau! Promising to send a bottle of my oil over from Greece I bade him farewell before parting from my wife as casually as we both could manage. It's better that way for both of us. I followed them down the drive to start the next stage of the journey – into the mountains.

Chapter 4. Through the Savoie Alps

I expect readers of this story will be familiar with that conflict of emotions as freedom beckons in middle life. The undeniable attractions of agency, lack of compromise and to be honest self indulgence initially beckon countered by the loss of companionship and the risks of abandonment which loom up like the inevitable monster encountered in any quest. As a "work hard, play hard" type one of the challenges of my transition to a third life was always going to be handling the move to 'moderation in all things' long advocated by my father, most of the philosophers and certainly the world religions. The opposite corner however make up for their lack of numbers and, lets face it, low life expectancy with a sang froid that was encapsulated for me by my lapel button during student days reading 'Je ne regrette rien' around a central image, not of the author of these lines the Little Sparrow, Edith Piaf, but of Rolling Stone Keith Richards. The siren attractions of excess played out with predictable consequences in that rock and roll generation with some notable exceptions amongst whom 'Keef' himself of course ranks.

Some years ago I sat cross legged at the back of a prayer hall in Kathmandu listening to the sage advice of my friend Greg's guru Chokyi Niyma Rinpoche at his annual seminar for foreigners. In the pause during which questions are invited I found myself enquiring what advice he had for those of us in the west who struggled with the temptations of our materially wealthy society. Rinpoche leaned in to hear his Danish translator's version of my query and after a brief exchange the Dane sent Rinpoche's responding enquiry neutrally but precisely aimed back down the hall to me....'Alcohol or Drugs?'. 'Alcohol' I responded and after a theatrical pause, during which the audience seemed to hold its breath waiting for the sage's all seeing wisdom, Rinpoche responded 'AA'. Now I have enormous respect for Chokyi Niyma but I have never bought into the 12 steps and in particular step 3 to make 'a decision to turn our will and our lives over to the care of God as we understood Him'. I could readily see how this maps well onto a Buddhist conception of sentient beings. But after half a lifetime's introspection on the whole issue of spirituality I concluded on a later visit to Kathmandu that Buddhism did indeed require the sort of 'leap of faith' I had first heard identified as the defining difference between the epistemology of science and religion in a seminar series I took back in Cambridge days. And my rationally trained mind doesn't accept leaps of faith. So I can't say I heeded this particular piece of advice and continue to fall prey to temptation from time to time. Returning to the theme of the quest of course temptation plays at least as big a role as 'the Monster'.

In terms of the European alcohol consumption pattern the planned life journey entailed a move from the Northern 'Scandinavian model' of binge drinking (think Glasgow.......or Liverpool for that matter!) to a southern 'Mediterranean model' of sipping. Message to self as I set out down the greenway that morning could be summed up as 'sip don't gulp'! So it seemed strangely appropriate that having regained the main north-south cycleway through southern Burgundy that the first stop should be Cluny. Monasticism did much to take forward viniculture and its proponents attempted to teach us all to sip whilst falling guilty to the odd gulp themselves within those cloistered walls!

The Catholic centres I had encountered to date had been satellites founded by the Benedictine mothership Cluny. Today's ride led straight to the heart of that institution which wielded enormous influence in the credo state of Christianity during the early Middle Ages between the 10th-12th centuries CE. All the Carolingian institutions left by Charlemagne's Holy Roman Empire came under its patronage. With a reach extending from Spain to England Cluny recruited and controlled a vast network of appointees ensuring influence across the continent. Not sure what to expect I arrived in the small town nestling in the fertile Burgundy vale and following signage to the Centre de Ville found at its heart an enormous void with a single transept - all that remains of the largest church in Christendom through the middles ages. The building would not be bettered in size until the Italian Renaissance by St Peter's in Rome. But what faced me was just like visiting English monastic centres such as Tintern Abbey. What Henry VIII did in the late 1500's was finally achieved in France in 1790 as a revolutionary mob destroyed what had over 800 years decayed into a symbol of the 'ancienne regime'. I filled my water bottles from an attractive medieval public drinking fountain beside a shady square where I ate some bread and cheese and contemplated the dust of once great institutions. A local arts cooperative offered their shop space as a meeting place but in the mid afternoon heat it was deserted. I had enjoyed the distraction of visiting a place of historic importance but a sense of decay amplified the pangs of loneliness which life back on the road alone was channelling with renewed vigour after so pleasant a conjugal interlude - it was time to hit the road.

The cycle route soon thereafter plunges into the longest cyclable tunnel in Europe – the 3 kilometre tunnel of Bois Clare. Our recent host Bertrand, a self-confessed bat lover, had expressed some concern as to whether the tunnel would be passable given its local reputation as a bat refuge. As I blogged a sign at the entrance informs riders that it closes in the winter months when the bats hibernate; a reasonable compromise it seems to me....I hope Bertrand would agree! As I plunged into the darkness on came my light sensitive LED front light – a gizmo that seemed a luxury at the outset of this ride but which would come to be an essential safety aid in the weeks ahead.

Emerging into dense woodland at the end of the tunnel I started to refind my own tempo and lose myself in the traverse of increasingly hilly countryside. Stopping to consult the map I realised I was approaching the valley of the Saone proper above which rear some high bluffs of which none are more dramatic than the one I was looking across at, Solutre, a limestone outcrop made famous by President Mitterand's annual ascent to commune with his resistance past. Below these outcrops and dating back to the Romans are vineyards climbing the steep short slopes around the neighbouring villages of Pouilly and Fuisse. I was feeling strong and a little under challenged on my flat cycle path still following the line of a railway across the southernmost marches of Burgundy. The outcrop looked very do-able about 5 kilometres to the west of me. I had little desire to negotiate the sizeable town of Macon ahead and with the famous Chardonnay appellation of Pouilly Fuisse calling to me I decided, on a whim, to head up towards Solutre.

It was a stiff climb on minor D roads through beautiful manicured vineyards and quiet prosperous villages. Stopping at one for directions I took a refreshing glass of beer whilst checking on accommodation options up ahead. There appeared to be a chambres d'hotes in Pouilly which sounded the perfect solution and I powered up the final climb into an idyllic village perched just below Solutre only to find it shut. Merde! Walking the village I found a high-end wine tasting outlet which was just closing. Michel, the laid back lad on the counter was unphased by the sweaty Englishman in cycling kit enquiring as to the cost of a tasting sample. For €10 he then proceeded to introduce me to the delights of the local Pouilly Fouise working our way down the slopes between the twin villages, sipping vineyard by vineyard. A route I then mirrored largely freewheeling on my bike with the late afternoon air whistling by my senses filled with the light glinting off the great limestone bluff above where it used to be (mistakenly) thought palaeolithic man chased wild horses to their death below. It was indeed an important hunting site for Cro Magnon people but the copious animal skeletons attest simply to the scale of the feasting not the means of hunting.

Around a corner I happened upon an idyllic bistro in a village whose name remains a mystery but suffice to say the poulet plat du jours mopped up the wine and supplied the calories to get me safely down to the banks of the Saone, south of Macon. There, beside a bridge, I found a municipal campsite where I gratefully got my little tent back out and returned to my cycle-tramp life tout seul!

The next morning I woke early (reacquainting myself with the rigours of sleeping on my skeletally minimalist mat) and went the few strides across to the river bank to get my first daylight sighting of this week's riverine companion. Quietly flows the Don they say – an epithet that could have been coined for the Saone. Yet as I gazed across the sluggish river I was reminded that this river formed one of the fault lines which continue to define a European border. Following a period of instability on his death Charlemagne's Carolingian empire was split three ways between his three grandsons by the Treaty of Verdun in 843. One grandson was awarded West Francia which would become France. Another grandson took East Francia around which Germany would eventually coalesce. But the eldest grandson Lothar was granted the central swathe and the title of Emperor as befitted his status stretching from his grandfather's court headquarters in Aachen to the north all the way down to the ancient imperial capital of Rome to the south. This unwieldy and diverse strip of Europe subsequently split again three ways leaving Lorraine in the north and Lombardy in the south. Burgundy in the centre was itself split three ways within 50 years of the treaty. The area to the north west of the Saone persisted as the Duchy of Burgundy with the rich monastic tradition and associated viniculture which I had been enjoying for the last week and remain at the heart of what we now know as France. To the southeast across the river the kingdom of Lower Burgundy would form part of the medieval kingdom of Provence with its administrative centre a long way south at Arles. Whilst to the north-east Upper Burgundy coalesced around the local power base of St Maurice and would after many centuries morph into modern Switzerland. So here was another frontier river crossing marking a border both in space but in some sense in time aswell.

My quest was taking me back in space and time as intended. The river was wide, slow moving and cloaked in a morning mist hinting that the summer would not continue forever. I found a fishing platform on which to do my morning Tai Chi then packed up, shaking a heavy dew off the tent which hadn't been necessary since England. Crossing the river I soon came to the cross-roads I had been looking for where I turned right to head south towards Lyon. There, on cue, was a café offering not only coffee but also a bag of baguettes which had been delivered from the local boulangerie. As I chewed on my baguette washing it down with a large café au lait I enjoyed a Proustian moment as the smell of fresh bread and gallic coffee took me back to family holidays down in Ciboure across the river from St Jean de Luz where for several consecutive years we spent a week staying in a chambres d'hotes. Every morning we took breakfast on the rooftop terrace overlooking the harbour sipping chocolat chaud and café au lait out of steaming bowls chewing on croissants and baguettes. Suffused with these pleasant memories I got back on the bike determined to get some miles under my belt. After a very pleasant hour or two on quiet lanes loosely following the left (East) bank of the Saone southwards I realised the lane I was following was drifting eastward into the Dombes, a region of hundreds of small man-made lakes sitting on clay which had been dug for fish farming. The villages were picturesque and cycling signage indicating preferred quiet lanes kept tempting me too far east. Stopping for a refreshment stop at a village café I was chatting in my schoolboy French with the personable girl running the place when a middle-aged businessman dropped in for a coffee. He was quite intrigued by my mode of transport, and after a short conversation (inevitably about my route), he wished me 'Bon Route..... Courage' in the exceedingly warm and encouraging way I was getting used to across France. As I got back on my bike this word 'Courage' started a line of linguistic thought. One of the many reasons for learning languages other than ones' own is for the insights it gives into what is otherwise the automaticity of the native tongue. 'Courage' in French, though sounding rather different because of the length of the 'a' obviously maps onto the English 'encourage' – both deriving ultimately from the Latin for heart, 'cor'. Now I know enough Greek to know that καρδια is heart. So does cor relate to καρδια? Not directly – there are plenty of Greek loan words in Latin (eg amphora) but cor isn't one of them.

The 19th century world of comparative linguistics traced a family tree for human language much as Darwin was busily tracing the tree of life. This traced linguistic commonalities back to a Proto Indo-European language originating, according to one hypothesis, on the steppes of Asia between the Black and Caspian Seas. This theory points to *kerd as the common root for both. Linguistics formed an important strand in my anthropology studies in the late 1970's, language being considered an exemplar for culture more generally. In reaction to the sort of 19th century diffusionism which generated the Indo-European tree of language and of course has uncomfortable echoes of the Aryan master race and other such racist Nazi rubbish there was a lot of interest in Chomsky's work on generative grammar and programming of the central nervous system which tied in with the structuralist ideas my chums studying English were playing around with. This all feeds into the nature / nurture debate which underpins so much of our never ending struggle to better understand ourselves.

During my doctoral studies in which I describe the epidemiological challenge posed by newborn infants who suffer brain injury during birth in the low income setting of Kathmandu I became fascinated by the emerging science of neuroplasticity. Having started the day with a language class in Nepali (surprisingly manageable due to it being an Indo-Iranian branch member of the Indo-European language family just described) I would then walk to the neonatal unit of the main maternity hospital working with babies who had suffered brain injuries to learn how to prevent them. In my reading I came across microradiographs of complex synaptic webs which demonstrate beautifully the pluripotentiality with which we are born. Those connections which are used and encouraged strengthen and become habitual. Those that we don't use whither away and die through a rather chillingly named process of 'programmed cell death'. A nice example I have used to illustrate this to a generation of medical students brings us back to language. We are all born with the ability to speak any one of the current 6,000 human languages as a native speaker. Beyond about the third year of life those 5,998/9 languages we weren't thoroughly exposed to will never be available to be mastered as a native speaker – if we come to them in later life and devote ourselves to learning one or two we will always speak them with a foreign accent. Those synaptic control mechanisms which allow for the marvellous palatal contortions so as to produce a Khoisan click consonant for example will simply not be there. Experience really does shape the connectivity within the brain. My fellow coffee drinker and I do have different synaptic connections through nurture which led him to wish me Gallic 'courage' which I took as English 'encouragement' but we were born with similar pluripotentialities.

Having rediscovered universality through particularity in this case of language I resolved to stick to my plan of heading south to Lyon and reverted to the Saone via a fast and relatively quiet D road (D933). This smoothed the meanders of the river and regained the bank at Beauregard which was as pretty as the name suggested. The Saone here was wide, a deep blue mirroring the light blue sky studded with fluffy white clouds. Riverside villas of the well to do 19th century bourgeoise seemed to have organically grown out of the manicured riverbank. Forgoing a side trip across the river to Anse I stuck to my D road which cut across another meander of the Saone before regaining the riverbank once again towards Trevoux. By now I was well into the extended French lunchtime and riverside terraces could be glimpsed from the path where lunch was being taken by the bourgeoise. There is something about the French middle class which does make this descriptor apt. Are they any more bourgeois than the English? Maybe we simply see the class foibles more clearly when we look across the channel? Cultural anthropology is premised on the idea that by studying the other we better understand ourselves. Suppressing my hunger pangs and class consciousness I pressed on gratified to find a wide gravel towpath along the bank of the river which solved the routing issue thereafter. I had spent fruitless hours researching route options on this leg unable to confirm a riverside cycle friendly route. Well dear cycling readers there is, I used it and a very good route it proved to be leading me directly to the outskirts of Lyon along the Saone!

As it approaches Lyon the banks get progressively more built up as you might expect. Soon I was riding into the city proper with magnificent vistas across the river over into the old town above. Having rushed through Paris I was determined to explore what Lyon had to offer and rode directly to the huge Place Bellecour (another take on 'heart' I noted) where I orientated myself learning that the Saone's confluence with the Rhône was just round the corner. The plan was to follow the Rhone upstream which meant I would come briefly back on myself in a northerly direction. But that would wait a while – for now the priorities were a bed and a shower after a couple of days on the road. Booking.com took me to a low cost but fairly smart hotel in an unfashionable quarter near the train station. As I booked in the manager recommended a nearby barber's offering a massage that he professed would be beneficial for the spine. Feeling stiff from my night's camping and long day in the saddle I showered and took up his recommendation. The barber was a smooth swarthy looking guy who gestured me into a back room with massage couch. A few minutes later one of the hairdressers I had seen cutting old ladies' hair in the front arrived to pummel me. And pummel me she did, adding in some stretches out of the Thai massage manual, which did the trick. Feeling the proverbial new man I was ready to hit Lyon and immediately happened upon a medieval hospital quarter newly renovated and now buzzing with the after work crowds thronging the cafés. Taking a turn around the extensive restored hospital courtyard it had clearly been a powerful institution and I soon learnt that it had indeed been an important centre of medicine in the Hippocratic and Galenical classical tradition. Galen, a Greek speaking inhabitant of Asia Minor ends up as physician to the Emperor in Rome. Despite his undoubtedly empirical investigations most successfully into anatomy he bequeathed us a theory of medicine limited to the four humours which stayed with us for 1600 years! Francois Rabelais, physician I learnt at this same Lyonais Hospital de Dieu, helped propagate this prevailing paradigm of clinical medicine in the sixteenth century through his own translations of Galen. In addition to translating classical texts he performed anatomical dissections himself, corresponded with Erasmus and wrote some powerful allegorical novels of which the two best known extol the merits of Pantagruelisme as an "eat, drink and be merry" philosophy whilst describing the only rule of the Abbey of Theleme to be 'do what you want'! I didn't hang around in the hospital quarter long enough to discover whether it remains Rabelaisian in the modern era and retreated to the old town in search of a characterful dinner. Sadly, the old alleyways were now sanitised and filled with tourist traps so I kept going until I broke out of the medieval town into a student quarter where I soon found a large café bar serving platters of Lyonais charcuterie and bread washed down by micro brewed ale. Suitably refreshed and revived by friendly banter with locals who were almost too admiring of my endeavour I happened upon a late bar back in the old town on my way back down to my hotel which was the characterful venue which had eluded me earlier in the evening. Having reconciled two drunken lovers who had been having a tiff (not quite sure how that came about!) I managed to tear myself away and retreat to my bed somewhat the worse for wear.

The next morning was devoted to the museum of the confluence which is an architectural gem literally on the Rhône/Saone confluence. Spectacular! Why do the French make such a better job of their public architecture than the British? I dedicated a Tai Chi session at the confluence to my Buddhist friend Greg, cremated at the confluence of the holy Bagmati with the Vishnumati in Nepal earlier in the year, and then decided to push on after all. City life is distracting but interestingly lonely for the solo traveller in a way country travel rarely is. Why should this be? Possibly something about being by oneself when the urban masses play in groups around one!

The afternoon ride took me out along the Rhône through a new, prestigious, environmentally friendly development which was very whizzy and where I encountered a bike packer speeding into Lyon from Geneva – clearly I had joined another Eurovelo scene again – this time the via Rhôna Eurovelo 17! It felt like I was now in the heart of Europe as Mr Whiz explained he had left Geneva the previous morning! It sounded from him that this section was going to be relatively straightforward and I was soon out of the city back on a river bank. But unlike the Saone or Loire here the River Rhône was cold and full, with an immensely impressive flow of snowmelt water pouring off the Alps - a harbinger of trials ahead!

I stopped to enjoy a swim at a lakeside water park as river swimming was clearly not going to be a possibility on the Rhône unlike the Saone in which I had enjoyed an idyllic dip on the ride into Lyon a couple of days before. The swimming lake was crowded and noisy – refreshing but not conducive to lingering. I did however linger on the lakeside long enough to identify suitable out of town accommodation just up river in Loyettes. Pressing on I then had to force the route which on this section suffers from poor signage squeezed away from its natural path by the Lyon golf club to the north hugging the river bank and Lyon airport to the south. So it was with some relief that I pulled up at the delightful rustic terrace of the Hotel de la Place just down from the old bridge across the river.

Over the arrival beer whilst taking in my surroundings I realised I was sat under my first fruiting olive of the journey. 'The noble fruit' can withstand brief frosts which is why you do see ornamental olives north of the Alps but the buds are damaged by temperatures of -5° Centigrade for any length of time and -10 °C can be fatal for them. To encourage fruit production the trees like a cold couple of months with temperatures below 10 °C but thereafter the sunnier the better with persistent warm temperatures required above 7.5 °C. Certainly the tree shading me from the summer evening's still warm rays looked healthy and was clearly in fruit. I think this was the first time I really accepted I was Mediterranean bound. But that cold full river came from mountains ahead which would first be demanding of my attention. In the meantime I could pick the brains of fellow cyclists, a middle aged French couple cycling the other way who were sat at a neighbouring table and were happy to trade cycle experiences. They also had come from Geneva (at a rather more leisurely pace than Mr Whizz encountered earlier) and were headed south from Lyon towards Avignon. It was only studying their map that a memory of camping beside the Rhone at Avignon came back. I must have been 22 years of age, a recent graduate and working to pay off my overdraft. I had spent the early summer in Holland doing agency factory work kidding myself as a student of Marx that it would do me good to experience 'alienation'! I stuck it out for a couple of months, before heading south, suitably 'alienated', with the plan to find seasonal agricultural work before heading onto Nice where my linguist friend Ian (admirer of Montaigne, Voltaire and Sartre) was enjoying a year as a teaching assistant in a French Lycee. Having hitched down as far as Avignon, I found myself headed for a riverside campsite in early September. There I encountered a young, equally clueless, Egyptian guy with whom I teamed up in our search for employment. We ended up at the weekly market where we were told to report to the announcer's van. Having given in our details we were duly announced by name, age and country of origin whereupon the assembled French Farmers looked us over with many a shake of the head! Eventually as the market was thinning out a gendarme came over, checked our papers and then directed us to an apple farming friend of his up the road who had been let down by a couple of his Moroccan regulars. Sure enough he was hiring and allowing us to camp in the farmyard, informed us work would start the next day at 7 am. And work us he did from dawn to dusk. After picking apples all day the last job involved stacking the crates of picked apples on a flatbed truck. The speed he drove thereby determined the rate at which one had to pick up the crates. He had a finely judged sense of just how much energy one had left pushing me, in particular, to my limit. Never again would I harbour romantic notions of field work. So alienated by factory work and exhausted by field work I was ready for medical school! Now, after half a lifetime of medical work, I am returning to fieldwork but in choosing olives I have since congratulated myself more than once that my chosen crop are at a good height (and am less of a taskmaster than that unforgettable pied-noir apple farmer).

Once the French couple retired for the evening I struck up conversation with the gang of young tradesmen at the next but one table. It turned out they were contractors working away from home at the massive nuclear power station just up river at Bugey. They were naturally up for 'le crac' and by the time we had exhausted football and cycling as topics of conversation my magret de canard had arrived and my last words in the blog that night asks 'how can it taste so good?'.

As I looked at the map the next morning over croissant and coffee on the now deserted terrace (long after other cyclists and tradesmen had made a start) I did question whether the heavy red accompanying the duck had been a wise decision but rapidly concluded that it was a price worth paying for the excellence of the previous evening. A couple of kilometres down the trail my head cleared as the circulation pumped the blood through the liver a few times and I felt as good as new. I was now leaving the river bank and the massive cooling towers of the nuclear plant, where yesterday's companions were no doubt hard at work, heading south towards a striking plateau high above the Rhone referred to on the information board as the Isle de Cremieu. As I paused for water I could see the high plateau with limestone cliffs towering above me whilst the Rhone rushed through the valley below. At the top the village of Hières-sur-Amby promised an archaeological museum with findings from the plateau where habitation goes back to the Neolithic period. After a steep climb it was sadly closed but the village was pretty and the setting dramatic. A fully kitted out veloist came racing round a bend through what was now classic cycling country and I soon found myself sweeping down the steep curving road too admiring the escarpment towering above as I regained the river bank. As the morning progressed I found myself on an idyllic new via Rhône riverside cycle track with limestone cliffs towering above the Rhone on its southern left bank as I headed upstream on the northerly right bank. I knew I was beginning to tire at the morning refreshment stop as a passer-by called my attention back to my wallet which I had left on the wall beside the bike as I put on my helmet and begun setting off. Whoops! Small acts of kindness from quest helpers like her made the whole trip possible. As it was I had already left a trail of minor belongings across Europe but it would only take one serious piece of forgetfulness to bring the whole enterprise juddering to a halt. Thanking my lucky stars I followed the trail once again away from the river following the recommended route. This diversion took me into reforested mining spoil – not unattractive but obviously less 'wild' than the limestone country I had just been enjoying. The cause of the surface mining became apparent just ahead as I started to track a working conveyor belt which marched across the landscape beside the cycle trail in a concrete conduit leading to a massive cement factory.

Cement requires clay and limestone which are here in abundance. Louis Vicat a local engineer is credited with inventing an artificial cement which lay the foundations for what is now a massive multinational concrete company still called Vicat with a major plant right next to my route. There had clearly been company input to the cycle routing which allowed coexistence and indeed attempted to make a virtue of the plant with information boards educating the passerby (me!) on the process. For the record the huge kilns heat the core materials along with catalysts to produce red hot clinker which must be cooled and ground down to form cement powder. Once this is combined with an aggregate of sand or gravel and water it will set into concrete. Once again I found myself admiring the French way of celebrating their industry in a socially conscious way.

As I passed by the conveyor belt maintenance crew had paused for lunch and asking where I had come from shared their sympathies over the ongoing Brexit crisis. In the ensuing discussion the nuanced ambivalence towards Europe felt more sophisticated than the simplistic in/out debate I had left behind in the UK. My summer in France was proving a salutary reminder of progress at every turn here in France in my lifetime – a progress which currently felt harder to discern back in the UK.

Pressing on the rehabilitated landscape beyond provided for another (overcrowded) swimming lake in one of the now disused clay pits and at a calmer neighbouring fishing lake I ate a late lunch in the shade before stretching out for a siesta. On waking refreshed and reinvigorated I followed the trail 10 kms to Morestel where in search of a café I found myself drawn to the ancient centre of the old town where in a Dauphinois mansion a beautiful art gallery, Maison Ravier, stands in the name of the 19th century head of the Lyonais art school. With the delightful happenstance of the life of an itinerant cyclist I was drawn to the work on display of Yvonne Cheffer-de-Louis, the daughter of Renault's first engineer, whose delightful paintings on display caught my mood with their garden scenes in attractive post impressionist style. Her handwritten elegiac poem 'Adieu' was genuinely moving in my sensitised state capturing something about the transience of this life.

Finding a café back in the 'real' end of the little hill top town I returned to the noise and petty concerns of this life as a harassed woman with child came in to collect a swaggering flash drinker who had been holding forth with his cronies. Happy to jump back on my bike after the fortifying caffeine I raced down the hill and didn't slow down for an hour until I was transported back into a bucolic Rhone valley landscape with golden wheat fields, a tall church spire around which a hamlet gathered all overlooked by a magnificent chateau. According to a sign there was a campsite nearby but first I was ready for more substantial refreshment and sure enough at the heart of the village was a café bar with terrace to die for. As so often on this trip it all came together at the day's end. In the evening sunshine I enquired as to the inhabitant of the Chateau and Monsieur le Patron explained with some gravitas that this place had been the residence of Stendhal. I looked suitably impressed and persuaded myself I had heard of him but I had to admit to myself for what I had no idea – there were certainly no honorific clues on offer! So he didn't appear to have been a general, or a professor or even a doctor so what was his contribution? Whilst waiting for dinner I looked him up to learn that having been born of modest beginnings in this very village he rose through selection by the local priest for education in Lyon and thence with service under Napoleon to be 'a man of letters' and French ambassador. His literary reputation was gained for applying an acute understanding of human nature to romantic novels (he was an inveterate womanizer and serially in love, frequently unrequited) which earned him attention amongst the literary giants of the day who celebrated the realism he brought to the genre. Reflecting over my poulet and chips on another great day I concluded it was the sheer range of cultural references encountered along the banks of the Rhone in the Lyonais hinterland which had made it memorable. In the dying light I had some difficulties locating the 'campsite' which turned out to be a farmhouse field where I was the only guest. It was a self-service sort of arrangement with an honesty box and shower room accessed from the field. Perfect, a reasonable night's sleep and away at dawn all for less than the price of my dinner. I left a nice message of appreciation in a visitors' book provided by my (unknown) host who must have thought me a fanatic arriving so late and leaving so early. If only they knew the truth of it - a slow traveller and late diner keen now to get amongst the approaching lakes and mountains.

I hardly bother mentioning weather simply because it was still unchangingly warm and bright. Indeed I overheard several heat warnings being issued on French TV at café stops but was grateful for the cooling effect of the massive flow of ice-cold water in the Rhone which was substantial. People also forget the cooling evaporative effect of air movement on a bicycle. The mere fact that traditionally it's been a warm weather sport of the southern Mediterranean countries should tell us something! So heat wasn't my motivation to get to the mountains. Having been basically following rivers for a month across France I was ready for something a little more undulating. If all ran according to plan this was the day when I would abandon the Via Rhona Eurovelo 17 to begin my own chosen traverse of the alps via Mont Cenis. To do this I needed to navigate round Le Lac du Bourget.

My research had involved nights on the net over the winter when I would explore a particular pass examining its profile and occasionally even viewing a go-pro video of someone's descent (people never post films of the slow and painful ascent....watching paint dry!). My specifications was a minor (quiet, preferably traffic free) road climbing up and over (without a tunnel) with a manageable gradient up. I was looking for a slow and gentle ascent with a dramatic descent straight down into Italy. For some reason Mont Cenis came onto my radar one evening and it seemed to tick all the boxes including as a bonus feature a summit 'tarn'. This turned out to have been damned and hence technically a reservoir but nevertheless it added to the romance of the high pass. It is one of three potential routes historians argue over for Hannibal and the elephants, it is certainly the route Charlemagne took when he pushed south for Rome and it was none other than Napoleon who converted a mule track to a carriage road over the pass to smooth communications in his empire. All this history persuaded me that it was the one for me!

A superb map of cycling routes furnished free of charge by the Savoie Alps tourist board indicated I was entering a much cycled region with a colour coding system reminiscent of skiing. The easy blues, the hard reds and challenging blacks suggested that routing was crucial. On either side of the Rhone the landscape was getting progressively more vertiginous and it was not hard to see that a wrong turn could lead to a painful half day long digression. One of these routes known as the Mont du Chat lies high above Lac du Bourget and had just featured in this year's Tour. Judging from the TV coverage it wasn't one for novice laden cycle tourers! So I knew I wanted to get to Aix les Bains on the south east shore of Lac du Bourget but it wasn't entirely clear how I was going to do it.

An increasingly dramatic morning took me over a barrage on the Rhone with an impressive volume of water pouring down to the Mediterranean several hundred kilometres away hemmed in by increasingly high hills on either side above me. Now I was approaching the pretty riverside town of Chanaz complete with canal basin which would unlock my route South. My map indicated a boat service from here to Aix-les-Bains and seeing the canal link between the Rhone navigation and Lac du Bourget this all now made sense. All I had to do was get a ticket from the boat trip booth doing brisk business beside the canal lock and I would soon be heading on. 'Non', explained the lady in the booth – the suggested itinerary on my map was in process and for now whilst possible it would not be quite that simple. The day trip boat from Aix having traversed the 4km Canal de Savieres from the Lake turns upstream on the Rhone but doesn't quite reach Chanaz. It takes a refreshment stop at the hotel and neighbouring craft outlet a kilometre away on the far bank of the Rhone before returning via the massive river lock to the lake navigation. I would be able to cycle over to the hotel and catch the one boat of the day later in the afternoon.

So after an enforced canalside lunch, siesta and fruitless search for the padded inner briefs from my courier pants which had been drying on my cycle rack (probably nicked for a laugh by some school kids hanging around my bike I concluded) I headed hopefully for the boat stop. Having cycled back onto the Via Rhona, I crossed at the next bridge before coming back down the far bank where the old riverside hotel was clearly visible. It was closed and deserted as was the neighbouring landing stage and I started to doubt the instructions. But then I watched the river lock open for a substantial pleasure boat to bob across the current towards the landing stage. A mixed touristic party came down the gangplank to mooch around on the hot dusty shore past the closed pub for the requisite 20 minute turn-around time during which I was loaded and befriended by the captain's mate. In his early 40's he knew his cycling, was interested in my journey, and pointed out the various climbs along our route sanctified by inclusion in the Tour over the years. He explained he was a ski instructor by winter and worked this pleasure boat to keep him going in the summer. Mountains, lakes, Geneva up the road and Lyons down the road he suggested he lived in the best area in Europe for its range of options within a 100 kms radius. Who was I to question this conclusion surrounded on all sides as we were by magnificent and dramatic scenery. Like a big Windermere combined with the

Buttermere fells...I mentioned previously that the English Lakes remain my yardstick in mountains. Leaning on the stern rail with my bicycle beside me, the air rushing by laced with occasional spray from the glinting deep blue water through which we were ploughing enroute to Aix I allowed my eye to dawdle on the vertiginous contours of the Mont du Chat. Luxuriating in my decision to hang on for the boat I arrived in Aix in some style!

This was just as well as Aix en Bains was ready to receive me in some style. A favoured hangout in a previous generation of British Royalty it retained that air of a well-heeled and still stylish watering hole complete with Casino. I cycled up from the lakeside into the heart of the place where big terrace cafés lined the main boulevards just as the early evening show of seeing and being seen was under way. I probably was a slightly dissonant note still in cycle shorts quaffing a beer with a laden bike beside me in one of the larger terrace cafés. But the beauty of this whole journey was that I was so beyond caring what anybody thought of me that I had entered that sacred land of the mad (or egomaniac) who feels they are the arbiter of style! It was perhaps more accurate to reflect that I seemed to be practically invisible as a 60 year old bloke with a bike. It was Leonard Cohen who warned that men apparently became invisible to members of the opposite sex around 60, only to re-emerge if they make it to eighty as a much loved treasure. Oh dear I had just donned the cloak of invisibility! Well so be it!

I checked into the old spa hotel which was big and grand enough (if somewhat faded) to cope with a bike ('lock it in the ballroom, its not in use tonight sir'), got scrubbed up and putting on my one leisure shirt over my (stylish) courier half length cycle trousers hit the town. Aix it turns out has some attractive pedestrianised old streets where stylish bistros turn out pretty reasonable dishes and plenty of elegant wines. I ate my fill but didn't linger - the holiday crowds weren't interested in me nor I in them. I had an Alpine pass to find my way too!

The next day I was loading up at the Saturday market before even the locals were there in force. Mmm poulet roti with curried potatoes again! And fresh fruit for the snack pouch. I was still experimenting at this stage and on a mission to find the perfect cycle snack fruit. Strawberries had been fun, but I was now far enough South to try the peaches. The problem is of course the juicier the fruit the more it drips down your chin, getting onto the cycle grips and making everything sticky as the day heats up. I was to learn that apricots are the perfect fresh fruit snack on a bike – just enough bite to give you something to chew on and deliver that sugary boost without being too hard work to chew, whilst having enough juice to refresh without being so juicy as to lead to sticky grips!

Anyway I was soon heading south admiring the Saturday morning sporties out along the lakeside of whom the roller skaters were probably the most alien and impressive – especially the guys using ski poles on the side moving at a serious pace. I passed several lake swimmers but it was too early for a dip especially as I had my brakes on my mind that morning. They had been gradually working loose as the weeks had slipped by since their adjustment at Emsworth in Hampshire. Basically bike cables stretch ever so slightly and thus they become less responsive as you have to pull further and further on the brake lever before they start to bite. The Thorn has a disc brake on the rear wheel and standard V brakes on the front. It is conventionally cabled with the right brake lever controlling the front brake and left for the rear. The logic is you apply gentle pressure with your left hand to control the disc brake which reliably determines overall speed reserving the right for sharper applications of braking pressure via the front brake pads on the rims. Some people have moved onto hydraulic systems but I was very happy to keep it relatively low tech and simple. That way when it starts to fail there should be an easy fix. Now, whilst tightening up the cables was something I understood in principle I was keen to seek professional advice to ensure 100% reliability before the big climb and even bigger descent ahead. I had identified upcoming Chambery as the last place of any size and checking with a fellow cyclist out with his kids on the trail that morning he suggested what turned out to be a cycle superstore on the outer fringes of the town called DVélos. There Piet, a cool Belgian who cut his cycling teeth touring Britain by bike, wheeled me into the workshop area and gave me a master class on cable adjustment. At the end when I asked him what I owed he said a postcard from Greece. I commented how cool things kept happening when riding my bike to which he signed off with a wink and the inclusive throw away 'That's why we do it huh!". Another quest helper this time from the brotherhood of all things bike!

Newly tightened up and back on the road I soon managed to get lost again on the outskirts of Chambery. I had now left the world of major transcontinental routes (the Eurovelos) and was picking my way into the Savoie Alps with the assistance of my Hautes Savoies Cycle Map. As I was standing besides a promising looking minor road orientating the map a woman cyclist coming by screeched to a halt to enquire if she could help. I explained my next destination was Montmélian 20 kms away which seemed to be a good response as she said follow me and we were off. Wow, the minor roads she took me on were her back yard and this was her head clearing route with enough undulation to keep it interesting as we whizzed along the winding lane with panoramic mountain views in all directions. I was just able to ride in her slipstream and on the less demanding sections she shared the recent loss of her mother and coming funeral and I gave her the bare bones of my adventure whilst sharing my own recent fraternal bereavement. Well, if it is possible to make friends in an hour whilst snatching a few moments of conversation at speed then Marion and I are officially friends as we embraced at the end of the hour with no need for more words apart from the obligatory Bon Route! This is what happens when two human beings establish some common ground. It requires an ability to be mutually intelligible to each other and very little else. Sometimes it's more rewarding than other times - but the first two ages of my life have taught me it's always worth a try! Would it happen travelling as a couple? Well it didn't in the 10 days Susannah and I were crossing France yet here I was just over a week later and I'd had some really heart warming random interactions but my ride with Marion was especially memorable.

Indeed it presaged a magical stage of my journey - the crossing of the Alps. Long a necessary evil it was the grand tourists of the Romantic era who really put the Alps on the map so to speak. Robert Macfarlane (Macfarlane 2009) captures the mood of these early forays with Shelley and Byron pausing in the mountains to seek out the 'sublime', a slippery concept which filled them, as it continues to do us, with unspeakably forceful emotions verging on, but short of, true fear. The most straightforward expression to capture the sense of the sublime would be 'awesome' if this word hadn't been reduced to the throwaway hyperbolic response now preferred to its more low-key predecessor 'really'! The eighteenth century 'discovery' of the Sublime and the awe it gave rise to in the traveller crossing the Alps was contrasted with the Beauty which would trigger pleasure in the traveller at his Italian destinations. I was heading for the Sublime via the long winding transverse valley terminating at the Col du Mont Cenis which would be my home for the next three nights - the Maurienne. But to get into the right valley was not straight forward and having briefly discussed the options with Marion I was swung by mention of a swimming lake up ahead if I were to head East on a minor road on the valley side above the river Isere (of Val d'Isere fame)!

By this time we were well into the heat of day and the steep climb up the valley side from Montmelian to take the scenic minor road looping through the farming villages of the lower north slopes was hot work. So much so that an hour later a local homeowner emerged from his Savoie cottage to find me drinking thirstily at his pretty refurbished animal drinking trough supplied with fresh mountain water from a fountain. He seemed amused by the scene and I was far too hot to be at all self-conscious as I poured my bigger 1.5 L bottle of the beautiful cool Alpine water over my sweating head to drip down my open cycle top. The next hour was incredibly picturesque and horribly hot as I attempted to hold out on lunch until the swimming lake. This could not be achieved and half a still warm poulet from the morning market back at lakeside Aix was wolfed down in the shade of a bush high on the north bank of the Isere river. I was enjoying the views but needed to get to the lake and wasn't sorry when my minor road turned down hill rushing down towards the Isere below and just before, amidst signs of parked traffic and a nearby major road interchange turned into a lakeside park. I barely locked the bike before I was in the still cool water – the second lake swim of the trip. It was delightful, far fresher in feel to the Etang near the Canal de Orleans, and clearly a significant summer hang out for all sorts of people. Nobody was that interested in a lone cyclist and having cooled down and eaten the remains of my Aix market lunch I was ready to push on.

I negotiated my way out of the lakeside amenities via a minor road which rapidly led towards a motorway signposted Torino. It was exciting to see my next major staging post appear on signage but I was less enamoured by the motorway. The only obvious way forward led across it and up the opposite southern side of the valley on an inviting minor road. Keen to push on and unable to easily locate myself on the map I entrusted myself to the Garmin and up I went. I was soon in serious hairpin territory but feeling good for the midday stop felt it was within my range and stuck at it. My gut instinct was proved right as the climb levelled off after 500m or so and the route started plateauing across the higher ground between the two valleys of the Isere behind and the Arc ahead. In effect I was bypassing the valley route beset by a motorway and a major road for the traffic free higher alternative with the added benefit of shaving off a few kilometres in theory. There were roadside vines to admire, craggy mountains all around and soon my first glimpse of snow in the shape of a north facing cornice high on a rocky ridge towering above me. Encountering not a soul with whom I could check my route I plunged down a lane, through some fields and emerged back on a main road with a large sign announcing the 'praticabilite des cols' and proceeding to list seven cols including Mont Cenis to be 'ouvert'!

So I was now in the valley of the Arc and the gradual climb up towards Mont Cenis was beginning in ernest! How exciting...the afternoon was cooling down now, the mountains were all around me and the route was once again clear with a helpful cycle sign ushering me across the Arc off the main road to a glorious minor road on the southern bank direction Argentine! Lightheaded with the excitement of it all I was off racing along my lane flanked by alpine meadows chuckling to myself that my detour over the hill had mysteriously transported me to South America! I was back on the eve of my 21st birthday in an open truck between Huancayo and Satipo in the Peruvian Andes with only a bag of coca leaves for company (my mate Mike was snoozing in the cab with our kind host Alberto behind the wheel taking us down to his brother's coffee plantation in the Amazon below) so the light headedness was not an unpleasant association. However when light headedness deepens into a full-blown hypo as any cyclist will tell you the legs rapidly go and progress grinds to a shuddering listless halt. Keen to avoid this scenario I spotted the perfect grassy knoll in a field through which the now unfenced lane wound and had one of the most memorably perfect refreshment stops of my life. There was a quality to the cooling afternoon air, a clarity of the light, greenness of the grass and a backdrop of silence that filled me with emotion (was this sublime or merely beautiful?) as I emptied my snack bag and bottles in that search for calories that is undiscriminating (if it can be consumed it will be). I think a week-old morsel of bread was my record on the trip...surprising what can be resurrected provided there is water to swill it down with!

Recharged spiritually and calorifically I rolled up the valley alongside the Arc until the cycle signage I was following indicated my minor road was crossing the river to rejoin the main road at the village of Branafan. A rather tatty settlement which seemed little more than a pit stop for the transalpine traffic squeezed between the main road and the river, it consisted of a supermarket and alpine inn. Ready for refreshment as I was it was novel to enter the sort of large chalet inn one encounters on a skiing holiday. Bizarrely there were two young women running the bar under the supervision of an older woman whom I took to be their grandmother who were downright flirtatious – not invisible after all Mr Cohen! Seizing the chance to get invaluable local info I asked them of the villages up ahead - where would they head for if they were planning on camping with opportunities for refreshment. They were clear that my best bet was La Corbiere, as it had a swimming lake with a bar/restaurant. Well that sealed the deal after my earlier experience of mountain swimming lakes.

Back on the bike and onwards, not too far up the valley road before the turn off for Corbiere....and soon enough there was the lake – hmm not as nice as the lunchtime place, murky looking water but there appeared to be a café of sorts on the far side – closed! Merde! So up into Corbiere I ride, and when I say up I mean up, and then I reach the heart of the village, but of a swimming lake there is not a sniff. On my way back down passing a row of affluent looking villas I became aware of signs of life, people in the garden behind a high hedge. Tired, thirsty and frustrated I really needed to establish whether those girls had sent me on a wild goose chase so in I strode and, thankful once again for my schoolboy French, enquired that I had heard there was a swimming lake here but the lake below their house looked closed. Oh, they laughed not unkindly, "that's the fishing lake, you want the Swimming lake!" Pointing me back up the hill they gestured I would soon be there. How soon I somewhat niggedly responded. 'Dix minutes'. Well, now I could join in the general merriment and thanked everybody most sincerely for their helpful directions. Result! I jumped back on the bike and rode that 10 mins like a man possessed. Once up and over the road gently ran diagonally down to a beautifully manicured lawn surrounding a lake with a bar/restaurant perched on the bank. Pulling up outside 5 minutes later I strode in and requested a table to be told they were full. Well crestfallen probably wouldn't cover it but however you would describe my face in French the Madame proceeded to announce that if I didn't mind sitting inside I could be fed. My eye ran to the wide open sliding windows with tables nominally inside but virtually sharing the crowded terrace in all but ambience. Mais oui merci! Armed with a beer I went for ablutions in the lake which in the circumstances were most easily concluded by walking into the water in full cycling gear thereby killing two birds with one stone – the 'shower' and the 'clothes wash'. Suitably refreshed I was soon back at my table dressed for dinner (in my 'civvies' of zippy trousers and one decent shirt) at the 'Café Gourmand' for a slightly over the top meal memorable for the alpine cheese which hit the spot. Madame having enquired as to my route insisted on plying me with alpine liqueurs after dinner 'pour le courage' (that heart word again) and no one batted an eyelid as I wheeled my bike down to the lakeside as they locked up. I had my tent up in two minutes and was asleep in 5 after a full day!

I awoke on a deserted lakeside sward of grass with a young man litter picking and generally preparing the lake for its Sunday visitors. I had left my swimming trunks and towel to dry down by the waters edge and he casually handed them to me as I emerged with the sun already up. After a refreshing morning swim I was ready to pack up and continue my ascent of the Maurienne. I soon picked up cycle signage which kept me on the opposite bank of the Arc from the main road as I cycled through a series of small settlements nestling in the valley keeping my eye out for breakfast options. The second village had an all-purpose general shop/bar-tabac serving coffee and croissant which I took with an eclectic mix of men ranging from mountain farmers in pickups through to retirees who strolled down for their coffee and paper. Suitably refreshed I was off for another hour or so to St Remy de Maurienne which was a more substantial town with a smart bar-restaurant where I joined a Lycra-clad cyclist for morning coffee. He was on his way as I sat down, a Sunday leisure cyclist with no particular kinship with me, the tourer. There are subtribes amidst the cyclists as there are in all human populations – our need to distinguish and differentiate just as strong as the common need to discover joint ground!

In the back of my mind a plan was forming. If I kept going the pass might be coming into today's range. I knew I didn't want to do the ascent in the heat of the day so the window to go up would be later on that day or the following morning. Fuelled with this, the second coffee of the day and gee'ed up by these thoughts I held out for lunch until I had covered the 20 kilometres up to St Jean de Maurienne, the capital of the Maurienne and launch pad for the local warlord Umberto to found what would become the House of Savoie. Norman Davies (Davies 2011) in his magisterial works on European History includes two pertinent chapters in his book Vanished Kingdoms dealing with the history of Burgundia and Sabaudia. The interested reader is referred to these excellent pieces if they wish to do justice to the complicated history hereabouts. The short version tells of Umberto Biancomano, (Humbert the Whitehanded), who appears to have been a highborn ally of King Rudolf III of Burgundy, in his role as commander of the March of Maurienne on behalf of the Holy Roman Emperor dealing with a rebellion centring on the Bishop of St Jean de Maurienne by razing the town to the ground in 1035. Humbert was rewarded by the Holy Roman Emperor Conrad with a county including the high passes of Mont Cenis, St Bernard and Simplon. This powerbase controlling the passes as the Count of Maurienne gradually grew into an expansive political entity rebadged as the Count(y) of Savoie with its capital moving as a result of the political expansion initially north west down the valley to Chambery.

However that Sunday afternoon in a deserted St Jean lunch rather than history was on my mind and a large well-run cycle friendly establishment called la Tour hit the spot with mussels and chips. At the next table I was joined by a Dutch cycling couple who were doing day rides up into the mountains. That morning they had been over a 2000m pass and were pleased to be down as they seemed confident that rain was coming. I had enjoyed virtually unbroken sunshine since leaving home a month before. I hadn't so much as glanced at a weather forecast in that time. The nearest I had got to a weather report was overhearing a heatwave warning on a TV in a bar-tabac over breakfast coffee. My new Dutch friends were very clear that rain comes in the afternoons in the Alps and you didn't want to get caught on your bike up in the mountains when it came. Hearing this I paid up and got cracking with 40 kilometres ahead of me to the pass. Just as I was getting on the bike my phone rang, which was a novelty and it turned out to be my nephew and niece at home in London wanting a Sunday afternoon family conference call about plans for the flat they had inherited from their father. By the time we had finished and I looked around me the clouds were gathering. There was nothing to do but push on as the routeways started to converge in the narrowing valley of the Arc. There seemed more traffic about that Sunday afternoon in August presumably transalpine traffic to and from holidays. A further 10 kms up the road the rain started, rapidly building from first drops to thunder and lightening by the time I pulled up in the next town, St Michel de Maurienne. The sky was dark and threatening adding to the gloomy uninspiring atmosphere in this pit stop of a place and I sat drinking tea at a roadside café watching the weather and checking out my local accommodation options. The café patron intimated that I should forget about getting any further that day as the rain would now settle in. I identified a hostel round the corner and the decision was made. There was space in a vacant family apartment at the hostel which I was lent at a knockdown rate and a local supermarket was pointed out for supplies. I had a domestic evening cooking up some pasta, preparing supplies for the big day and repacking the bike. The view at the hostel was that the weather would be good first thing but rain would come in later on. Little did I realise it but this new weather pattern was to take over for the next couple of weeks.

So given that there remained 20 plus kms before the climb would start in ernest I set the alarm for 4 am and fell asleep fighting a sense of mounting excitement.

Typically on such a big day I awoke without need of the alarm at 3:30 am. All was dark and quiet as I layered up including for the first time on the trip my yellow windproof rain jacket, got all my lights on including head torch rigged up on the cycle helmet and set off at 3:55 am. I covered the first 10 kms without seeing another vehicle sticking to the main road. Desperately hoping for a coffee I was delighted to come across a 24 hour service station where the main road met the motorway just before it entered the subalpine tunnel signposted Torino. As I enjoyed the hot coffee and croissant the first bleary eyed truckdrivers started to drift in from their overnight cab stops to do likewise. With a new surge of adrenaline I set off along the quiet road signposted Mont Cenis which tracked the river Arc up into the pine woods. The dawn light slowly filled the sky over head though dawn's rosy fingers were hidden behind the trees. After an hour or so views started to open up of forested ridges and rounding a corner I broke free of the trees in an upland river valley with grazing meadows below rocky slopes leading up to the heights above. There were sporadic signs of roadside commercial building but little habitation until the head of the valley when Lanslebourg came into view clustered around the river with a fine church tower and a high street lined with chalet hotels. Picking one which looked active in the quiet summer season I found a handful of guests enjoying a buffet breakfast whilst I took coffee and surreptiously munched on the apple tart I had just bought from the neighbouring bakers. Pinching some orange juice to lace my refilled water bottles I didn't linger so as to stay ahead of the heat. As I climbed out of the town I was immediately faced with a series of hairpins which lead up at a steady 6-9% gradient over the next 10kms to the Col.

I pushed back on my saddle to ensure maximum leg power, engaged second gear (always keep one back in case of need – good psychology!) and started 'spinning'. I have found this laid back approach to climbing to be the most sustainable way of progressing and I was soon high above the town looking back over its church tower as the hairpins looped up the pass. I realised there was a cyclist up ahead on a bright red recumbent with a rear flag which acted as the perfect target to gauge my progress against. It was hugely encouraging 20 minutes later to realise I was definitely gaining ground on him.

By this time I was passing ski lifts beside the road – a new cycling experience! The views were becoming ever more expansive as the Graian Alps opened up all around me. To the north beyond Lanslebourg (which was now a toy village down below) I could see vast snow fields leading up towards Mont Blanc which was hidden from me by a complex series of intermediate peaks all glistening in the morning sunshine. It was 9:30 a.m. as I reeled in the recumbent and wished him a good morning in as steady a voice as I could manage between the grunting gasps! A little further on the magnificent views meant I just had to have a break to take some photos. Sure enough as I snapped away the red recumbent came steadily into view and duly returned my morning pleasantries. However, no sooner had he gone past than I realised there was another rider coming up steadily. His was a contrasting style of ascent standing on his pedals in an intermediate gear on a classic old road bike. I jokily reached for the toblerone I had packed as my climbing treat and breaking off a couple of segments held them out, Tour style, as a mid-climb treat. I hadn't meant him to but the cyclist smilingly stopped, accepted the proffered snack and immediately started quizzing me 'Where had I started? Where was I going? Wasn't it a fine morning to be climbing this Col'. Well having fallen into conversation we both agreed that momentum should be maintained so off we went now together with my new found friend holding a half wheel lead modulating his pace to mine.

In shifting media of communication between English and French I learnt that Michel had last climbed this particular Col by bicycle 40 years ago. As I ground out the last 500m of ascent he seemingly effortlessly stood on his pedals on his 40 year old classic using the middle ring of his front cogs reflecting that the pleasure he took in the climb hadn't changed over that 40 year period. As a member of the Club des Cents Cols he had actually climbed 5500 cols, he informed me, 354 of them over 2000 metres -this by the way is the definitional threshold for a Col to be Grand – I was relieved to hear Mont Cenis qualified! What an extraordinary guy in his late 60's to be cycling my first Grand Col with - I couldn't have been following better wheels this morning! I remember being in some pain just before seeing the 3 kilometres sign when we were on a hard 9% section but of course the wonderful distraction of maintaining my conversation with Michel saw me through the pain barrier! And suddenly we were there posing for our obligatory photo beside the summit marker at 2083m! There was my recumbent acquaintance needing his photo taken which I was happy to oblige amidst a quick chat about the machine (which was still new and so far so good – I had newfound respect for its rider when up close I realised how heavily laden he was). And of course to be fair Michel was carrying virtually nothing. Anyway we all had different days ahead with the other two peeling off for upland off road adventures whilst I was Italy bound and with everybody agreed that rain was due later we all were keen to make the most of the morning sun.

For me that was a coffee at the little summit café admiring the high altitude lake in the hanging valley below the road now dammed and therefore quite extensive. Suitably fortified with caffeine I carried on around the lake until the barrage was visible below and a group of paragliders provided the perfect entertainment for a morning brunch. I sat on a rock with panoramic views munching still high from my first Grand Col. The weather remained sunny with little wind, perfect conditions, to begin my descent into Italy and I literally pushed off down into the first hairpin not too sure what to expect. The answer was a whopping 25 kms of hairpins as the road wound down virtually to sea level at Susa. The occasional motor bike whining down at speed was the only interruption to an experience of harmonious banking turns with the air whistling by. I had to stop twice just to relax my fingers gripping hard on the brakes. My second stop entailed a coffee ordered in halting Italian – I really had crossed the mountains into another country.

Susa came into view far below, a sizeable town filled with churches from above. Closer inspection revealed an attractive place at the foot of the pass with piazzas and churches galore. I was struck by the contrast with the mountain villages I had been in the last few days. I was soon down and went into the main church finding myself at the main shrine silently thanking somebody for safe passage through the mountains. But I was still far too high on adrenaline to think of stopping and pushed on, setting course for Torino. I was adamant that I wanted now to reach the regional capital city and have a day off and wasn't to be distracted by seeking out a cycle friendly route. So I ground out the 50 kms to Torino that afternoon inevitably tiring a little towards the end. As I approached the city I identified a central 'bed and breakfast' which looked well placed and arriving in the city centre had a sense of the weather breaking around me. Having identified my lodgings down a side road off one of the main city shopping streets I was aware of the first drops of rain as I rang the bell in the wall of an imposing palazzo gateway. A lady answered and gestured me upto the top floor. As we emerged onto a roof terrace with rooms the heavens opened accompanied by thunder and lightening...it had been a 120kms 2000m of ascent sort of day!

Chapter 5. The Foot of the Mountains and Some Unexpected Hills

Taking stock of my surroundings in Turin the lodging occupied the top storey of a newly restored Renaissance palace – the Palazzo Scaglia di Verrua. The walls of the central courtyard were painted with allegorical figures against a terracotta background which gave the place an authentically Renaissance atmosphere. My hostess spoke no English and seemed to live in a tiny storeroom beside the capacious guest rooms. She was charming and welcoming but probably a little confused by my babbling effusiveness of the 'bonissimo bicycletta des Alpes' - my great ride over the mountains. However crucially she was able to recommend a local restaurant to which I repaired famished and enjoyed my first (of many) fine Italian meals, beef agnolotti (the Torinese take on ravioli) with the local Barolo red wine. Before passing out I dipped into a history of my lodgings and found reference to the extensive makeover of the building in the early 1600s when Filiberto Gherado Scaglia (1561-1619) did a spot of match-making. It turned out that the descendants of Humbert the Whitehanded had flourished, expanding their role from 'guardian of the Alpine passes' to 'Counts of Sabaudia'. They retained one foot on the North West side around their early capital Chambery but over the years expanded their territory to the South taking over much of Piedmont, literally the 'foot of the mountains'. In 1563, following a period of turbulence, Duke Emanuele-Filiberto moved the capital down to Turin, where he refashioned the family firm into Casa Savoie, the House of Savoie. Incidentally as a measure of the extensive political machinations the family had pursued over the centuries the Savoy Hotel in London stands on a manor granted to the Savoyards in return for the hand in marriage of Eleanor of Provence by Henry III in 1246. It turns out my 'B and B' was in quite such a magnificent palazzio because Scaglia Senior was richly rewarded for having arranged another dynastic marriage, this time between the Duchies of Savoie and Modena.

Inevitably, therefore, once I had completed an important kit purchase (replacement of my spare padded cycling shorts with a new pair complete with a blue 'go faster' azurro hoop on one thigh) my day off was devoted to the cultural treasure house of the House of Savoie, the Palazzo Reale fronting the enormous Piazzetta Reale. A baroque wedding cake of a building the entrance hall and grand staircase form one of the most over the top displays of wealth and power I have ever seen. Exploring the collections in this treasure house I found my first classical statues this side of the Alps. And not just a few – an entire gallery devoted to classical sculpture. From the sublime alpine crossing to my first taste of classical beauty the tour was living up to its reputation.

One room in the vast museum complex was given over to an exhibition illustrating how the great powers in the nineteenth century fought over these classical treasures - the House of Savoie after 1815 (and the fall of Napoleon) made representations to post imperial France for the return of classical booty taken by the imperial army over Napoleon's new road over Mont Cenis. But it was role of the Savoie family in the making of modern Europe which proved to be most revelatory. The Dukes of Savoie stepped up to the champions league with acquisition of a kingship of Sicily, which they then swapped for that of Sardinia. This put them in pole position when nation building led to the 'need' for a King of Italy. However, there remained the problem that the oldest part of their homeland around the original capital Chambery was aligned closely with France. , In a twist of history which had echoes of current concerns, a plebiscite, or people's choice was arranged in 1860 giving the inhabitants of Savoie the choice of 'oui' or 'non' to the question 'Does Savoie want to be reunited with France?'. 99.76% selected 'oui' in an open ballot with all sides keen for the people to give 'the right answer'. And thus the House of Savoie ditched their original power base for the greater prize of the newly invented Italian throne which would itself end in the referendum of 1946 which turned out 54% republican to 46% monarchist. Modern referenda can mould history on narrow margins as we have recently learnt in the UK! Italy remains to this day a loose confederation of people who retain fierce regional loyalties.

Almost too late I remembered I had decided on having the insurance of a paper map for my next leg across Northern Italy, and diving into a book shop as it was closing settled hurriedly on a Michelin map of Piedmont. It wasn't ideal as it didn't cover the southern belt of land around Genoa where I was dimly aware route complications might lie. But that was a problem for another day. Over an early evening beer I learnt in the local paper despite my lack of Italian language that Torino were playing a football friendly against Liverpool that night. The evening was turning thundery and a brief but heavy shower suggested it wouldn't be a night for piazza dining! So I raced around Turin to find a bar to watch the game. Now if you are not a keen football follower you may be forgiven for not knowing that there are two teams in Turin and my team Liverpool were playing the less fashionable team Torino that night not Juventus. What I didn't know was that the rivalries were sufficiently intense that the centre of the city was solidly 'Juve' and in denial that there was even televised football being shown that evening! It was only when I had crossed the railway tracks into San Salvario down by the Po that I found what I was looking for. A working-class district now in the process of getting the hipster vibe but still authentic enough to have a sports bar with a couple of dozen men of my age devoting their evening to watching a pre-season friendly. I learnt something of the passion with which Italians follow football as their team went down 3-1 with my fellow viewers screaming at the TV as if their lives depended on it! They welcomed me as a fellow footie supporter (there was only one of me!) but I kept celebrations muted in respect! The area had a pleasantly bohemian feel after the rather upmarket city centre and I had the best pizza of the trip in a funky bar round the corner. I managed to wander into a drug dealing zone on the edge of a park on my way home but was sufficiently street savvy to work it out before anybody got on my case and I walked back through a wet city centre, skidding across the smooth rain soaked ancient stone pavements in the treadless crocs donated by bro-in-law after the sandal loss debacle hoping for better weather for the next leg of the journey.

I was now entering my pilgrimage leg and the question was which road of the many should I take? This has of course an allegorical quality which was not lost on me. My life to date had been a journey along well travelled routes with less travelled interludes. After those early adolescent hitch-hiking trips exploring Southern Europe at 19 years of age I took off for the East on 'Budget Bus' following a well travelled route which still could be characterised in those days as the hippy trail. 'Are you on the bus or are you off the bus?' Ken Kesey had famously asked in 1964. Well it was 1977 and I was off to do my thing. Having abandoned Budget Bus in Kabul I was on a local bus crossing the Khyber Pass that spring when I recall meeting a lone Italian cyclist on a road bike who could be said to be taking the road less travelled. He nonchalantly told me the kids threw stones at him as he passed by – cyclists were made of tougher stuff back then!

I wended my way via Peshawar up into the Swat Valley where I spent a week as a guest of the local schoolmaster in a village high up amidst the ridge top Pathan villages between the Swat and the Indus Rivers. His son was memorably called Neil after Neil Armstrong of the American moon shot fame. A reminder of just how far the battle for hearts and minds has swung in this part of the world since. Back on the Grand Trunk Road at Rawalpindi after pausing at an expat compound at Islamabad where I had a contact I spent a memorable night at Taxilla under the stars on a rope bed smoking dope with the site custodian who recalled Sir Mortimer Wheeler's summer school 30 years earlier. This was all part of my rather romantic scheme to sleep over at ancient sites along the silk road. I got as far as the military checkpoint just beyond Hemis Gompa, past Leh in Ladakh, the furthest point East one could venture on this particular axis in those cold war days. China and India were still squared up to each other and the risk of conflict had only just cooled enough for India to allow foreigners into Ladakh that summer. Highlights on the way back West included Bamiyan, the Buddhist site in central Afghanistan. This necessitated leaving the 'hippy trail' to take the northern route leading to Mazari Sharif, the remains of Balkh and eventually after a week of hard travel Herat. Once across the border at the holy city of Mashhad I chose to head for Yazd across the Dashti Kavar, the great central desert of Iran. En route memorably trapped in a caravanserai in sand-storms I felt I really was on the old Silk Road. Last year I was bouncing along a potholed lane leading down from friendship bridge and Nepal's northern border with Chinese Tibet when my colleague Professor Sunil turned to me nonchalantly to say they were expecting a four lane highway down this route as part of China's beltway scheme. A hint of the latest version of the Silk Road still to come! As perhaps you have detected dear reader I remain of the view that a good narrative should leave room for digression just as a good journey should allow plenty of time to explore scenic diversions off the main route!

Applying this slow travel philosophy to what, in effect was the western leg of the silk route back in the winter I had identified the Via Francigena a route following that described by Sigeric the Serious, the Archbishop of Canterbury, which he took to Rome in 990 in order to receive his pallium, an ecclesiastical vestment which acted as a badge of office from the Pope. This has now become an official pilgrimage route which is being promoted by the Italian church no doubt with more than half an eye on the popularity of the Camino to Santiago de Compostela in Spain. However like the Camino there are several variants described particularly relating to the route taken across the Alps. Having set my heart on Mont Cenis I was pleased to find one variant of the Francigena took this pass. The question that preoccupied me as winter turned to spring was would it be possible to follow the Francigena, particularly the Mont Cenis variant on a bike? It was relatively late in the day that I found reference to a crowd funded signed cycling route following the Francigena down to Rome – perfecto – but it followed the main variant across the Great Saint Bernard Pass which lay 70 kms to the north east of Mont Cenis.

One option from Turin was to head out east along the Po valley on a dedicated cycle route which eventually meets this branch of the Via Francigena coming south east. However this appeared two sides of a triangle on the map and I had read comments about long hot sections of the Po devoid of settlements which had been off-putting. I was dimly aware that alternatives would be hillier but now I had proved to myself I could handle the Alps – what could possibly be more challenging? I had been heartened to see Via Francigena signage for walkers back around Susa as I came down off the pass so the Mont Cenis variant clearly existed and I had found a blog by a chap who had certainly cycled part of it which was the clincher. So my plan on leaving Turin was to go for this variant which would eventually lead me to Lucca (one of my favourite Italian towns) and thence into Tuscany (where I had honeymooned 10 years previously). So using my trusty tablet to access the interactive map of the Francigena on the internet I transposed the towns through which the route passed onto my new map of Piedmont and set off.

My route took me through the grand piazzas of central Turin to pick up the Po and follow it briefly upstream round the city centre and out through industrialised suburbs to the south. Turin is described as post-industrial and there was a fair degree of regreening evident along the riverbank. Reflecting on my two night city break I thought Turin had a lot going for it, combining history and elegance of course but still a real city with plenty of gritty areas. All too soon my cycle path turned off over a bridge and left me attempting to negotiate a cyclable route through a major road interchange on the outskirts of a satellite town called Moncalieri. I got away from the traffic by heading up into the old town centre where I paused to admire an imposing fortified palace which unsurprisingly turned out to be another trophy home of the uber successful House of Savoie. Whilst staring at my map a road cyclist stopped, admired the English touring bike setup and kindly enquired where I was trying to get to. The next town circled on my route map was Chieri and my new friend told me to follow his wheels. I was still new to riding in Italy and hadn't as yet got the measure of the road system. Strada Regionale (SR) the regional roads seemed busier up here in the north than the D roads of France so I was pleased my friend had a leisure route along minor back roads through what was still a busy peri-urban area with plenty of commuting traffic. He peeled off leaving me to it and I managed to pick my way along increasingly rural lanes to Chieri, once an important medieval city state to rival Genoa now a sleepy backwater. I spent a few minutes seeking out an historic church which proved elusive and made do enjoying morning coffee trying to apply half remembered Latin to read a plaque on a baroque archway and clocktower in Italian commemorating the towns illustrious past. With midday almost upon me I needed to see more progress before lunch, wending my way on minor roads across the rolling Piedmont countryside through a series of small towns direction Asti. This was my first real taste of the Italian countryside which here was a patchwork of relatively small-scale arable farms. The towns, situated on low hills, with their pantile rooves lent a pleasing terracotta dimension to the yellows and browns of the midsummer fields. The sun was hot and with no river to follow I was working hard crossing undulating country. Around two in the afternoon with my legs going I pulled up in one of these small towns outside a promising trattoria for lunch. Inside was what seemed the entire rural workforce gathered in groups of four to six at tables enjoying a hearty home cooked lunch. I enquired hungrily at the counter only for the serving girl to look with concern towards her boss – a rather imposing woman clearly in charge of the kitchen and all else it would seem. No, she firmly shook her head, too late for the set. Feeling miffed as food was being brought out all around I asked for the sorry looking pastry in a glass case and took a vacant table.

My neighbours watching all this enquired after my route in a friendly enough manner...but I did feel a little aggrieved pointedly meeting the Madame's eye on departure and thanking her ironically. But the great thing about cycling is that it's impossible to be aggrieved for long as you have to give the ride your energy and attention and I was soon rolling on past fields, over streams and at one point passing an enormous modern monstrosity of a basilica – a pilgrimage sanctuary to an eminent Italian missionary called Don Bosco. Beyond this Cortazzone sticks in the mind, a real hill-top town in deep red terracotta brick perched above fields of maze reminiscent to me of the small brick built Newar towns of the Kathmandu Valley. Through my work there I had become intimately familiar with those little Newar towns in the Southern valley like Bungamati, home to Raato Machhendranath, a raingod in the little tradition who morphs into Avalokiteswara, bodhisattva of compassion in the great tradition. Walking through these Newar urban centres in the Valley, historically vying for control of the Tibeto-Indian trade route, the analogy with the great trading cities of medieval Italy had always struck me. Now here I was confirming this impression with the reverse comparison.

I managed to navigate a route under the A21 autostrada and continued wending my way east with Asti up ahead. Mindful of the navigation difficulties posed by towns I decided to stay to the South of Asti as I needed to hit the main road bridge over the River Tanaro just South of the town, to gain the south bank along which my route lay. On the map there appeared to be a track I could follow which stayed low instead of which I could find only a lane which climbed steeply up the vineclad hill of Vaglierano. Picturesque it was but in the afternoon sun also rather draining. Finally negotiating my way through this charming but infuriatingly hilly corner of Piedmont I descended to the road bridge which was the crux of the afternoon's ride. As I crossed the bridge alongside a rail line to finally gain the southern bank I became aware of a thunder cloud coming down fast from the north. These afternoon thunderstorms were proving to be a regular afternoon feature as I made my way across Piedmont, the 'foot of the mountains'. With a great peel of thunder the heavens opened and I sought shelter in a café bar by a level crossing. A couple of grizzled locals were watching life go by nursing coffees whilst young African street sellers caught making a run for it sheltered under the awning where I had balanced my laden bike. There was nothing for it but to take a bar stool, order a coffee and let the thunderstorm pass over. After half an hour or so of dramatic thunder and lightening the storm front had passed but the rain felt like it was settling in so I started to look for accommodation options of which the best and closest was an agriturismo some 8 kms beyond at Azzano d'Asti, complete with rave reviews describing it as a 'little gem'. On that prematurely dark and stormy afternoon it seemed to offer the promise of superior shelter with foodie overtones which was exactly what the situation called for. My call to book a place for the night was answered by a woman who sounded helpful but before any details could be confirmed the electrical storm (presumably) caused the call to be dropped and despite repeated attempts I failed to reconnect. The rain seemed to be lessening and I decided to make a break for it. I put in the location details of the Agriturismo 'Ilfiordaliso' (the 'Cornflower') into the Garmin and bidding farewell to my brief companions with whom I had shared shelter in the storm I got my (Italian) rain jacket on and setoff. Almost immediately the road started to wind up into thickly wooded hilly country. Whilst there was plenty of water about from the thunderstorm the rain was now light and intermittent with occasional brighter shafts of sunlight illuminating swirling mist. Birdsong rang from the trees and occasional vistas through the treetops below suggested I was climbing onto a ridge. I paused to check my route and was struck by the magical atmosphere of these mist clad wooded hills shimmering in the light. I dropped to a farmstead and then saw up above me a ridge top town which had to be my destination. A little downcast at the prospect of another biggish climb I dug in and reached the top only for the Garmin to indicate I should start descending the other side. At this point, always wary of losing altitude, I sought a second (human) opinion from a passing pedestrian. Yes, he knew Ilfiordaliso and gestured down an equally steep descent different to the one I had been considering with clear instructions that my destination lay only a third of the way down. Sure enough there was a pull off heading into the woods which in a few metres opened into a clearing with a delightful chalet style house with balconies at the upstairs windows and a spacious conservatory leading from the back of the house into the pretty gardens falling down the slope of the clearing back into the woods.

I pulled up at the front door and my knock was greeted by a petite, serious, dark haired woman whom I would come to know as Piera. So I was the person who had tried to ring her with whom conversation had been inconclusive. Well the problem was she did have one spare room but it was booked for the following day. Well I pressed upon her that I was seeking only overnight accommodation and attempted to present myself other than the wet bedraggled cyclist with whom she was faced. To her credit Piera, another Helper on the Quest, thinking aloud persuaded herself that she could make up the room later after dinner if I didn't mind! I responded that if a shower and dinner were available all else could follow in its own sweet time. So it was that I was sat in the dining room clean, warm and dry half an hour later greeting the two middle aged couples at adjoining tables who were my fellow guests.

Piera started to bring out the food and I began to appreciate just how much of a one-woman operation she was running. There was a rich soup flavoured with truffle, agnolotti the small square packets of pasta I had come across in Turin, a sweet cake-like dessert and a selection of local cheeses all washed down with a bottle of Monferrato Red wine. The wine like all the food was local and I was able to relate the Monferrato wine region in Piedmont to my day's cycle having, I now learnt, crossed the Basso (lower) Monferrato that morning between the Po and Tanaro rivers and entered the Alto (higher) Monferrato which chimed with my experience since crossing the bridge down by the railway that afternoon. I retired to my newly made up room overlooking the woods below and fell into a blissful sleep to the backdrop of owls hooting in the damp summer's night air.

Morning Tai Chi was atmospheric in the garden clearing below the house surrounded by the beech, ash, sycamore and oak of this typical Piedmont woodland with the bleating of young goats coming from a neighbouring loafing shed. After a delicious breakfast notable for the wide variety of bread and pastries Piera suggested I accompany her to the neighbouring town where she had some essential food shopping but which also had a bank machine so I could pay in cash as required. I had the unfamiliar experience of being a motor car passenger as we drove over to the neighbouring larger town of Rocca D'Arazzo listening as Piera shared her story. This opened (and would close) with the observation that she had been cooking since age 5. Her parents ran a farm in the valley below Azzano which she had left with some reluctance to pursue a career in the city. After 10 years of work in commercial offices she followed her heart and put together her love of cooking, houses and flowers to start the agriturismo and open it to visitors. I complemented her on the commitment and integrity which came over in the care with which she fed the guests. I was then given quite an insight into the importance of locality in the slow food movement which has now spread far beyond Italy. Piera was clear that to do what she did you had to come from the area. Indeed from the immediate locale. A sense of the place was integral to the authenticity of the whole proceedings and was acquired by birth through family and land. An interesting take on Italian regionalism. So for an authentic Piedmont experience the Agriturismo Il Fiordaliso can't be too highly recommended and taking an unexpected call from Susannah, as I repacked the bike to set out that morning, I promised her a visit in the future.

My route for the morning tracked the Tanaro river Eastwards and as I had already experienced the ups and downs of Alto Monferrato I was delighted to descend to a riverside cyclepath. The wooded slopes above me to the south of the Rochetta Tanaro Park would have to await a return with Susannah and I made steady if less spectacular progress for the first 20 kms or so until morning coffee at Oviglio, another medieval Italian town on a minor prominence above the river. From there I abandoned the Tanaro cutting eastwards heading for another bridge across the Bormida and thence across the Orba, all three Piedmont tributaries of the Po draining this rolling wooded region. What was beginning to dawn on me that all this water had to be coming from somewhere significant! As I headed due south in the early afternoon heat on a deserted minor road I passed a tumbledown farmhouse with an elderly man sat outside preparing vegetables. Gesturing behind me he made the unmistakeable gesture of rain and turning I could see the now familiar dark thunder clouds crowding the sky to the north. We exchanged gestures as he suggested it was coming quickly and I set about pedalling to see what shelter lay ahead. Round the corner and under a major trunkroad underpass I reached my crossing point of the Orba which was more of a slow flowing lake than a river at this point. A sign indicated some sort of café down on the river bank to which I duly descended. This turned out to be more of a down at heel inland resort complete with dance floor and booming Italian pop. There were a few families sat around having lunch and a friendly barman reassured me that there was a set lunch available all day. Having found shelter I whiled away a couple of hours over lunch enjoying the Italian pop music and keeping a wary eye on the thunder clouds which in the event slid by to the south west. After some agonising I decided that for the first time since my arrival in Italy I was going to be spared an afternoon downpour.

The afternoon session was a delightful rolling 20 kms through more wine country and I started to set my sights on a town up ahead called Gavi. With about 8 kms to go I was stood at a minor road junction agonising about which of two routes to take when a young man came racing round the corner on a proper, sleek looking Italian road bike. I hailed him to ask the way to Gavi to which he instructed me to follow him and off he went. Now this lad was of an age where humiliation of the more mature cyclist was something to cherish. So I'm sure he took me the hilliest route pushing on with hardly a backward glance as I laboured behind. Having just about found enough in my legs to keep him in sight we reached the last stretch back now on the main road into Gavi when he burned off into town leaving the old man for dead!

The town of Gavi turned out to be a memorable overnight stop perched on a natural routeway between two hills dominated by medieval Genovese fortifications guarding the approaches to Genoa's 'backdoor'. Gavi has quite a name for its wines made from the local Cortese grape variety which produce a dry white which I learnt is considered the perfect match for seafood from the Ligurian Mediterranean coast. So after finding myself a rather anonymous hotel room I headed for the wine bar I had ridden past after checking out the medieval church which turned out to be an important pilgrimage stop and its neighbouring bar where the friendly owner recommended my return later for salsa night! Wow, Gavi appeared buzzing after my night with the owls in Piedmont. The wine bar was crowded with locals taking an aperitif and when I informed the husband and wife owners that I had come especially to sample the famous Gavi white wine well I had clearly come to the right place. Over the next couple of hours the Gavi DOC was thoroughly explored much of it while in conversation with an impressively erect and goatee bearded gentleman well into his seventies who introduced himself in fluent English with hardly a trace of an Italian accent. When I commented on this he explained that his father had owned a Genovese shipping business and when they had needed a new ship his father and uncle had gone to Glasgow to procure one. The visit must have gone well because they came back with not only a new ship but also a wife for his uncle. This Glaswegian lady spent the rest of her life in Genova and ensured most of the nephews and nieces spoke good English. As the wine bar started to slow down I bade the gentleman and his wife farewell as they toddled up the single main street and I headed back down it, grabbing some pasta en route to the salsa dancing. In the little piazza off the Main Street an authentically Latin playlist was blasting out over a dance floor surrounded by seats for the elderly and infirm. I was somewhat surprised to be introduced by the friendly patron to a couple of UK based Peruvian sisters hanging out there ...one had married locally and her sister was over visiting. Emboldened by the Gavi and feeling neither elderly nor infirm I suggested a dance and didn't make too much of a fool of myself. One of the more surreal evenings of the journey

Knowing the next day would be a big push I extricated myself and headed to my room in reasonable order. Grateful for a decent buffet breakfast I was up and out by 7am to begin the climb over the Appenines and down to the coast. At this point I was forced to admit to myself a fundamental error in purchasing a map which stopped at Genoa (which I had no intention of entering) as I would be riding off the south-easterly corner of the map. So, ill equipped navigationally and under researched geographically, I set out on the final push for the Mediterranean to the south. What could possibly go wrong!

The first climb to the south of Gavi was a slow wind up through forested hills which in the cool morning air was positively enjoyable. The slowly looping ascent topped out at a 600m col above Voltaggio which felt fine as I took a selfie against the summit sign. The descent was not as steep as from Mon Cenis and with my growing confidence leaning into the curves I came down fast and smooth to emerge in the busy urban centre of Busalla for morning coffee amidst the busy Friday morning housewives doing the weekend shop. It was getting hot, dusty and busy as I battled through the first traffic I had encountered since Turin, in what I realised was a bottleneck river crossing point just north of Genoa. Most of the traffic was headed south for the city which I was keen to avoid so my route to the east on a minor road was once again relatively traffic free and soon started to wind up into hilly terrain. By this time I was off my map and totally reliant on the Garmin into which I was punching way mark villages I had copied off the Via Francigena. The terrain started to get exceptionally hilly with ever steeper inclines and a complex pattern to the ridges which made navigation challenging. After winding up a twisting and turning valley for some time I was relieved to reach the next village of Montoggio, which had the air of a minor hill resort as I pulled up for some much-needed food. Families were parading along the bustling main street in a holiday atmosphere. One of the two main café bars was clearly going for the passing cyclist trade with bike memorabilia much in evidence...the bubbly patroness presenting me with a branded key fob as a momento of my visit. I must say as it was now hot and the way forward was uncertain I was concerned with cracking on so I extracted myself with effusive thanks, pushing the remains of my sandwich into my pannier. The main street ascended sharply from the café and kept on climbing steadily for the next 10 kms. Hilly wooded ridges surrounded me as I topped out at Scoffera grateful to find a bar with a wonderful terrace view (but still no sign of the elusive Mediterranean) and locals enjoying a Friday afternoon session. Tempting though it was to join them for once I resisted the siren call of cold beer, I got online and consulted the online map of the Mons Cenis variant of the Via Francigena for the next waymark. I was immediately struck by the fact that the pilgrim route traversed along the ridge from Scoffera and looking from the terrace could see that it would not be cyclable. The idea of pushing/carrying my bike plus 10 kgs of panniers along a wooded mountain ridge did not appeal in the afternoon heat and so I had to find a way through these final ridges of the Apennines and down to the coast. Studying my Garmin and experimenting with different way marks I found what looked like a reasonable route on minor roads crossing the col here at Scoffera and not losing too much height before looping back up and over a final ridge to a long valley descent down to the coast.

Never one to prevaricate too much before a challenge I filled up my water bottles and headed on. The first section was actually great cycling, descending gradually on a winding well surfaced road with the reassuring sight of a road cyclist in full kit swooping by in my direction with a grunted greeting. On arrival at the next village I headed off to the left for what I hoped would be the final ascent. Thank God it did indeed prove to be the final climb as it was the steepest of the three and I had to pull every trick I knew to cycle it whilst keeping my front wheel in contact with the sticky melting tarmac. I got through all 3 litres of my water in the space of an hour and a half's toil up that final section. At the top of the climb from Hell was the village of Maxena clinging to the sharp ridge with a tiny plaza ringed by iron railings to protect the local inhabitants from falling off. And yes, thankfully, a narrow lane zigzagged down the other side presumably headed to the valley below. As I caught my breath taking all this in a bored young lad sat watching me as if I had descended from another planet. I smiled and gave him my stock Italian phrase 'Va Bene' – 'its going well'– which for the first time that afternoon I really felt wholeheartedly – now surely the Mediterranean was within reach.

With a whoop I set off down the zig zags only to slam the brakes on at the first switch-back – this really was vertiginous and demanded care and control. Fortunately I didn't meet anyone attempting the ascent in a car until towards the bottom when I was beginning to relax my grip on the brakes and had a rather close shave as we squeezed past one another and suddenly I was speeding along a gently descending valley lane. As the valley opened up my lane joined a more used thoroughfare and thence joined the main road emerging at Lumarzo, a little town set back from the coast, where a major bowling competition was in full swing under the trees complete with a big crowd of spectators. I paused and took in the scene. Kids watched by mothers on the playground whilst the men focussed intently on their bowling. Lumarzo's claim to fame is the village of origin of Frank Sinatra's mother. Dolly 'hatpin' Sinatra emigrated as a baby, grew up to be a midwife in New Jersey and as a Democrat and Suffragette activist earned her nickname by her readiness to break the law and supply abortions on demand. It was funny to think in another version of history Frank would have spent his life practising bowling here. Having sat taking in the scene for a few minutes the draw of the sea propelled me onwards. Briefly trying out a local off-road bike route signposted and promoted as the Ciclovia dell'Ardesia (Ardesia is the name given to the local sedimentary rock) I realised my energy had been spent crossing my three ridges of the day and the additional demands of a circuitous rolling off road path were more than I could deal with. So retracing my route briefly I got on the main road back at Lumarzo and started to track it down to the coast ...until a 'hypo' struck. When the demanding muscle cells have depleted the short term energy store of glycogen in the liver (1-2 hours into moderate intensity exercise) the body adapts by switching to the oxidation of fat which generates all important glucose for the brain. Although endurance (low intensity) training encourages this fat burning pathway I sometimes experience low sugar symptoms presumably at the switchover. My mind loses focus, I become lightheaded and strangely semi-detached from the task in hand. I became more sensitised to the symptoms (which initially are quite subtle) when I started to dabble in triathlons and several times experienced a hypo half way through the bike ride around an hour and a half into the event having burnt lots of energy in the swim. In the unforgiving world of competition the subjective symptoms of listlessness were objectively measurable as people I had been comfortably ahead of started overtaking me! The quick fix, if you want to keep going, is carbohydrate in an easily burned form to supply that missing sugar. So pulling up in a lay-by I stuffed the remains of my lunchtime sandwich, an old piece of cheese, a dry crust and some half melted fruit chews in, washed down by warm water and observed the magical effects of refuelling on my mind and body. Fine dining never tasted as good! 10 minutes later I resumed the push for the sea emerging on the coastal flats by Lavagna towards the eastern end of the Genovese Riviera. And suddenly I found where all the Italians had been hiding – they were all at the coast. The strip from Genova was lined with a wide promenade providing access to bathing off stony beaches broken up by breakwaters and cafés set above on the promenade all backed by a suburban railway. And there were people, people everywhere. I stopped at the first café with a spare table, locked the bike and had a reviving swim off the beach before taking a celebratory cold beer up at the café with Italian pop pulsing out over the turquoise waters of the Mediterranean with a feeling of having made it! Strange how little I had preconceived what the seaside would be like in these parts– I was living in the present and knew only that my way south east lay across the Appenines to the sea. I had made a classic error due to my lack of geographical research which would come back to bite me the following day but for now I was content to explore this stretch of coast and find a suitable lodging for the night.

The vibe on this stretch was still pretty urban as I was still in effect in the suburbs of Genoa so consulting Google maps I noted 'the Bay of Silence' a local beauty spot round the corner and thought this might offer beach sleeping opportunities. How wrong could I be? The world and his wife (and their kids, uncles and aunts, grandparents and cousins, lots of cousins) were all packed in at the Baia del Silenzio doing what people do when they are having fun in a group, but especially people of Italian origin, shouting, laughing and surprisingly frequently crying. This was the Bay of Cacophony and I needed to keep going. I set off round the coast through the pedestrianised crammed restaurant lined streets backing the Bay to regain the coast road here with cycle path alongside. Perfect...I was soon making steady progress until the main road started to climb away from the coast. Fortunately there was a minor road which branched off at this point and stayed low alongside the rail line. After a kilometre or so this disappeared into a tunnel with a set of traffic lights on red. It was all strangely quiet given how busy the coast road had been. There was a long sign in Italian issuing various warnings beside the traffic lights which I couldn't understand. No matter my way lay along the coast, my legs were nearly spent and here was a flat route heading in the right direction. Well the traffic lights went on and on until I started to think they were broken. By now three or four cars had joined me in our wait which seemed to me to have exceeded ten minutes when suddenly the lights changed and we all roared into the tunnel....or at least I hung back as the cars roared into the tunnel and I silently and rather gingerly followed them. Well talk about entering the inferno....I was in a narrow single lane roughly hewn tunnel, unlit with no evidence of the proverbial 'light at the end of...". Fortunately my light sensitive front light system had come on and provided enough light to both see and be seen. What I had not reckoned on was the length of the tunnel....approximately 8 kms with two short breaks when it emerged briefly onto a coastal platform. The 10 minutes or so of the traffic light cycle allowed for cars to traverse the route fully before the next cohort was allowed through from the opposite end. Of course this does not allow for cyclists who are therefore caught out on the single track lane in the dark by the oncoming cohort of cars when the inevitable traffic lights change occurs. This was unnerving but I had identified refuge bays cut into the walls where one could shelter and keep out of the way of passing traffic. So that's what I did, and then pushed on with renewed vigour to ensure I didn't have to repeat the experience. Halfway, at the first break in the tunnel, I admired an isolated café, and a family taking a rocky coastal path but I was sufficiently unnerved not to dawdle and complete my journey through the underworld. Once again I got caught with oncoming traffic who this time hooted me and perhaps more unnervingly a few minutes later traffic coming from behind me who were taking no prisoners hooted me more insistently to get out of their way. At the second break in the tunnel wall there was a sign saying 'Camping' like a message beamed from heaven reaching into the inferno and I swung off barely believing my luck. There crammed in against the rocky bay walls was a narrow strip terraced into a series of platforms above the sea on which were perched tents and campervans. Yes there was a pitch for a one man tent I was told at reception – at a cost of €25 – ouch welcome to the Mediterranean- but with relief I followed the easygoing lad to my stretch of gravel perched atop the sea defences. A little bay had been created for swimming and sunbathing so once I had pitched (about 3 minutes later) I was floating on my back relaxing my hardworked legs admiring the impressive mountain scenery climbing up behind the bay of Moneglia. I idly wondered about the route on towards Lucca – it all looked impressively (worryingly) mountainous to the south but heh that was for another day. Every quest involves a visit to the underworld and I had survived mine! That evening I had one of the best seafood dinners I can remember at the campsite restaurant on a balcony overlooking the sea. My phone went and George from Bristol touched base to check I was doing OK... a very kind touch much appreciated given the crux of a day I had experienced. The pair of Italian ladies at the neighbouring table seemed completely at ease with me filling my guts in my cycling gear. Afterall we were all at the seaside in August in Italy – La Dolce Vita.

Chapter 6. All Roads Lead to Rome

I felt I had mastered the art of my skeletal sleeping mat the following morning as I awoke refreshed ready for a morning swim despite the gravel platform on which my tent was perched. I was swum, packed up and setting off as the sun broke the horizon of the ultramarine bay. Re-entering the tunnels of hell I was grateful for the brevity of the section into the seaside town of Moneglia where I encountered a fellow early morning weekend cyclist. As I was still 'off the map' I thought I would ask him the best way to Lucca. Gesturing up at the roadway on concrete stilts way above us he said the only way was up....or take the train (no progress with the planned cycle route beside the railway yet). So up it was...and it certainly was a memorable climb. Engaging my next to bottom gear (always keep 1 in reserve- it helps psychologically) I started 'spinning' – a mind and body set I had mastered crossing the Alps and Liguria. There was a particularly demoralising moment an hour and a half in when I realised the roadway I had believed the chap was gesturing to wasn't my road but the autostrada...the SS1 which I wanted was some way above! I was beginning to hit empty when I encountered two Saturday morning road cyclists and asked in somewhat of a desperate tone about the whereabouts of a café. 'Just round the corner but the second one is better' came the most helpful and understanding reply. And glory, glory suddenly I had made it onto the Corniche Road SS1 and was replenishing myself with the best cheese toastie and coffee I can remember tasting. This was becoming a trend in catering superlatives. I was beginning to 'get' Italy! Taking stock of my situation I was now some 500 meters above and around 5kms back from the coast with fantastic views south-west down across steep scrubby hills to the coastline far below. The road I had been directed to, the SS 1, was a well surfaced main road which seemed virtually traffic free as all the through traffic was on the Autostrada below. Also referred to as the Via Aurelia after the Emperor Aurelian (270-275CE) who built it to improve an important Roman route north into Etruria and Liguria and extended later as the empire expanded into Gallia Narbonensis (modern day southern France). There was a steady trickle of road cyclists out this Saturday morning coming past the café and I started to realise having put in the graft I might be in for a classic ride. Sure enough the rest of Saturday morning was spent swinging around the hilly contours of the Riviera del Lavante as I learnt this section of the coast is known. The terrain pushes the route somewhat inland over the Passo dei Bracco (615m) and I wasn't remotely tempted to sacrifice all my height gain to head back down to the coast to see the reputedly beautiful but busy 'Cinque Terre' or five villages region.

Instead sticking doggedly to the marvellous cycling route of the Aurelian Way I dropped somewhat into the village of Brugnato where I drank more coffee, bought packed lunch and admired a sculpture 25 metres high of old bikes welded to each other in somebody's (eccentric) front yard. Heading on in the heat of the day

I heard the unmistakeable sound of children larking around in water and realised I was now following the banks of a significant river (the Vara as I later worked out). Stopping to check out a possible swim spot I could see an old trestle bridge across what was a reasonably sized river, deep enough to allow for some swimming. Bingo! I pushed the bike across the bridge, down under its shade on the shingle river bank and rushed into the inviting water. Sea swim at dawn followed by river swim at lunchtime – now this cycle touring was settling into a very enjoyable rhythm! I took the opportunity of having ready access to water to do a bicycle wash and maintenance check. Spinning the front wheel with my front lamp activated should have caused it to illuminate but there was no response. Remembering the words of my set-up mechanic that the connections can work lose over a journey I fiddled around tightening things up and got the front lamp working again. By which time another crew had arrived on the river bank complete with guitar and had attempted some desultory singing. The guitarist was clearly kean but his crew rather too laid back. A mixed age extended family group I assumed – very chilled. For some reason after a final swim I took it into my head to suggest a go at 'Mr Tambourine Man' to the guitarist. Without hesitation he pulled out a harmonica, blew a couple of tuning up notes and indicated he was ready. Gulp, now as everyone who knows me will attest I am not a singer having been dubbed a 'non-singer' in my school days back in a more brutal era when underperformance was considered a natural bar to participation. How the world has changed in this regard as in a more inclusive era we rightly celebrate every child's efforts. Anyway here was my chance to prove that music master wrong 50 years later!

The first three verses went well and with confidence growing I even found myself encouraging mass participation in the choruses. But then I dried up, we all laughed enjoying the moment (I think) and I packed myself up and started pushing back across the trestle bridge. Then, as is the way with memory, the words suddenly returned and I found myself launching back into that final spine tingling stanza from the bridge

And take me disappearing through the smoke rings of my mind
Down the foggy ruins of time
Far past the frozen leaves
The haunted frightened trees
Out to the windy beach
Far from the twisted reach of crazy sorrow
Yes, to dance beneath the diamond sky
With one hand waving free
Silhouetted by the sea
Circled by the circus sands
With all memory and fate
Driven deep beneath the waves
Let me forget about today until tomorrow

I had memorised the song to perform at my departure birthday camp fire in memoriam to brother Geoff and it felt good on this glorious sunny day to be minstrel like 'with one hand waving free' from the trestle bridge down to my newly met Italian friends below. My accompanist waved back and then I was off again, like a rolling stone, refreshed in body and soul, heading south east. At the afternoon coffee stop the bored English speaking café guy asked whether I had lights on the bike. Yes I replied thinking of my lunchtime maintenance effort with satisfaction. 'Good coz you're gonna need them' came the fluent reply. 'There are three tunnels between here and La Spezia,' (the port ahead where I was due to regain the coast); 'the first is the longest - 3kms, the last is the shortest and they are all downhill'. I thanked him and headed off digesting this information. I had already tasted a tunnel but of course that had been single lane and whilst I technically shouldn't have been cycling it the speeds were relatively low. What would a Strada Statale tunnel be like? Whilst still chewing on this I came round a bend and there lay the opening ahead...a mouth-like opening in a vertiginous rocky hillside. I paused to survey the gloomy unlit opening ahead - one lane in either direction, a white line along either side with perhaps a further half metre of tarmac apron non of which could be described as in good condition. Oh well, my lights were in good order, and it wasn't busy so it shouldn't be that bad I thought. Pushing off I remembered the café man's comments 'all downhill' as I gathered speed and suddenly I was engulfed by the darkness as my fantastic front light cast a powerful beam illuminating the road ahead sufficiently to steer round the potholes. But what nobody could have adequately forewarned about was the noise. It was a loud, deep booming noise emanating from a vintage ventilation system which suggested the deep breathing of a Minotaur like monster lurking in the labyrinth. And then came the traffic. Having enjoyed a peaceful Saturday ride now that afternoon was turning to evening there seemed all of a sudden to be a mass return to town in process. Odysseus like I clung to my bike trying to keep my ears shut, my eyes focussed on the road, holding my line so as not be pushed off course and into the perilous edge by insistent car drivers. The incline meant at least I was keeping up with the traffic but by adding speed into the mix reduced the margin for error yet further. White knuckled I emerged blinking into the afternoon sunlight, took a few gasps of fresh air and steadied myself for the next tunnel a few hundred metres ahead. This was at least less of a shock and shorter, again with a short breather before the third, last and fortunately shortest dive into the inferno. Maybe this, the third circle of hell, reserved by Dante for the glutinous would have been an apt end but anyways I escaped once again back into the light and suddenly I was descending into the sizeable port of La Spezia.

The town, a busy working port bustling with ships loading and unloading, was quite a shock to the system. I hadn't really paused to consider where I was headed having made better than expected progress on the downhill run here. Finding a café with Wifi to review my map of the Via Francigena I was excited to realise that after an extensive hiking section through the eastern Ligurian hills the Mon Cenis variant descended to the village of Sarzana 3 kms from La Spezia where I could rejoin it before pushing South along a flat coastal plain. I checked out Sarzana and there was a camping there so the decision was made. Punching Sarzana into my Garmin a route was rapidly generated and with nothing to detain me in this industrial port I was off following the purple route line on the Garmin into an industrial estate, out the other side and up towards what appeared to be quarried hills.

Onward and upward following the Garmin I headed up a lane which seemed a little 'off the beaten track'. Sure enough around a corner the asphalt surface ended at a new house's driveway and beyond lay a mule path climbing up a steep slope to disappear round a bend above. Now I must admit that my Garmin had been set for quiet cycleways including off road options – but a mule path climbing too steeply to ride? Not for the first time cursing the machine Basil Fawlty like I decided to reconnoitre the route ahead on foot. About 200 metres further up the track levelled off, reaching a much older house and then became a perfectly cyclable track through olive groves. As I portered my stuff and bike up the steep slope in two trips this felt like the final ascent required on this leg of my quest. My exhausted brain summoned unbidden the words of my old prep school teacher Miss Barrow reading to us of Christian's quest to reach the celestial city. Onward and upward, overcoming all obstacles came the message as I toiled with first panniers then bike up the final slope.

And final slope it turned out to be. I had forced my way through Liguria and below me lay the delightful hillside town of Sarzana with steep winding streets and a little square onto which I emerged gratefully for refreshments at the 'Bar Pizzeria Centrale'. Once rehydrated I headed down to a delightful camping where I found enough space to sling my little tent before returning on foot through the old town back to the pizzeria for dinner. As I tottered back down the hill through the winding narrow streets breathing in the smells of dinner long eaten, sounds of families enjoying a summer Saturday evening, exchanging furtive glances with adolescents sneaking cigarettes and dodging groups of noisy kids having a last play before bed it felt like I had reached a semi-mythical Italy glimpsed in the movies.

Camping without a flysheet once again, now the reliably fine summer weather had returned, led to an early start the following morning and I picked up my first cycle signage for the Via Francigena almost immediately. The hills finally swung away from the coast to the North making way for a coastal plain over which they glistened in the early morning sunshine like the white cliffs of Dover – however this wasn't chalk but the famed marble of nearby Carrara. Quarried since classical times the modern port of La Spezia was still shipping the stuff continuing a tradition dating back to the Romans. The flatlands stretched away to the South and soon I was cycling past my first pilgrim striding along the pavement. I was so excited I stopped to confirm this bearded chap with pack and staff really was on the Via Francigena. Indeed he was and he seemed not in the least surprised by my enquiry but more so when I responded he was the first pilgrim I had encountered. 'But there are many of us on the path'. Well maybe on the walking route but not so far on my cycling version of it. 'Good road' was mutually murmured and I cycled on.

Not far beyond the Via Francigena route was signed off to the right of the SS1 taking an ancient route across the plain through the ancient Roman port of Luna, now stranded a couple of kilometres inland but initially founded as the port for an early Roman colony in 177 BCE. It was my first Roman archaeological site of the trip and I savoured it to the full, exploring the low walled outline of the town, marvelling at the well preserved statuary depicting imperial family figures in the little site museum before taking the obligatory walk across the fields to a well preserved amphitheatre. My classical education was patchy, strong on language but weak on history, so I had very little idea of the timeline of Roman expansion. I was amazed to learn the Romans were only colonising their own backyard so to speak 100 years before the Gallic wars were fought by Julius Caesar. Do all empires expand exponentially to decay in more leisurely manner? No, the British Empire was a gradual 400 year expansion followed by a rapid collapse over barely 50 years. I wonder if anyone has looked at this systematically across the ages? Meanwhile here at Luna the site included all the now ruined trappings of a Roman town (theatre, amphitheatre, temples, fine houses) and an intact drainage system – a humbling reminder that after all else has decayed our waste disposal systems live on as our epitaph.

I pushed on re-enthused that this journey would improve my Roman education at the very least. On arrival at the next place of any size, Massa, I found it deserted on this Sunday lunchtime. The Cathedral was a relatively uninteresting 19th century edifice situated in a fine square notable for high cloistered sides. Neighbouring the Church was a welcoming looking restaurant just setting up tables in the now shaded cloister and I was pleased to settle in, taking a late coffee before the lunch sitting. The trendy waiter had worked in London and recommended the pasta with black truffle as, he added, 'now it is in season'. 'Fantastico' I responded and settled in for a lazy lunch. Just as I was tucking in who should walk past but none other than my bearded fellow pilgrim. We hailed each other and he didn't need much encouragement to join me, laying down his pack and staff and pulling up a chair. Gijs turned out to be a Dutchman walking from Copenhagen to Rome. 'Why add a northern leg to what was already a 1900 km pilgrimage from Canterbury to reach Rome?' I asked. Well he wondered what it would be like to walk it from an area that had escaped Roman colonisation – to cross a cultural fault line so to speak. I sensed a kindred spirit. Like many he had already walked the Camino and wanted more. He proved excellent lunchtime company as our conversation ranged over historical and cultural dimensions of our respective journeys. Gijs was tolerant of, but amused by, my range of digital gizmos which enabled me to capture my trip both visually and verbally and transmit in the form of a blog. He explained he eschewed recording what he was up to and indeed since the Camino had stripped down his life to be as minimalist as he could (in all but his choice of walking routes!). I could tell he thought I had some way to go in this regard but of course he was far too non-judgemental to say anything. But he did recommend I sample pilgrim accommodation for which I would need to pick up my 'credentials' - evidence of a witnessed self-declaration to be travelling under one's own steam though I noted in a Medieval hangover horse-riding remained acceptable. As if to providentially evidence fellowship amongst pilgrims just at that moment we were joined by a father and daughter who had walked with Gijs a day or two before. They were pleasantly surprised to have caught him – he clearly had everybody's respect on the road for his prodigious effort.

Having stood Gijs, the minimalist, a nice lunch I felt he had more than repaid me with his story and advice...not that anybody was counting. Feeling the need to now make some kilometers I soon crossed the plain heading South-East and started climbing again more gently than in Liguria to cross a low col at Piazzano in the Appian Alps before dropping down in a wonderful swooping series of wide hairpins through forested slopes to the river valley of lovely Lucca. I had booked ahead remembering my favourite piazza from our honeymoon visit when we stayed outside the town in a country house hotel. This time I wanted to be in the heart of the action. As I negotiated my way by bike to the Piazza dell' Amfiteatro I had surely found the action. Just as Massa had been deserted so Lucca was teeming. Lucca's biennial public art exhibition was in situ with intriguing installations dotted theatrically through the town. What a herd we are when we go mass travelling! I enjoy a buzz (for a bit) but spending your entire vacation fighting for air, airtime and a seat at a café would get me down. However the Piazza didn't disappoint being based on a 10,000 seater Roman Amphitheatre dating from the 1st century BCE it can accommodate a crowd without losing its sense of theatre. I was soon checked in as requested to a room with a view over this majestic space. Now I had just one more important task before I could relax. On the advice of Gijs, my minimalist pilgrim lunch companion, I registered my own journey as a pilgrimage via the Lucca Tourist Office and received in return my pilgrim credentials – a small booklet with room for stamps. This was my passport to official pilgrim resthouses on the route south to Rome.

Wandering the town to find refreshment I was suddenly feeling lonely. Had it been a mistake to head through Tuscany with its honeymoon associations? More specifically how did Lucca in August without Susannah compare with Lucca in May with her? The answer seemed to be infinitely poorer – more people, less of the laid back 'icecream' atmosphere that had made it so attractive then. Fixing on a midrange restaurant in a piazza with a free outside table I ordered some pasta and was drawn into conversation with a neighbouring couple of diners, Grad and Louise from Liege in Belgium. The wine was flowing by now on both tables and more sympathetic dining partners one could not have invited. They were half a generation younger than me working hard raising their family now enjoying a long weekend away in the south. But they 'got' what I was about and described their own dreams in turn. As we hugged and parted, best friends for the night, all thoughts of loneliness were banished and I took a last turn around the now calmer late night theatrical streets and piazzas of lovely Lucca reassured that we are not alone with our quests and dreams.

Running around in my head were the famous lines which I had first come across on reading Hemingway's Spanish civil war novel 'For Whom the Bell Tolls'. There on the frontispiece the quotation continues "do not ask for whom the bell tolls – it tolls for thee". Confirming my recollection on arrival in my room I found the original Olde English text which continues 'No man is an Iland, intire of itselfe; every man is a peece of the Continent, a part of the maine;'. Donne was an educated Tudor cleric and metaphysical poet who blew his inheritance travelling for some years in Italy and later Spain. On his return to Elizabethan England he remained somewhat of a (catholic) outsider – I recognised the paradox of the semi-outsider stressing the importance of communitarian collectivism. But that night mildly intoxicated by the companiable evening I slipped into the arms of Morpheus feeling part of the continente – mixing metaphors as I dived into the deeper metaphysical conceits of dreamland.

Back in the wonderful 'B & B Amfiteatro' the following morning Mario served up a hearty breakfast platter and over coffee kindly loaned me the house laptop. After a couple of false starts I managed to upload a series of GPX files detailing the 'Via Francigena' route to Rome into my Garmin. Eureka – I now had the all important route map for the next leg! I did a celebratory circuit of the famous medieval fortified walls of Lucca by bike before following the Garmin route out across the valley of the Arne downstream from Florence. Superb information boards en route did nothing to downplay the importance of the Via Francigena suggesting its creation around the 10th century by the Lombards and its maintenance through the early middle ages with associated hospice/hospital networks to aid travellers was instrumental in creating a peaceable network which in its own right allowed Tuscan hill towns to flourish. The fact that Sigeric had recorded the 79 stages of his journey to Rome in his diary thus preserving his route for the modern pilgrimage movement to rediscover I knew but this wider historical significance was exciting news to me.

My quest to follow the route 'in reverse' of the transmission of classical ideas from Greece to Britain had just deepened significantly. Now the 10th century is a long time before the fall of Constantinopole in 1483 which I was taught as a boy triggered the Renaissance. The story went that the fall of the Roman Empire's eastern capital to the Ottoman Turks triggered a great exodus of people and ideas westward bringing with them the 'rebirth' of classical civilisation and its reinvention via the great outpouring of works of art. Thus the Tuscan hill towns in general and Florence under the Medicis in particular become pivotal to the story. My mother, an amateur artist, had studied the Italian masters at night class and introduced me to some highlights at the Walker Art Gallery back in Liverpool. So it was very much part of my coming of age that as a young man hitchhiking south across Europe I should choose to hang out for a fortnight in Florence absorbing the art in the day and rough sleeping in the Cascine Park at night. But the very route I was now following played an important part in the story of the transmission of ideas westward....hundreds of years prior to the fall of Constantinopole.

Constantinopole is central to the story but the 'Renaissance' is part of a longer and deeper story most recently told superbly in the transformative world history given to us by Peter Frankopan's 'Silk Roads'

(Frankopan 2015). Constantinopole is indeed a pivot point on the series of routes linking the east and the west of the old World. Whilst the term "silk road' awards an apparent primacy to the transportation of goods along this route its role in the transmission of ideas is equally as important. Lucca was an important early centre of silk trading in the 1200's. Frankish Crusaders travelling east to the holy land not infrequently were drawn to Constantinopole in search of financial opportunities to better resource their campaign. One such adventurer was Edward, Prince of England, who in 1271-2 sailed with a small force of English men at arms to Acre to relieve Marmeluke pressure on the Hospitaler stronghold of Krak de Chevaliers. After a spell of middle eastern geo-politicking during which he forged an alliance with Abagha, the Mongol ruler of Persia against the Muslims, the ever-impressive Edward returned home. Accompanying Edward on his holy land foray was one 'Luke of Luka', or Lucasio Natale, as he was more correctly known silk merchant to the king and partner in the Ricciardi Company of Lucca (Kaeuper 2015). In the context of the Italian medieval company, the Corpo was the starting capital contributed by its founding partners. The English word "corporation" is descended from the Latin corpus or body. These Tuscan merchant-bankers were in the process of developing a collective enterprise for financing trade with 'geographical spread, temporal depth, and corporate liability' (Padgett 2012). Here we find the roots of a trading system which would develop into the system of limited liability companies underpinning capitalism.

Add an ambitious, ruthless king like Edward I, who having taken a loan in Genoa on his way back to his investiture, had just discovered an independent means of financing military expansionism and the result is the subjugation of the Welsh. What is more Edward realised the Italians would take wool in payment for their loans. The folllowing year 25% of licensed English wool exports were controlled by Tuscan banking corporations. So here is another strand to the thread linking our remote island to the Mediterranean world. As the grandson of a native Welsh speaking Welshman who had migrated to Liverpool I knew the results of Edward's campaigns from long ago childhood visits on sunny Sundays to the mighty castles he built to control the defeated Welsh.

So it wasn't just monks who took this road to Rome. As the afternoon shadows lengthened the route started to positively ooze history. A beautiful arcaded medieval bridge which led me across a swampy outlet known as the black Arno was commissioned by Cosimo Medici of the famously powerful clan that ran Florence and therefore it's clear resemblance to the Ponte Vecchio is no coincidence. I passed another information board in a cutting above the Arne telling about Leonardo da Vinci 's interest in the marine fossils to be found there causing him to speculate on a pre-existing geological marine phase....not for nothing labelled by my father as 'the last man to know everything that could be known'! With all these historical currents swirling around in my mind I found myself following the Arne East for a few kilometres with a prominent tower visible on the horizon to the south. As I started to climb up the valley slopes towards my destination for the night, a pilgrim hostel in San Miniato, it gradually became clear that the hostel must be near the foot of the tall tower high above me – they aren't known as Italian hill towns for nothing. Having used up my last reserves on the steep climb I was rewarded with a richly decorated piazza, an ornate church, some outbuildings newly converted into a small hostel all topped by a park on the crown of the hill on which stood the imposing tower.

This park would prove my saving grace later that evening. On arrival I was informed by the young hostel keeper that though the hostel was full (there seemed to be several groups of young Italian holidaying youths in the small communal area) I was welcome to use the shower and self catering facilities. I still had some food bought that morning in Lucca so I gratefully took him up on the offer. Having satisfied immediate needs I headed up for the sunset from the park and realised that I would be able to put up a tent there after dark and that such was its popularity as a sunset viewing spot there was a small bar embedded in the walls below the tower. Alessandra the bartender was charming and as it quietened down was keen to use the English she had learnt working in London the previous summer. Joined by her boyfriend I heard all about their travails growing up in Tuscan paradise and why living in shared squalor in Stratford London was far preferable. Given the setting I found this one of the more outstanding examples of the 'grass appearing greener on the other side' that I have ever come across.

The night was memorable for the tower under which I slept (one of many monuments across Italy that is attributable to the energy and vision of the Holy Roman Emperor Frederick II to whom I will return in Puglia to the far south), the hippy sing along that serenaded me to sleep and the thunder and lightning storm that raged through the pre-dawn hour. I managed to get back off to sleep for a final hour before waking to another world of cool, damp, swirling mist.

The weather would transition that day from a Scotch mist on wakening complete with pine forests to a brilliant Tuscan sunny afternoon and back to a Siennese rainstorm all in 12 hours. My colleague at work who told me to take an umbrella when honeymooning in Tuscany in May was not wrong – this is hill country with weather to match. As the morning progressed the hills became more pronounced and wooded and the cycling harder going. Above the woods I broke out into mixed farming country. Beside one field of brilliant yellow sunflowers I watched sheepdogs working a flock of sheep who shone with a yellowish sheen as they picked up the luminous Tuscan light from the flowers against the brown stubble backdrop of the hillside. I was working my way south largely on

Strada Bianchi by this time, unsurfaced limestone chipping covered agricultural lanes largely avoided by cars as the chippings are lethal for paintwork! They aren't great for the knees either. If one attempts to freewheel its quite 'technical' (ie tricky to maintain control) without specialist fat tyres and the consequence of a wheel wrenching suddenly to one side is typically a fall. On the flip side climbing on loose chippings is much harder work than on a 'blacktop' surfaced road. The bonus is the lack of other vehicles and the views. Taking a Strada Bianchi out of San Gimigagno after an overcrowded lunchtime stop there memorable for a fortifying white bean and boar stew the route looped all the way round the town giving stunning views of the 'mini Manhattan' towers across the fields with not a soul in sight. Bliss in the brilliant bright sunshine after the morning rain. The afternoon slipped by as I wound my way via less crowded yet still achingly beautiful Renaissance hill towns of Poggibonsi and Colle di Val d'Elsa before dropping onto a welcome 10km stretch of flat ex-railway and beginning the approach to Siena which had come into focus as my next destination. By this time the weather was closing in and I reluctantly bypassed a sign pointing to an Etruscan megalith. On the horizon above me a remarkably well preserved battlemented castle caught the eye whilst a sign on my cycleway was the first indication of Rome (300kms to the south) ahead. This region was so rich in cultural treasures it was hard to take it all in. The final ascent was a hard climb through forest which spat me out on a busy road approaching Siena thankfully along a ridge. I had found an edge of town villa which sounded superb on an end of day deal so was feeling my way towards the town hoping my tired legs wouldn't have to attempt a further climb. Then the thunderstorm which had been threatening broke around me. In inclement conditions I am especially defensive so I was riding down the middle of the single lane in a busy underpass when I suffered inconsiderate Italian driving - to be fair for the first time – at the hands of a guy in a Fiat who swung out dangerously to pass me. My very clear positioning was of course designed to prevent exactly this manoeuvre - I guess in his head bikes could never be allowed to occupy the place of a car. Anyway as he veered round me sounding his horn I snapped and put in a 100m sprint worthy of a Tour de France finish on the up-side of the underpass, caught the Fiat and flicked him the Vs with a heartfelt cry of 'FU Tosser'! As I put on my blog that night I thought this was worthy of bonus 'General Competition (ie all round)' points for the effort plus expletive though my readers' responses suggested the effort might have got lost in translation.

It was with some relief I arrived at my villa destination in a magnificent setting just south of the historic centre only to realise I had just come all the way round the town of Siena on the busy circular main road bypassing the historic centre! The lovely guy on the desk having confirmed I could park my cycle in the outbuildings beside the ornate gardens (very upmarket) went on to congratulate me for timing my arrival on the eve of the

Palio. What? 'Oh yes sir, the famous horse race in the square you can't possibly miss it...there will be training tomorrow night and the real thing the following evening!' An interesting issue for the morrow but for now I was all in! Having enjoyed the passing of the thunderstorm in the magic of the sunset hour looking out on the red Sienese walls I ate locally and passed out in my lovely bed!

The following day I took a few things in a cycle bag to enjoy the day in Siena and check out what all the fuss was about. The Piazza del Campo is shaped like a giant scallop (think of rival Florence's iconic painting by Botticelli of the Birth of Venus from a giant shell) with the hinge at the lowest point climbing quite steeply up either side to the elevated rim. The result is a highly theatrical space permitting a large standing crowd good lines of sight whilst temporary seated galleries lining the perimeter medieval buildings provide perfect vantage spots for the great, the good and those willing to part with hundreds of euros. For the rest of us the shell-like piazza provides a large toiletless unshaded space overseen by the tall pencil like Torre del Mangia (which standing to the south-east is no help with the sun in the late afternoon) in which to mingle during the interminable pre-race hours.

I spent the day in the town memorably visiting the hospital (now museum) complex of Santa Maria de la Scala founded a 1000 years ago to serve the pilgrims on the Via Francigena headed for Rome. Descending from the modern street level several storeys one can wander the medieval passageways deep under the city. Siena's urban geography remains medieval and down in the bowels of Santa Maria amidst the religious relics you can really taste that atmosphere which remains dense, dark, and oppressive. Re-emerging into the light I headed back to the Campo where officials were testing the temporary tufa track (earth laid on the ancient cobbles) for moisture levels after the previous day's rain. They were satisfied it was dry enough for the training race to go ahead and I watched a 'training session' with a few thousand locals and passing tourists on the Campo. The horses and their jockeys cantered round the track on the perimeter of the piazza amidst a buzzy atmosphere which was exciting after my quiet days on the bike and I instantly decided to stay for the main event the following day. I rang my hotel who regretted to inform me that they had no space (unsurprisingly) but would be happy to house my bike and pannier until I returned. I managed to find a room there and then in a B & B right in the heart of the old town and headed back out for dinner. Everywhere was busy (Siena, August, the night before the Palio) but I found a tiny free table towards the back of a traditional Tuscan restaurant where the young guys running the place made me welcome thanks to our football banter (always a marvellous bridge builder in my experience). So much so that I reserved my little table for the following evening which I figured would be even madder. Before turning in for the night I was drawn back to the Campo where I fell into conversation with the off-duty security guys in town for the big event. Members of an elite parachute regiment the three guys I fell in with were intense in an outwardly laid-back way. Hearing my tale I was gratified to be pronounced to be 'on a soul journey'. There was something Homeric in the chance encounter with these impressively vigilant warriors. From these fellow questers I could ask for no higher compliment! On that note I took my leave and headed to my bed.

Having sought and received advice from a variety of sources the consensus next day seemed to be to ensure I was on the Piazzo by 5 p.m. I therefore headed for the cathedral in the early afternoon (shortly after paying my respects to our neighbourhood horse stabled just behind my B & B!) only to find the narrow streets jam-packed with sightseeers as costumed locals followed banners and drummers towards the cathedral. It seemed like the whole town plus a vast party crowd in town for the Palio were all attempting to head the same way. Reaching a good vantage point at an open intersection of lanes around the corner from the cathedral I stopped to soak up the scene. Each of the seventeen neighbourhoods (*contrade*) of medieval Siena had six representatives in the parade led by their banner and drummers. After a blessing which included their horse and rider they processed out behind various representatives and symbols of the city. In their costumes amidst the medieval streets with all the heat and dust of the crowds, squinting against the brilliant sunshine, I managed momentarily to filter out the mobile phones and the surrounding chatter and caught a glimpse of the medieval pageantry underlying the glitzy modern show. As the clocks of the town struck five p.m. I hastily beat a retreat cutting ahead of the parade back to the Campo. Disaster, as my planned route was blocked and I suddenly realised the entire Campo had been closed off and the crowds were being redirected round the outside towards the western corner. I moved as quickly as I could arriving in a large holding area at the back of the Campo where large numbers of the paratroopers with whom I'd enjoyed a drink the previous evening were now running a large and efficient security operation to process the crowds and filter us through into the Campo.

My earlier concerns were calmed as this seemed a well practiced operation and presumably they knew there was still plenty of capacity. So at 5.30 p.m. I emerged into the still hot afternoon sun of the Campo and reconnoitred for my 'spec' as we used to say on the Anfield Kop. I settled on a point roughly two thirds up and midway round the banked 'shell' adjacent to the 15th century Fonte Gaia fountain where a complex long system of conduits deliver water to the heart of the city. As the Campo filled up around me over the next hour or so I became aware that the scattered tourists like myself were in amongst more solid blocks of locals sporting one of the neighbourhood colours. It dawned on me that the Campo's human geography for the day mirrored that of the medieval town. 'My' neighbourhood i.e. that of my room in the Albergo

Centrale lay to the immediate North of the Campo in the Civetta neighbourhood of the shoemakers guild, symbolised by the owl in red and black colours. But immediately around me the predominant colours seemed to be the green and white which I learnt represented Oca, the dyemakers, to the west of the Campo. Many tourists were touting the coloured neckerchiefs of 'their' adopted neighbourhoods. An Italian father and son beside me in green surprised me by admitting to being southerners who came up to Siena regularly for the biannual Palio. They explained there were two annual runnings but this, the August Palio falling on the Ferrogusto, the Assumption day of Mary which is a big feast day throughout the catholic Mediterranean dating back to the Romans was the bigger one.

A buzz in the crowd and the sound of trumpets heralded the arrival of the main procession led in by standard bearers, with each contrade which had been selected by lot to run (the track is just wide enough to accommodate 10 horses) represented by a flag holder with horse and jockey (in their contrade colours by now) having been blessed at the cathedral by the Bishop. Those 7 contrade not running were also represented as was the town council in suitably costumed medieval splendour. Bringing up the rear of the procession was the ox cart, bearing the Palio itself plus more trumpeters. Every few metres the procession paused to allow the flag holders to throw their flags high into the sky before expertly bringing them back under control by catching them as they fell back to the ground. The entire procession then had to be seated in the temporary gallery with the best view of the opening and finishing strait down at the bottom of the Piazza below the Tower in front of the Palazzo Publico.

Finally, we were getting to the main event. An extraordinary hush settled around the piazza observed by the huge crowd of 30-40,000 onlookers as 9 of the ten horses lined up in order of their allotted places from inside to outside. One horse, the rincorsa, hangs back and only when he finally enters the space between the ropes the starter activates a mechanism that instantly drops the canapo (the front rope). This process (the mossa) can take a very long time, as deals have usually been made between various contrade and jockeys that affect when the rincorsa moves,. After 5 or so attempts the tension was becoming unbearable. So perhaps the starter was ready to allow a slightly wider margin – but on this occasion the 'overexcitable' rincorsa with his 'struggling rider' came from behind the pack to hit the starting line perfectly accelerating into a gallop as he did so thus stealing a march on his more static fellow 9 contestants. Given the race itself involves tearing around the scallop shaped 'track' hanging on for dear life (no saddles!) if your horse is fast and you stay on the leader has an immense advantage which is exactly how it all fell out in this race with the aforesaid horse winning for Lupa, the bakers, also to the north of the Campo. Lupa as the name may suggest to those who have studied Latin has the symbol of a she-wolf marking the association of Siena with the founding of Rome. In myth Romulus and Remus, abandoned at birth and famously reared by a she-wolf went on to found Rome and after Romulus murdered Remus bathing Rome in the blood of fratricide, Remus's two sons Senius and Aschius fled Rome to found Siena.

The respectful silence disappeared once the race started to be replaced by a deafening guttural roar. The actual race seemed to last all of 2 minutes after an entire day of preparations. As a standing spectator in the Campo I spun round catching glimpses of the galloping horses with their riders visible as flashes of colour above the crowd. Whips were being whirled willy-nilly as the riders urged on their own mounts and attempted to interfere with their rivals. This was no holds barred racing. In the manner of all gambling events all those intimately involved with the action instantly grasped the result and the significance for their neighbourhood reputations and their pockets. The Palio, a painted banner handed to the winning contrade (and like Sigeric's papal 'pallium' derived from the Latin for cloth) was immediately dispensed to the winning jockey whose supporters rushed round in wild celebration to form both an honour guard and defence force. Simultaneously belligerents from other contrade feeling slighted or worse cheated by the manner of the victory rushed over to vent their spleen at the victors. The resulting melee is short lived as the victorious contrade head for their geographically appropriate exit from the Campo. As an unitiated newbie I left the Campo thoroughly bemused by the race unclear as to the victor even misbelieving for a moment that my neighbourhood had won as the merriment seemed to be heading towards my quarter. However carefully skirting the more vociferous groups on the narrow lanes and reaching my restaurant I was able to watch the endless TV replays and have the tactics explained. So what I had mistaken for gamesmanship by one horse over the start to rig the race turned out to be a 'legitimate' tactic in this peculiar and unique event.

Millions are won and lost on each running of the Palio I was reliably informed. That, and the confirmation of bragging rights for neighbourhoods for the following year combine to create the heady mix of pageantry and competition that is the Palio. The highest compliment I can pay it is to compare it favourably with the Merseyside Derby. The passion is just as intense and the colours a far greater spectrum than simply red or blue! The other comparison from my own travels is with the binary neighbourhood ritual competitions whereby two neighbourhoods of Newar communities in Nepal including Kathmandu, Patan and Bhaktapur compete in a giant tug of war to pull a juggernaut bearing an idol through the city. What these festivals have in common, with their mix of the colourful and chaotic, the sacred and the profane, are the recognition of urban rivalries transforming them in the process into something to be celebrated. Just as I compared Newari towns with their Tuscan counterparts I would go so far as to compare the civic space of the Durbar Square in Patan with the Piazze del Campo in Siena as the most atmospheric urban spaces I have been fortunate enough to hang out in.

The following morning I walked through the old town savouring its sights and sounds one last time as I retraced my steps to the villa hotel beyond the walls where my trusty bicycle awaited. Reunited with my stead I experienced such a strong sense of attachment I instinctively found myself reaching for a name with which to personalise my 'Thorn'. The messenger of the Olympian Greek Gods was an obvious choice and so that day Hermes was christened. I was soon heading south stopping every now and again to look back at the terracotta coloured town on the ridge behind me. It felt like Hermes and I were crossing a Renaissance painting with a backdrop of light blue skies, rolling hills in shades of yellow and brown studded with reddish terracotta buildings and green elegantly tapering Cyprus trees. The Via Francigena here picks up the Arbia, a seasonal torrent which is said by Dante to have flowed red after the battle of Montaperti on the ridge outside Siena in 1260 when the Sienese, with the aid of German heavy cavalry supplied by Holy Roman Empire allies scored a decisive defeat against the Florentine army, with more than 10,000 dead. This conflict was one of a whole series between the Guelphs and Ghibellines, rival factions that took the parts of the Papacy and the Holy Roman Empire, respectively, in Italy in the 12th and 13th centuries. My route on the Via

Francigena picked a path between the warring factions on the path of neutrality.

On a short steep section of strada bianca I came a cropper, failing to control Hermes adequately on the descent. Bizarrely as I lay grazed and feeling sorry for myself a jogger came by and we exchanged gruff 'mornings' in English! There were ex pats tucked away in these hills I realised. I found myself pushing the bike on the next uphill due to the uneven surface that makes climbing harder and downhills dangerous. I resolved to come off the strada bianchi at the next opportunity but in the meantime was charmed by some handsome horses in a field on the ridge. I realised there a was a chap on the other side of the fence tending them and unlike my previous encounter this guy was a friendly foreigner from Belgium. Falling into discussion with Carole he was amused by my tales of Siena and the Palio. He ran a horse riding operation and was knowledgeable about the Palio, stressing the specialist nature of the horses run in the race. He emphasised the value of the race to Siena and made me realise how I had been sucked (willingly) into a much hyped event! However his best information from my point of view was that he felt the Via Francigena missed an opportunity in these parts and he directed me instead to deviate onto the ridge where he took pony trekking tourists. This route kept high with good views before dropping back down to Buonconvento, where I would rejoin the official route. Following his advice I stopped for morning Tai Chi on a wonderful vantage point surrounded by what seemed endless flowing Tuscan ridges lined with Cyprus trees, receding into the far distance to the barely perceptible ochre smudge of Siena.

Picking my way past abandoned farm buildings the track led into the cool shaded streets of Buonconvento, yet another charming medieval stone-built town. Quiet after the hustle and bustle of Siena I enjoyed a late morning coffee, found a supermarket in which to buy supplies and headed out of town on the beautifully surfaced SR2, the main road to Rome. My rationale was that as we entered the heat of the day paradoxically sitting on a moving bike is about the coolest place to be and unlike this mad Englishman the Italians are long since off the road enjoying a siesta. So I settled into the rhythm of some road riding and watched with satisfaction as the kilometres rolled by. The country was very rural, with increasingly high rocky slopes to either side of the route as the rolling Tuscan Hills gave way to volcanic country all reinforcing the idea of sticking to the main road for now. I was well into my rhythm, thankful that I had left the strada bianchi behind for the present at least. The psychologists call these 'flow' states when you are in the moment, pushing yourself sufficiently to lose oneself in the activity. The burr of the chain, the sensation of wind on your cheeks, the heat 'out there' from which one feels strangely sheltered beneath the old fashioned peaked cycle cap (under my helmet) behind sun glasses. As the afternoon wore on I could just about make out the unlikely figure of another cyclist up ahead. Of course this spurred me on to catch him up if only to find out who else would be mad enough to be on the road at this time of day. The fact that the cyclist was in a bright red shirt only reinforced the sense of a target. I gradually reeled him in over the next half an hour or so and as I reached him and exchanged greetings we immediately realised we were both English ('mad dogs and Englishmen!'). A few minutes later by chance we were approaching a short tunnel and as we paused for light adjustment (my new companion lacked a front light and therefore tucked in behind Hermes with our automatic LED!) we picked up the conversation to establish that James from Dulwich, like me, was headed for Rome. Unlike me James had been following the the Via Francigena all the way from Canterbury and having loitered less, was pretty focussed on his destination. After my unscripted Palio days in Siena I was happy to be on the move again and we passed a vigorous afternoon's cycling together pushing south on the SR2. As the sun started to cool little wispy clouds started to coalesce and briefly gave us a light shower during which we stopped for tea at a rustic wayside café complete with Italian beauty in the shape of the rugged proprietor's daughter. This led to some good natured banter about abandoning the journey to take up residence here with the beauty, bonding laddish humour which sounds corny at this remove but was at the time entirely in keeping with our slightly hysterical mind states induced by a long day of cycling in the hot sun!

The question of our evening destination was beginning to enter the reckoning. We were both packing tents so camping was the obvious choice and where better than on a lake shore given the heat we had absorbed all day. The massive Lago Bolsena lay within range (thanks to our afternoon efforts) and looked promising. So, decision made, we had a final hour up to the town of San Lorenzo Nuevo where we crested the hill to find a Gnocchi festival in full flow complete with the Madonna of the Gnocchi specially brought out of her church for the occasion. Of course we were starving and thirsty so having bought our tickets we were soon tucking into gnocchi and tomato sauce washed down with a couple of beers, eaten on trestle tables as we exchanged tales of the road surrounded by gnocchi worshipping Italian holidaymakers. Perfect! With darkness rapidly descending we had a steep descent to the lakeshore and the camping identified on the map before we could relax. So leading the way as the one with lights we made a surprisingly chilly descent (the first hint of autumn), located the campsite without difficulty and found a pitch in the dark (not hard given our two miniature tents). Over a glass of wine in the campsite bar I heard more tales of James' colourful life most recently in the guise of a vintage car enthusiast and trader following in his father's footsteps, a Formula 1 engineer from the early days in the 1950s. I have previously encountered this genre of romantic motor car enthusiast during a brief sojourn in Wareham, Dorset and can't claim to 'get it' myself...but each to their own and it certainly made for entertaining stories of travels halfway across the world to inspect vintage Alfa Romeos with a view to import, restore and resell them. The Via Francigena was for him, like Gijs, a follow up to a Camino pilgrimage and he more than I deserved the soul journey tag I suspected. There was a previous Italian girlfriend caught up in the mix and talk of another Italian friend of a friend in Rome who was proving elusive but with whom he might stay on arrival. What was clear was that he had 'done' the road the hard way pushing on alone at speed and was ready to arrive in Rome. Having enjoyed the catch up ride on the main road I, however, was in no rush and we agreed to part the following morning. Having exchanged phone numbers we took to our separate coffin tents and when I woke up the next morning he was gone.

I enjoyed my day by Lago Bolsena which slipped by swimming, doing Tai Chi, reading and relaxing in a camper van neighbour's hammock. But I was ready to hit the road early the following morning following the eastern shore of the lake as far as Bolsena before climbing into the hills above to reach Montefiascone high above. The Via Francigena leads straight to the medieval church of San Flaviano, which proved to be an unusual architectural gem. The lower 11th century Romanesque interior with round Roman arches, is encased within a somewhat later 12th century 'gothic' shell i.e. less rounded and more pointed arches to the exterior. The great age of gothic cathedral building to the north in France and Britain was already well on the way when these modest but interesting stylistic modifications were being made to San Flaviano. Unsurprisingly this close to Rome the Roman building style or 'Romanesque' would persist here longer than elsewhere. The Byzantine style had meanwhile developed in the eastern empire and would come back to influence Italian design particularly through Venice and what has become known as the Venetian Gothic!

As so often I was enjoying my church refuge despite being an atheist. For this my father must shoulder the blame! As an engineer who had run the family building business he took a keen interest in historical architecture. Many are the churches visited during childhood with an abiding memory of him striding past the altar rail in search of a particularly richly described architectural feature. This disregard for the sacred made an impact on my then more vivid childhood imagination which had a lasting effect. The fact that he always escaped divine consequences added to my growing realisation that there was indeed nothing empirical to enforce the demarcation between the sacred and the profane. He left me with this habit (like so many) of rooting around in old churches taking in that timeless sense of history of the place.

My eye was caught by a medieval wall painting featuring three well dressed young gentleman and three skeletons. Here again was the medieval morality tale of the three young gentlemen faced by their deaths ('Dit des trois morts et des trois vifs' as it was known where I had first come across it in a medieval French church north of Orleans). Proof indeed of the transmission of ideas up and down the Via Francigena and the then monopoly of the church in the spread of ideas around the credo-state of Christendom!

San Flaviano turned out not only to be blessed with surviving medieval wall painting but also with historic tombs. Of particular note I discovered that of a previous traveller on the Via Francigena in the early 12th century, a German bishop called Johannesburg Defuk, who enjoyed his wine so much , we are told, that he sent his valet ahead to research which lodging had the most drinkable wine. Once identified he proceeded to inscribe EST (here it is) on the door as instructed. The story goes (as told by the good people of Montefiascone) that the Moscatello wine hereabouts was so good that the valet inscribed EST EST EST on the door of a local establishment in his excitement. The Bishop didn't get out alive but left funds for his tomb to be toasted with wine annually and the local vintage earned the name EST EST EST! Musing on the personal relevance of this cautionary tale I found myself surrounded by a large Italian walking party and decided it was time to leave them to their potted account of the church. Pausing on an airy terrace with magnificent views out over Lago Bolsena back towards Tuscany now to the North the walking party caught me and greeted me warmly as a fellow traveller (and church visitor!).

No sooner had I escaped the madding crowd for a second time than I found myself pouring over my map on the edge of the town trying to check whether the Garmin was right to take me down a vanishingly small lane steeply downhill when up behind rode a young Italian woman also apparently seeking the Via Francigena. Camilla, as I soon learnt, spoke excellent English fortunately and having both concluded this was the correct route we careered joyously downhill exchanging shouted comments about the joys of multiday cycling. Having got to the bottom we realised we were lost and Camilla immediately put her local language skills to good use getting a detailed account of how to recover the route without (crucially) having to go back up the hill. We knew we were back on the trail when our minor road ran alongside a stone paved track on which my erstwhile Italian walking party was making steady progress. This third meeting now elicited effusive greetings as if we had all known each other for years though I must admit the walkers were perhaps especially enlivened given my apparent good fortune of meeting up with an attractive cycling companion. Picking our way gingerly down the ancient paving stones it seemed rather churlish to complain about the state of the road given that we were on the original Roman paving of the Via Cassia.

This antique stretch gave way after a while to a dirt road on which Camilla and I made steady progress, her insisting she was holding me back and I equally insistent that '*piano piano*' (slowly slowly) suited me just fine today. I was enjoying her company and when the conversation turned to naming of our bikes I realised we had both given this serious thought. I secretly delighted in an ernest conversation of suitable bike names with this astrophysicist in training. We were aware that there were thermal springs somewhere ahead and were independently planning to stop and sample their delights. Sure enough after an hour or two a simple rustic wood cabin beside the path indicated the entrance (free for pellegrinos!) and that afternoon I couldn't quite believe my luck to be lounging in an outdoor thermal pool, surrounded by relaxing Italian bathers, chatting with Camilla and later a couple of other walking pellegrinos. But all good things must pass and I dragged myself out as the afternoon shadows started to lengthen, as I was aiming for Sutri still a good 30 kms away. I made my farewells to the lovely Camilla (who needed some thinking space on her pilgrimage to decide what direction to take with her studies and her life) and enjoyed a fast leg though open country before getting a bit lost in woodland that eventually yielded a route out to Vetralla. This was the heartland of the Etruscans and later the scene of the first Roman expansion. But the weather was once again unsettled with electrical storms in the air coming down from the North clearly visible across this big open volcanic landscape. I had by now telephoned ahead and booked a room in Sutri after my last couple of nights camping and so needed to get there before nightfall. Regaining the SS2 I had a fast ride with a tailwind through wooded uplands as far as Capranica which looked inviting in the late afternoon light. But Sutri lay another 5 kms down what turned out to be a scenic river valley before a dramatic climb into the town itself. I collapsed at the first square and took a beer whilst getting directions from my landlady who said she would meet me in the next square! My hostess turned out to have a medical student daughter studying in Rome. I was made very welcome and her daughter was duly sent down with the sweetest red peaches from their garden I have ever tasted. Wandering back to the square I chose what I gleaned to be the more foodie of the two café bars and enjoyed one of those idyllic southern piazza evenings entertained by the local kids at play and various mini dramas of town life playing out in the public theatre of the square. The pasta was delicious (with rabbit I recall) as was the wine and I retired for the night satiated.

Sutri possessed a strategic importance as its fortified volcanic outcrop overlooks the road North between Rome and Etruria giving it prominence during the early Punic wars as Rome fought to establish itself against the then dominant Etruscans. The modern town gateway which carries single lane traffic up a backstreet sits on the original Roman stone blocks. Later the town became an important refuge for the popes who frequently stopped here and used it for their endless political meetings with representatives of the Emperor. Having explored its Tuffa amphitheatre (impressive and much older than the Colosseum) I tried its Etruscan tombs but unfortunately I couldn't get into the most interesting one which was subsequently used for the worship of Mithras, a cult figure derived from Zoroastrianism popular with the Roman army and prefiguring the more explicitly monotheistic Christian era with which it overlaps. When I repaired up the hill to collect my stuff I decided on a whim to drop in the local 'head' shop which I had noticed the previous evening, sat between the health food shop and the bank just round the corner from the town square. I had been aware of the legalisation of marijuana in Italy but I was still weirdly anxious as I slipped in to make a purchase. Oh yes sir, the shopkeeper smoothly put me at my ease – no skunk (the highly industrialised production from northern Europe) here we chiefly stock Californian St Semilion! Well of course I should have realised with partial legalisation in the US of course the Californians would corner the market! Good luck to them I reflected walking back to my room patting the €20 deal in my back pocket. Hmm this trip simultaneously back into my youth and forward into my third age was certainly living up to the billing – here was more evidence that 'the times they are a changing'!

I was now within striking distance of Rome but planned for one more night on the road and didn't really have any particular destination in mind. So after my Etruscan investigations I headed off late morning happy to take whatever would turn up by day's end. By late lunch I had traversed an extensive fig orchard (where I had been given more fruit by the guys

harvesting) and arrived at a local beauty spot called
Monte Gelato where the route crosses the river Treja
on a scenic stretch of stepped rock pools. Italians are
funny at beauty spots - instead of swimming in the
beautiful cool mountain water they were spending their
time posing for highly contrived photos (girls pushing
out bosoms and guys sucking in tummies). Having
myself swum my picnic lunch was rather hurried due
to unexpected light drizzle. This triggered a frenzied
mass exodus of the visitors in their cars fortunately in
the direction from whence I had come. Very
impressively a guy I had met with Camilla back at the
pools the previous day came marching through at this
stage. He had recently demobbed from the Italian army
so presumably was in the shape of his life. I pushed my
bike for a kilometre or so as we strode across another
stretch of Roman paving up beyond the Treja river, one
of tributaries of the Tiber. He could have been a
centurion in this timeless landscape. Wishing each
other good pilgrimages I remounted and enjoyed some
lovely riding in lightly wooded country on an obscure
backroad. The afternoon drizzle had settled into an
unusually grey afternoon as I made my way along a
lonely, marshy, lowland stretch. Up ahead rose an
impressive church tower and soon enough my track
started to ascend out of the minor river valley I had
been following up to a substantial settlement which
turned out to be Campagnano di Roma. As was my
custom I took the opportunity of refreshment whilst
taking stock of my situation. It was getting on time
wise, the weather wasn't at all promising and the next

place Formello (said to have a Renaissance pilgrim hostel) was another hour's ride down the road. Sat in the rather run down square the bar was authentically filled with men and the whole place had a rather out of the way feeling – very different from 'on the map' Sutri. Dithering as whether to stay or push on the die was cast when Bruno and his son piped up from a neighbouring table 'Are you a pellegrino?'. They had been walking since leaving their home in Switzerland and with his Italian roots Bruno took control of the situation. I was soon to realise this was his style but for now it was quite a surprise to have someone take over my accommodation search making enquiries in the bar on my behalf. Amusingly Booking.com beat the word of mouth approach and within half an hour my landlady had come down to the bar to pick me up! Tonight I was in a first floor apartment around the corner in the old town just across from that church tower I had spied out from the valley below. Hermes was safely installed besides my bedroom on his own balcony as I headed back down for a prearranged rendezvous with Bruno and his son. We then enjoyed what turned out to be a highly sociable evening as he single-handedly rounded up every pellegrino overstaying in Campagnano that night to orchestrate us all round one big table at the jolliest restaurant in the place where we all ate and drank and exchanged stories into the night. Admittedly as I learnt a cyclist has it easier than a walker, but as one of three solo travellers present we also had an intensity of experience at a personal level (the other two had actually teamed up platonically for the remainder of the journey) which I think for me more than made up for the lack of blisters! Anyway on this my last night before Rome (the walkers had a couple of days left which sounded like they could be a bit of a slog down city streets) I was now a fully-fledged pellegrino!

The following morning's ride took me through a pretty wooded hilly nature reserve before descending to the town of Formello. There I was curious to check out the 'renaissance palazzo' pilgrim hostel which I hadn't pushed for the previous day. Good decision! The lovely Nina proudly showed me the newly renovated palazzo library (closed), museum (closed) and the Hostel (closed). Over a picnic lunch in a wooded copse just outside the town I found myself musing on the general shut down across Italy around the August 15 assumption festival. Ferragusto it turns out dates from 18 BCE when the Emperor Augustus (of whom more in Rome) decided to join up several festivals in favour of a general shutdown referred in Latin as feriae Augusti. This coordinated summer break turns out to be a long running habit in these parts. In my Liverpool childhood such traditions as the builder's fortnight or the Lancashire Wakes Weeks expressed a similar concept of a general shutdown to allow a collective escape to the seaside. The idea that all the family can be off together is of course a good one. Maybe, what is strange, is how alien it feels to a northern European. Imagine a hostel designed for summer use closed for the summer holidays.

Setting aside these thoughts I set off for Rome in the heat of the day unsure what to expect. James had recommended a cheap hostel near the main train station which he had used before so I had a destination but I had little idea how the Via Francigena would enter the city. After a messy couple of kilometres negotiating a tatty path under the outer ring road signage indicated a much improved track which emerged onto the right bank of the Tiber. And that was that! I had a magnificent run in on a purpose built cycle track alongside the river known as the 'Way of the Resistance' in celebration of the role of women in opposing fascism during the 1940's often organising on their bikes. What a 'right on' approach to the Eternal City.

Chapter 7. The Eternal City

The outer suburbs with willows along the banks of the Tiber rapidly gave way to more gritty urban scenes which equally rapidly gave way to the casual elegance of central Rome. Suddenly the path left the river bank and I was negotiating multi-lane roads approaching the Vatican. Somehow I found myself outside the Castel Sant'Angelo amidst the touristy throng wheeling Hermes through the traffic choked approach across some traffic lights into the pedestrianised approach to St Peter's Square. And there was the destination of the Via Francigena towering in front of me. Feeling quite emotional I hopped onto Hermes to cycle the last kilometre of this leg of my journey with a surge of un-pilgrim like pride in my efforts. Having taken the obligatory selfie I then set about finding my way across to my hostel. Checking the map carefully I could hardly believe it – cross the Tiber, keep going past the Pantheon and the Forum as far as the Colosseum then head up left across the Park Dell Colle Oppio and I'd reach the quarter of my hostel! Blimey all roads lead to Rome and not just to Rome but to the heart of the ancient empire...once I had got myself sorted out I knew I wanted to pick up the story as close to the beginning of the place as I could.

But that could wait - first things first- to the hostel. On arrival it was friendly enough though I hadn't really got my head around shared rooms with bunk beds. I introduced myself to Tareq, the gentle guy I would get to know a little over the next five days who used this hostel as his base when in Rome. He ran a clothing business back home in Libya but seemed to commute between Germany and Rome when he wasn't home. Returning to the shared lobby area to make some tea and plan my evening I was delighted to hear the dulcet tones of James telling the student running reception the trials and tribulations of his attempted day out.

He seemed equally pleased to see me and before too long we retired to a neighbouring restaurant with which he was familiar and we were swapping tales. I had enjoyed a more scenic run from Lago di Bolsena than James who had kept doggedly to the Via Aurelia main road into Rome. His Italian contacts had been out of town so he had been spending his remaining days in the hostel. He was due home by plane the next day and so this was indeed a fortuitous re-meeting. We toasted our success in getting this far and wished each other well in our respective endeavours before creeping back and in my case climbing up over Tareq's recumbent and snoring figure into my top bunk.

I do not propose to give a blow by blow account of my five days in Rome. However staying with my theme I do intend to share those experiences which shed light on the role of Rome in the transmission of classical culture from ancient Greece to 20th century Liverpool. Having retraced my steps back to the river I dropped down to the river bank which had to be the heart of early Rome. There I enjoyed the ancient bridge piers and single remaining arch of the Pons Aemilius dating from the 2nd century. This bridge, whilst a remarkable survival, still dates hundreds of years later than the founding of Rome. The city grew out of hilltop villages on the left bank of the Tiber, notably the Palatine and the Quirinal hills where archeological remains of fortified settlement date back to the 8th century BCE have been found. By 500 BCE Rome had grown strong enough to exert some push back on the then dominant Etruscans to the North.

Having got a sense of the extent of the ancient city stretching from the river where I stood, past the outlying Field of Mars as far as the main railway station where I was staying close to surviving stretches of the 4th century BCE Servian walls (11 kms in length), I started to explore the riverside remains freely accessible to the public. Cutting in from the Tiber I immediately stumbled across a pedestrianised area containing a huge theatre complex (the Marcello Theatre started by Julius Caesar) and intriguingly the giant white Carrara marble columns of a temple to Apollo. This I reasoned might shed some light on the relationship of what was then not-so-ancient Greece to the early Romans. Reading up about the properly named Temple of Apollo Sosianus I found it to be an early temple built in thanks to Apollo the Healer, for deliverance from an outbreak of plague in 433 BCE and lay just outside the Pomerium, the boundary of the inner, sacred area of Rome proper. So in the early days Apollo, a Greek god was considered foreign and therefore could not at this stage be worshipped within the inner sanctum of the evolving city.

The Greeks weren't that far away with important colonial city states like Syracuse thriving in Sicily during this period. The Roman expansion South occurred in competition with the other western Mediterranean power Carthage who were to clash with Rome in three brutal 'Punic' wars as the two super-powers vied with each other for regional control. The wars raged intermittently for over a hundred years from 264BCE to 146BCE and Rome was of course the eventual victor but not before Hannibal in the second Punic war had marched an army from Spain, across the Alps to the (Servian) gates of Rome, swung round south-east of the city and annihilated the then biggest Roman army ever put in the field at Cannae pretty close to my final Italian destination Bari. The loss of life at Cannae has been compared to that of the Somme – this was war on a scale not previously seen. I was aware Hermes and I had been following in the footsteps of the great Hannibal and his elephants over the Alps down to the Po valley but I now realised we would be on his path again to the heel of Italy. Sicily was to become the first Roman Province run by a governor and Macedonia (modern North and Central Greece) rapidly followed after the battle of Corinth in 146BCE. A new province Achaea was annexed at this time containing the Pelopponese and Attica. So in this second stage of Roman expansionism Greece was transformed from a foreign source of ancient wisdom to a client province under Roman Control.

Moving on to the nearby Largo Argentina I looked down on four ancient temples next to which a plaque informs the visitor this is thought to be the site of Julius Caesar's infamous assassination in 44 BCE. These temples had been subsumed into a larger theatre and garden complex built by JC's great rival, the general Pompey, which included a Curia or meeting place for the Senate which being outside the Pomerium could be attended by those banned from entering the inner sanctum whilst still meeting the Senate stipulation of being no more than 1 km outside the ritual boundary. Caesar had been summoned to meet the Senate at this Curia on the edge of the city and was set upon by the conspirators as he arrived in a scene imagined so powerfully by Shakespeare that his version has triumphed over some sketchy ancient literary sources. Why let the facts (especially if sketchy) get in the way of a good story! The historical significance of these events were the unintended consequences that led to the demise of the republican senate as the seat of power in Rome and the rise of the Imperial era. I had been recommended the Cicero trilogy by Robert Harris (Harris 2016) which I was by now deep into reading and thoroughly enjoying. Here I was walking through the city - backdrop to such a tangled tale of conspiracy and treachery, truly a city founded on fratricide.

Having orientated myself I headed to the Palatine Hill, the heart of the Roman State, to educate myself on Roman imperial history as it was on the slopes of the Palatine that the leaders of each generation seemed determined to outshine their forebears. There in the excellent Palatine Museum I learnt that it was Julius Caesar's great nephew and adopted heir Octavian, once he had eventually chased down Mark Anthony and his Egyptian ally Cleopatra at the sea battle of Actium in 31 BCE (off the Ionian coast of Greece just south of Corfu) who consciously cloaked himself in all things Greek to legitimise his imperial reign as 'Augustus – the illustrious one'.

There had been a temple to Apollo at Actium which he presumably visited after his historic victory. He founded a town on the site which he named Nikopolis, marking his νίκη (victory). Returning to Rome he set about the construction of a temple to his protecting God Apollo, right there next to his private quarters on the Palatine, admitting this Greek god of light and healing for the first time into the sacred Pomerium. Renaming himself Augustus he ruled as 'first citizen', commander in chief, and de facto emperor for the next 45 years upto 14 CE. Expanding the empire North over the Alps, West to include Spain, East upto a negotiated border and diplomatic relations with the Parthians of South West Asia he left Rome as the undisputed power of the Mediterranean world, sowing the seed decisively of the outward facing expansionist empire that would dominate the Western old world for 500 years. And he achieved all this consciously manipulating Greek culture to such an extent that the great poet of the Augustinian age, Horace, wrote 'Graecia capta ferum victorem cepit' ("Captive Greece captured her rude conqueror").

A young student working at the Palatine Museum seeing my evident interest in Augustinian artefacts recommended the National Roman Museum situated in the Palazzo Massimo alle Terme back up by the train station. There it is possible to follow the changing fashions of roman sculpture through the imperial epochs. But that was for another day and I spent the remainder of this one wandering about the Roman Forum before finding my way through the afternoon crowds back round to the Arch of Constantine near the Colosseum. My reading of the imperial history on the Palatine had deeply impressed on me the massive influence of Constantine on the story I was pursuing and I was determined to try to get a feel for the man, or if not the man himself his impact on the world .

Born in the Balkans, the son of one of the four rulers of the Roman world, the Tetrarchy, instigated by Diocletian (284-305 CE) on his remarkable retirement to his newly built palace in Split, Constantine was stationed in York when his father died in 306 and he was acclaimed Emperor by his troops. There remained the tricky issue of three other claimants, two of whom he dealt with militarily in 312 and the last politically in 313 through a marital alliance which once again consolidated the Empire with a single emperor. Invoking the god of the Christians as having sent him a signal before the decisive battle, Constantine brought Christianity officially into the Roman world going on to convene an international conference to determine exactly what form Christianity would take within the Empire (the Nicene Creed). Oh and he rebased the economy on new gold coinage giving it a stable currency standard which would last for 700 years. Not a bad CV and that still hasn't covered the reason he plays such an important role in our story!

I had previously found reference to Constantine way back in France as Charlemagne's diplomat Theodulf was negotiating with the Byzantines in an attempt to bridge the great schism. The schism only existed because the great Constantine had the vision to realise the Roman world was expanding so far eastwards along the Silk Road that it needed a new great centre in the East, a city built at the strategic crossroads on the Bosphorus on the very border of Europe and Asia, Constantinopole – Constantine's city. Founded on the site of a small Greek colony known as Byzantium, we now know it as Istanbul but for Greeks it is to this day simply known as Ο Πολις 'The City'. And that is its significance for our story of cultural transmission from Ancient Greece to modern Europe. The Eastern Roman Empire was 'hellenised' from the beginning. The language of education was classical Attic Greek. The structure of education was modelled on the seven liberal arts of antiquity – three literary topics (grammar, rhetoric and logic) and four mathematical ones (arithmetic, geometry, harmonics and astronomy). As the Western Empire began to implode the Eastern Empire thrived. The Roman Senate sent the regalia of the Western Empire to the Eastern Emperor Zeno in 476 CE, acknowledging Constantinopole as the sole seat of the Roman Empire and Roman Emperor. What followed was a gradually intensifying process of political, cultural and eventually linguistic Hellenization. This culminated in the declaration of Greek as the official language of what became known as the Byzantine Empire in 610 CE. In a rich exchange with the scholars of Baghdad surviving copies of ancient texts held in the muslim and christian worlds were exchanged and transferred from papyrus onto more robust parchment. This learning would permeate the medieval christian world as trade increased under the Genovese and periodic crusader ventures brought high ranking feudal leaders to the city on campaign.

I retreated to the Piazza Navarone for refreshments as the procession of the ages marched through my head. But of course in Rome in the summer there is no escape and sat as I was in a first century Roman stadium now colonised by Bangladeshi touts flying gaudy neon toys to the backdrop of beatboxes amidst the babel of voices of the global travel circuit I felt like I was back to the future in a Bladerunner version of a post apocalypse Rome. Or maybe that was the effect of the San Semilion. Over dinner swapping pleasantries with the family at the next table, a woman infotaining her two teenage kids with a visit to the Eternal City, I reflected on the fact that human culture is transmitted across the generations in just this way. Some time back a Roman parent was no doubt telling their kids about the 'wonder that was Athens', a tradition which Rome consciously had inherited and made its own. As I wandered back to my hostel via the Quirinal I was pleased to finally find quiet dark streets and some space in which to process all the sights and sounds of the bustling city. Clambering up into my bunk above the sleeping figure of my Libyan neighbour I slipped effortlessly into the arms of Somnos, the latinised version of Hypnos, the Greek god of sleep and father of Morpheus – my regular night-time companion - the dream keeper.

The next day had been set aside for the Vatican, deferred on a previous family visit to the City when my daughters were young, the queues were long and pizza and ice-cream ranked higher on the family priorities. I would recommend people of a certain age to revisit cities they think they know as priorities are changed by their re-emergent freedom to explore selfishly. I have hesitated from attempting to weave the catholic church into the story of cultural transmission from ancient Greece hitherto. Partly because of my own ignorance and partly because roman catholicism and hellenisation have been uncomfortable bedfellows at times. However here at the Vatican I was going to finally grapple with this 'elephant in the room'.

The hellenisation of the orthodox tradition centred on what would become known from the 16th century onwards as the Byzantine Empire. But how did the catholic church accommodate itself to ancient Greece? With some intellectual gymnastics appears to be the answer. The superficial contrast of Christian monotheism versus classical polytheism soon gets muddied by the panoply of Catholic saints on the one hand and the supremacy of Zeus in the Greek pantheon on the other. Add in the reinterpretation of Plato's construct of the Good, Intellect and Soul of the world as God the father (Good), the word of God brought by his son (Intellect) and finally Soul as of course the Holy Spirit and the early church fathers got the show on the road. As I entered the vast nave of St Peter's the direct link back to Peter and thence to Jesus is of course hammered home. Here, one is told, is where it all began - because of course legitimacy and power flow from such a perception. Just as Octavian co-opted the tradition of Classical Greece to legitimise his position as Augustus so does the Pope, head of the Catholic Church, co-opt Peter as the central founding ancestor from whom all subsequent Popes have inherited their legitimacy. If the Palaeloggi of Byzantium lasted 1000 years well the Popes have been with us for 2000 years. So perhaps one should not be too surprised that the sound track through the visitors' headphones is a call to prayer as well as an appreciation of architecture and art history. Incidentally nine bone fragments from a 1960's dig beneath the Basilica were forensically adjudged to be consistent with a 61 year old male from the 1st century and having been claimed by Pope Paul VI to be relics of Apostle Peter were transferred by the current Pope Francis to the Orthodox Ecumenical Patriarch Bartholomew of Constantinople. I'm not sure what this says about relations between the eastern 'Greek' church and the western Catholic church apart from stressing their common heritage deep in the history of Rome.

Having come down the Via Francigena I wondered how I would find this visit. Knowing that Pope Francis was away in Eire had conclusively dissuaded me from hanging around until Sunday hoping for a welcome wave from the balcony! I figured that the Catholic Church in Rome had bigger fish to fry than putting anything on for a bunch of renegade pilgrims. Indeed proof of this was evident during my visit to St Peter's when we were ushered to the side so as to enable more important clerical visitors a clear run on the nave. As we were parked beside Bernini's housing of the Throne of St Peter the sun shone clear through an alabaster window illuminating, at its centre, the dove of the Holy Spirit. Finally I experienced a fleeting sense of the transformative calm I have come to associate with sacred power places. Stopping on the way back down the nave to engage with Michelangelo's masterpiece the Pieta I felt ready for the treasures of the Vatican Museums to follow.

They are of course overwhelming and bear witness to the role of the Catholic Church in acting as a vital link in my story of cultural transmission from Greece via Rome to Liverpool! Just picking two examples the Belvedere Torso is a Roman copy of a lost Greek original studied by Michaelangelo at the Pope's invitation. It's influence on his depiction of Adam, with his bulging muscular torso, in the Cistine Chapel gives a feel for its significance as an influence on how we once saw ourselves – and it was certainly how British people viewed Greek art until Thomas Bruce, the 7th Earl of Elgin, brought marbles he removed from the Parthenon to London in the early 19th century. Raphael's fresco 'the School of Athens' is instantly recognisable as a poster for Greek philosophy, a study in perspective, an exhortation to pursue first causes and the embodiment of our received version of the Renaissance. Through an archway we see a central apse like structure with stone porticos receding into the distance. Striding towards us from the vanishing point are Plato and his student Aristotle, locked in debate with the former clutching a copy of the Timaeus gesturing skywards as if to emphasise his underlying concept of idealism as opposed to Aristotle, carrying a copy of his Nicomachean Ethics – a treatise on how to live, of great influence in the medieval christian world - who is gesturing to the earth as if to emphasise the concrete particularism of his theoretical position. They are surrounded by a who's who of philosophy with a particular favourite of mine, Epicurus, crowned with vine leaves to signify his emphasis on the good life.

These two pieces amidst the biggest collection of commissioned art I have ever set eyes on stood out for me as exemplifying what I had been taught at school about the 'rebirth' of classical thought in the Renaissance and the way the church commissioned the great artists of the day to contribute to that rediscovery and onward transmission.

Of course one can spend all day in the Vatican Museums (as I did, unencumbered by children or indeed anybody) and explore all manner of treasures. I got to see significant Etruscan artefacts for the first time and particularly enjoyed tracing my journey through Italy on a set of wall maps commissioned in 1580 which fill a gallery the length of a football pitch. As I ventured out into the early evening light I was drawn to the Castel Sant'Angelo just up the river from St Peter's and indeed linked to it by a tunnel to permit Popes an escape route when temporal authorities threatened. But of course being Rome this apparently Renaissance military structure is actually the Emperor Hadrian's tomb. Where else would the layering of history be quite so rich? What else was there to do, on this my last evening, but partake of some St Semillion on the turret of Castel Sant' Angelo and enjoy some Tai Chi in the rays of the sun setting behind Michaelangelo's great dome on St Peters pondering on time, the continuities of history and the ultimate passing of all things. In this vein I eventually found myself with the late night visitors to the Trevi fountain where a wistful saxophone solo provided a soulful note to this last night in the Eternal City.

Having wished my Libyan neighbour good luck and rescued Hermes from the Hostel basement I set off in good order the following morning for the Italian south. This leg's route dilemma revolved around the Appian way. Having set my heart on leaving the city via the best preserved stretch of Roman road in Italy I was well aware that its continuation south towards Naples was too southerly and in any case was an urban concrete nightmare. The Amalfi Coast had been ruled out as it was August. Which left the still notional Eurovelo 5 cutting east south east from Lazio through Campania to Puglia. This looked pleasantly rural and was a fairly straight line to Bari where I planned to take a ferry across to Patras. Not at all sure how I would work out a link between the Appian way and Eurovelo 5 I got going.

The first bit retraced my route of the preceding days towards town but this time I kept going at the Colosseum down to the Circus Maximus where I knew the Via Appia Antica started. After a bit of faffing about I followed some likely looking cyclists (father and sons out for a Sunday ride) until suddenly we were on ancient paving. The next 20 kms ranked amongst the highlights of the entire trip. The paving had a shiny patina rubbed clean by the feet and wheels of the millennia. Even when it was built in 312 BC its surface was famously smooth with tight fitting, interlocking stones laid on a bed of gravel and mortar with a camber running down either side from the centre to allow water to run off into drainage ditches. It was built to speed troops to the front as Rome expanded southwards. In the modern era it forms the centrepiece of a carefully preserved linear corridor heading out of the city. Lined with elegant trees and wide grassy verges the impression is of parkland on either side punctuated by ancient mausolea of varying scales. The trees provided shade as the sun rose on a perfect Sunday morning and it felt good to be back on the road after my cultural adventures in the Eternal City.

Chapter 8. Into the Deep South

The calm beautiful surroundings came to a juddering halt as Hermes and I hit the ring road and the Way disappeared under a concrete four lane trunk road, the SS7, heading towards Napoli. Taking a morning cappuccino at a workers' café I studied the map to work out the best cut through to the notional Eurovelo 5 route. The only way avoiding the SS7 appeared to describe two sides of a triangle with a climb upto Castel Gandolfo, overlooking Lago di Albano. Looking at it again there must be a more direct route maybe by coming off the Appian Way a little earlier but I had savoured my Appian Way experience so much that a few extra kilometres felt a small price to pay for such a highlight. In any case I had a good stiff climb to focus on which always has the effect of driving unnecessary thought from the mind. As I climbed the views became more expansive until approaching the Castel a massive crater lake opened out below me. One of the advantages of being naïve to a beautiful country through which one is passing is that the landscape never ceases to surprise and delight. The lake glistening below with Romans clearly at play on its shores surrounded by impressively steep green hills was idyllic. Just as I was taking it all in a cloud crossed the sun and I felt some drops of rain which within minutes settled into a steady drizzle. Fortunately I spotted a restaurant up ahead, quite a bit ritzier than my usual roadside eatery but hey this was clearly prime Roman weekender land. Once I'd got Hermes locked up, my stuff safely out of the rain, pulled on some half decent over trousers and got a table under an awning on the back terrace overlooking the lake below I was beginning to feel rather chuffed with my decision. Around me Roman families were enjoying chilled out Sunday lunch and so I joined in, reading up on my tablet about this place which turned out to be the Pope's summer retreat. I had learnt enough at the Vatican for the generally ritzy atmosphere of the place to now make perfect sense as my fine seafood pasta arrived. The rain had thankfully now passed allowing me to enjoy the full vista from the veranda over coffee awaiting the bill. To get back to the Eurovelo 5 route would now require a north easterly leg to Palestrina, a promising sounding place far enough to the east of Rome to be a likely stopping point. As I stared out across Lago di Albano it appeared there should be a route contouring around the hills maintaining my height. Hermes was damp but sat where he'd been abandoned and with kit reloaded and my lightish pasta lunch onboard I was good to go as the sun broke through creating sunbeams through the wispy water vapour rising off the slick black road surface. Following the curve of the crater lake the road wound its way through the Alban Hills past a couple of hill towns which also provided summer retreats for the great and good of Rome before arriving well into the afternoon at a third little hill town called Frascati, which was instantly familiar for obvious reasons. I immediately liked the atmosphere on the piazza with local lads and lasses hanging out on a Sunday afternoon and I decided that a glass of wine would be in order. The Frascati arrived fresh but not so cold as to prevent the aroma adding to the enjoyment. It seemed to me to be on par with the other great white wines I had been privileged to taste in their place of origin along my way. My blog actually enthuses about the 'best glass of white since Burgundy!' but in retrospect that would do Gavi a misservice. Italy is the home of the slow food movement to which I would append the slow wine movement! The added bonus of being able to visualise the place of origin of a few of the world's great wines will forever add to my enjoyment.

Planning ahead I booked a room close enough to Palestrina (just below the town) to give me a firm objective just over 20 kms away. Breaking through the Alban Hills which had given me such an unexpectedly delightful Sunday afternoon ride I reluctantly turned my back on the big vista west back over Rome, exchanging it for the view east of a long wide valley whose southern wall I was now contouring along. Down there below was the busy A1 autoroute which would have to be crossed if I was to reach Palestrina. When the minor road I was following had descended to the level of the autoroute I was both pleased to see an overpass and alarmed to see it all closed off. I was aware there had been a disaster in Genoa just a few days previous when an overpass had collapsed crushing many people to death and surmised this was a precautionary measure whilst other concrete overpasses underwent engineering checks. Looking around there was nobody working on a Sunday in August so I sneaked Hermes past the barriers and crossed to the North side of the A1 where my route would lie all the way to Monte Casino 100kms to the south east. The remaining kilometres to Palestrina were uneventful and as I found my B & B on the southern margin of the town well below the upper town I congratulated myself on finding something suitable without having, on this occasion, to cycle up to the hill town proper.

My host, a pleasant youngish man who was helping his parents out by attending to the visitor, confirmed if I proceeded up the hill I would find places serving food into the evening. It was by now approaching the gloaming and hunger pangs were building. It had been a late night followed by an early start and a decent day's ride so I didn't waste much time before walking up and enjoying a rather pub-like meal of meat and chips served on an outdoor terrace of wooden tables, surrounded by families glugging beer. This wasn't Mediterranean drinking as I had over simplistically expected of the Italians – indeed there are plenty of aspects of the national character which are a close fit with the British! Going on walkabout after dinner I followed my nose up through winding cobbled streets before emerging in front of the Palazzo at the top of the town. Under researched as ever (I simply couldn't keep up) I learnt of the massive classical terraced shrine to Fortune where the resident personification of Lady

Luck threw lots as she foretold what lay ahead!), and that this Palazzo was in part designed by Maderno, the architect who took on St. Peter's from Michaelangelo. The house was later purchased by the Barberrini family (who were massively successful papal hangers on) and has been influential in the evolution of house styles in Italy. The town was the birthplace of a classical polyphonic music composer who was rediscovered by the German Romantics. Wandering the back streets I came across a plaque celebrating the long term stay of Thomas Mann and his brother in the town – a tangible link with German Romanticism summoning up memories of the movie version of Mann's 'Death in Venice' featuring unforgettably Mahler's music and cinematic images of youthful male beauty compared to Michaelangelo's sculptured forms. The layering of cultural history continued to emanate from this part of Italy long after the fall of Rome thanks to the power of papal patronage. On this summer's evening in 2018 it felt relaxed and convivial and a million miles away from either Rome or for that matter the Pope.

Getting up early I headed off along the SR 155 to Fiuggi. With the A1 well away down on my right (southward) side syphoning off the traffic this quiet old road contours above providing panoramic views with a reasonable road surface. With such beneficial conditions it was a fast morning and I was in Fuiggi for lunch. Re-named after a nearby spring that provided a well marketed water said to cure kidney stones Fuiggi was once supplier of water to the royal families of

Europe. These days it felt quite off the beaten track. The next place Ferentino, reached by following a lovely downhill stretch only to be faced with a climb of equal height upto the old town fortifications felt even further off track. Horace describe the place as quiet two millennia ago and not a lot has changed I would say. Dropping down to the main road I stopped in a café for refreshments and directions. The helpful woman in the café pointed out the way to Ceccano, by a country lane winding through the low lying agricultural land along the banks of the Sacco river. She lived in Ceccano and clearly considered it a far superior town to Ferentino though why she commuted over here was not something that was going to be easily learnt in my, now, pigeon Italian. So joking with her that we might meet later I dropped down to the Sacco and picked my way along quiet lanes, dodging a busy intersection and the sprawling commuter town of Frosinone, to reach Ceccano as the light was beginning to fade. Pushing Hercules up a particularly steep hilltop ascent I made it to the piazza which, by now, I had learnt is to be found (invariably) at the very top. There I found a café bar at which to take a reviving beer whilst looking into accommodation options. The best deal in the place was a two-star hotel around the corner so having got that organised I fell into conversation with a delightful local young woman accompanied by her brother and her Irish boyfriend. They were all just back from the beach in Puglia, raved about the area over the beer confirming my feeling I should aim to spend what time I could down there and not linger too much en route.

Enjoying the craic the early evening rather slipped by so when I tore myself away to push Hermes round the corner to the Hotel food options felt like they might be narrowing fairly rapidly. Hurriedly showering I needn't have worried. Going into the first trattoria I could find the family interrupted their own meal to prepare for me a light supper of pasta with buffalo mozzarella which was delicious. Having made me feel thoroughly at home in this casually civilised Italian way my hosts whiled away the remainder of the convivial evening in relaxed chat that sent me to bed feeling part of the place if not the family.

My hotel wasn't offering breakfast – unusually – so I took morning coffee and pastry at a neighbouring café where the locals were consulting over the papers. I was cycling along a minor road which appeared to be following the Eurovelo 5 route I was attempting to follow when a pair of road cyclists swept up behind me, overtook and allowed me (graciously) into their slipstream before greeting me and checking as to my destination. It is perhaps worth mentioning here that the slipstream effect is very considerable and increases with speed – a rule of thumb is that for every 1 mile per hour of velocity the drafting rider saves 1 per cent of energy expenditure compared to the lead rider – so at 25 mph that equates to 25% lower energy expenditure. So I was able to respond to their shouted enquiries that I was attempting to follow what one day might become a fully signposted transeuropean route Eurovelo 5. They nodded understandingly and told me to follow them. Wow, we slipped into a chain gang and an hour later almost 35 kilometres down the road pulled up at their morning coffee haunt where several other bikes were already drawn up. Ivano, as I now learnt the younger 'chef du peloton' was called, explained he ran a cycle guiding business so we had plenty to chat about over coffee. Before I pushed on I was introduced to all his cycle buddies and we all celebrated the cycling possibilities of the region, that underrated triangle I was now deep into which pushes east between Napoli and Roma. What is it about cyclists that makes for camaraderie? Well obviously the cyclist is IN the environment through which he or she is passing in a way a car driver (at least a saloon car driver) isn't. Then there's the physical effort involved. Finally there is the superior power of a group of cyclists over an individual due in part to the physics of wind resistance analysed above but also to group psychology.

I found myself musing on this, not for the first time, as I returned to my solo journey, not in a melancholic lonely way – anything but for such an interaction somehow carries one through the day. Lost in my musing I must have missed a turn because suddenly I was seeing signs for a cave system called the Grotte di Pastena which was a little south of the indicated route along the Sacco. At this point I should say unlike the Via Francigena I had been unable to download a route file onto my Garmin, so I was back to the daily exercise of matching my map with an online version of the still virtual Eurovelo 5, circling a series of waypoint towns to head between. When necessary these were then punched into the Garmin if the route was unclear or as now had been missed. What one then actually does after losing one's way is deeply subjective. For some the 5 miles retraced will always win out over the 10 mile detour. But others, like me, generally prefer to forge a new route even if it means a few miles extra rather than face the disheartening retracing of the route and the associated admission of error! This is the reason my wife will always insist on monitoring my map reading when we head out together. My argument that good things often happen when you forge ahead – a piece of pure Montainesque optimism – cuts little ice with her. Anyhow exercising the privilege of solo travel on I headed into the midday heat on what appeared to be the road that time forgot. Beginning to question my chances of encountering a lunch spot I was pleased to come across a sign advertising a Ristorante up ahead in the town of Pastena specialising in 'typical food' if my schoolboy Latin was any guide to modern Italian.

Arriving on the stroke of noon the place was hot and empty – a modest hill town with signage encouraging the hungry visitor upto the deserted plaza containing the Ristorante Matarocci. Inside the family were sat together eating and chatting before the lunchtime service, but I was welcomed warmly and the English speaking young adult son guided me through their lunchtime offering – I settled on bean soup followed by rabbit in olive oil and sage with aubergine on the side washed down with a glass of red. Fantastico, as I had acquired the habit of enthusiastically uttering when eating and drinking. The aubergines had been lightly pickled and as I sat enjoying the tangy result my eye was drawn to the rows of pickling jars filled with a wide variety of this year's produce. As I settled up mama came to the kitchen door to check out this Lycra clad addition to the usual clientele and I had the opportunity to thank her profusely for the best lunch of the trip! I even enjoyed a short post lunch siesta in their garden shelter – a design feature I keenly photographed for inspiration for our own Greek plot now coming more to mind with my south-easterly progress.

The climb out of the vale of Pastena was memorable. The road crossed the valley floor, dead straight to reach the valley wall at which point it climbed in a forgiving single switchback to a col on which stood an unusual octagonal stone building. Stopping to have a look around I could find no evidence to help with the building's historical function. I found it reminiscent of the Byzantine influenced Carolingian chapels I had encountered in Charlemagne's France. I speculated as to the history of this interesting monument noting that the Normans controlled all this area as part of their Kingdom of Sicily they adopted many features of Byzantine life as they sought to reinvent themselves as Mediterraneans. However online I discoverd it to be known as the Chiesa Madonna Della Machie, which at least confirms its status as a chapel but as to its date the only fact on offer reads 'Inside a tile bears the date of

1703, although the construction is considered to be earlier'. I rather like the idea that this Shangri-la home to the lovely people at the Matarocci should be timeless. It had indeed been a midday break out of time!

Once over the lip of the hidden valley I entered a greener hillier world which took me to a dramatic bluff on which sat yet another historic hill town, Falvaterra, overlooking the River Sacco regained down below. No time to linger now as I let myself go on a glorious descent all the way back down to the river, where light industry, a railway and the autoroute all squeezed together in a narrow corridor on the north bank that I was keen to avoid. Thankfully my way lay on this, southern bank, which remained agricultural and as the afternoon shadows lengthened I swooped along a quiet road wondering where I should lay my head. I was in the mood for a wild camp but the question was where. Every time a likely spot near the river appeared the intensity of the agricultural activity warned me off. Eventually the pleasant agricultural lane led into an unusually non-descript town by a river confluence where the Sacco joins the Liri. I found myself at a quayside fountain refilling my water bottles exchanging nods with a couple of bearded guys who looked like gentlemen of the road. Indeed I reflected that's pretty much what I had become.

Musing on this observation I found my way across a busy intersection and out on another agricultural backroad now tracking the south bank of the Liri. The fields hereabouts had been harvested and were in the process of turning a mellow yellowish-brown hue. The cycling was smooth following the gentle riverside contours, lunch was not a too distant memory, water bottles were full and my mind was wandering. Back to the tramps as it happened. I have always been a little in awe of people living outside the system. 'Down and Out in London and Paris' had such an effect on me, my very first night as a young traveller on foreign soil was spent under the Pont Neuf in Paris alongside '*les clochards*'. This French term is derived from the verb 'to limp'....which like the English word 'tramp' infers such gentlemen of the road to be walkers. Tramping becomes commonplace during times of displacement when populations are on the move. The Great Depression of the 1930s saw armies of unemployed men shuffling around the country in search of work. Here in Italy the term for tramp however is the less specific all encompassing '*vagabondo*' which would embrace an errant cyclist as well as those wandering on their own feet. After all here, south of Rome, I had little claim to *pelegrino* status on the Via Francigena though for the faithful the route on down through Italy towards the Holy Land is well recognised. No, I was that modern creation a Middle aged Man in Lycra (MaMiL) cycling the Eurovelos ....but for what? A question that passed through my mind from time to time but which usually slipped past, like the scenery, leaving a fleeting impression of flow induced well being without ever demanding an answer. Perhaps several answers were becoming clearer to me now as I headed ever southwards...to rediscover a Europe, to remind myself where I had come from, to find who I now was after half a lifetime of becoming what others demanded of me, to forgive myself my trespasses and salve life's sufferings.

Quite enough to be getting on with as the gloaming was fast approaching - no more time for philosophising - it was time to find a place to pitch camp whilst I could still see but the roadside fields consisted either of this year's stubble or had been ploughed ready for a winter crop. And anyway the perfect overnight wild camp included a pre set-up refuel. Up ahead I became aware of a hill town on a rocky outcrop rearing above the flat valley floor and I decided that would be my best bet. The Apennines to the north were beginning to glow as they caught the last of the sunlight and I settled into the steady rhythm of a thankfully shortish but steep climb. On a hairpin towards the top the local council had erected an unusual 4 foot high curving cameo of the town's history which I noted would provide the perfect cover for my small tent if pitched on the well mowed short grass behind. Just along the street there was the happy conjunction of a convenience store facing a view back down the valley to the west to die for complete with a public bench. Parking Hermes up I strode over, introduced myself and bought a starter of salty snacks and beer. I had missed sunset but as every gloamer knows the best bit is after the sun has gone down. This evening did not let me down and to a backdrop of yellow fading to pale blue above a patchwork of green and brown I swigged my beer and felt the glowing elation of a good ride nailed.

Returning across the road to the shop I engaged in a dinner conversation with the youngish couple running the shop. She suggested salami (practical) whilst he (Simone) talked football (Roma) and kept shaking his head in wonder that a red from Liverpool had cycled all the way to his shop to take in the evening vista and shoot the breeze over a couple of beers. Before darkness fell I tore myself away carrying a precious cargo of salami, bread, fruit, cheese and wine and slunk partway down the hill before slipping behind the welcome sign and throwing the tent up vagabondo style. In my view providing you get your tent up in the dark, are away at dawn and leave nothing behind then you are simply doing what people have always done and exercising your natural rights to see the world. Unfortunately I am well aware many do not see things in quite the same light. In my anthropology days we studied the often symbiotic relationships between pre-industrial sedentary agriculturalists and their semi-nomadic pastoralist neighbours. Capitalist economies have little place for nomads whilst paradoxically requiring Labour to be flexible. 'Get on your bike' Tebbit, The Chingford Skinhead, once famously admonished us northerners amidst the carnage of Thatcher's neoliberalisation of the British economy. Ironically when my brother Geoff did 'get on his bike' to 'the Smoke' it was with a relocation grant from the European Union then available for the unemployed of the wrecked northern cities of England to make their way down to the honeypot of the South East. Now we obsess about economic migrants, meaning workers who are flexibly meeting the demands of capital, and have recently started to fret about the 'stickiness' of people who don't behave as rationally as the economists predicted because, incredible as it seems, they feel a sense of attachment to place. If there's one thing one learns to appreciate touring across Europe on a bike is that sense of place and the attachment many feel towards the place they call home.

I think we all have this contradiction within us, the wandering hunter gatherer urging us onward and the sedentary farmer inveigling us to settle down. Having spent a bit of time hanging out with *sadhus* in Northern India over the years I celebrate how a bank manager in middle life can renounce wealth and stability for a wandering ascetic old age. One good friend after many years of devoted service to his clients and family just took off on a rented motorbike to tour South East Asia for a couple of months. I have been fortunate enough to live a life in which every now and then I get to take off somewhere. We all have multiple versions of ourselves inside of us, and that's ok provided each gets an airing. One way, and for me the easiest way of resolving these potentially clashing personas is to allow each their day in the sun. This was a night for the vagabond in me!

Waking with a mist in the valley below I rapidly packed up and headed down to negotiate a way across the main transport corridor below Monte Cassino. I knew of the battle for Monte Cassino because my father's friend Les had fought in it. Les walked with a limp which probably had everything to do with sciatica and nothing to do with the war. Somehow in my childish mind Les's limp became a token of the ferocity of the battle which, my father impressed upon us boys, had been one of the toughest of the war in Europe. As a result that morning as I negotiated a rather tedious section of main road my eyes kept flicking up to the glowering presence of the rocky outcrop 500 metres above me to my left. You could make out a large building on the top which I took to be the rebuilt Abbey. Having extracted myself from the main road, I stopped in the first village for breakfast and went online to read it up. As I was discovering the route I was following is the most easily passable corridor from Southern Italy to Rome and so the Allied armies were pushing North this way in 1944 as they fought their way up the Italian peninsula. The Benedictine Monastery at Monte Cassino was the founding monastery of the Benedictine Order which would go on through Cluny to build a European wide infrastructure to the medieval world. Rebuilt in the 15th century the monastery had not in fact been fortified by the Germans, as was feared when it was destroyed by American bombing. It was only after the bombing that the Panzer divisions dug into the ruins to great effect making it an extremely costly assault for the Allies to clear the approach to Rome. Gung-ho

American bombing - sounds familiar – however back in the present I had the more mundane task of finding a passable route avoiding the main transport corridor below. I fell into conversation with a young lawyer down from Milan visiting his family for the August holiday who was talking coffee next to me. 'I'm on my bike too' he commented by way of friendly introduction gesturing to a beat up BMX. I suggested he might want to join for a ride. 'Where to?' 'Bari!' He laughed but reassured me that this route from his parents' village would work well as just ahead there lay a 1km tunnel taking the road through the worryingly high rocky landscape up ahead.

Thanking him as I left for the useful information I didn't know whether to be reassured or alarmed by this news of another Italian tunnel! But regardless I had no choice when a couple of kilometres up the road I got to the tunnel mouth and thanking my lucky stars for an absence of traffic plunged in, once again downhill surviving the adrenaline rush to emerge high above the market town of Venafro reached in a freewheel to savour! This road junction town offered little to delay me and I was soon out the other side on a delightful agricultural lane towards Alife. At this point the public road entered an agricultural estate complete with barrack block worker housing now dilapidated and abandoned. Apart from a guy on a tractor the only real signs of life were some kids messing about on bicycles which lent the scene a Huckleberry Finn colonial New World character...but whatever time and space warp I had entered the cycling was blissful with not a car seen since escaping the sprawl of Venafro. Toying with an off-road riverside route variation the first sighting of a Eurovelo 5 sign kept me to the straight and narrow. The sudden signage evidenced the fact that I had just crossed a political boundary. The model for the development of cycleways is firmly routed in localism and even notionally trans-european routes like the Eurovelo 5 I was now following remain a project for local implementation. Campania appears to be more progressive than Lazio when it comes to cycleways!

I was now in the valley of the Volturno, running south-east with the Appenines, impressively daunting still on my left side and a complicated physical geography all around with large seemingly volcanic outcrops rearing up from the fertile plain. My route steered round these through corn and wheat fields long since harvested. It was getting noticeably hotter down here as the day progressed and I was getting hungry - my light breakfast in the café with the young lawyer was starting to feel a long time ago. By the time I reached the next town Alife I was running low on water, food and energy. My spirits lifted as I rolled through an intact Roman arch into a perfectly multilateral walled town just as the Romans had designed it. Unfortunately, I was knackered and all that was on my mind was lunch. Only one problem with this - where were all the inhabitants? On the beach, home in bed in the heat or had there been a zombie invasion? I said as much to the one lad loitering in the town square who responded, not unreasonably, with "non Capisco" as in 'I don't understand your ravings you clearly mad, red-faced stranger on a bike!' Persisting (me with him and more tolerantly he with me) the word restaurant triggered a positive response and waved directions out through another Roman gateway leading out of town and first right. How far I dejectedly asked? Oh the same distance as the span of Alife between the town gates he gestured in a brilliant piece of improvised communication. I set out more in desperation than hope as everything else (and I mean everything- even down to a corner kiosk) was clearly shut for the August holiday in Alife!

The asphalt road turned into a stony track which led to a compound where I found a long ranch style building. I opened the door to find an extended family just finishing what looked like it had been an excellent, vinous lunch. No, I was informed the restaurant wasn't open this lunchtime but after a pregnant pause faced with this dusty, red faced, figure of course they would feed me! I could have kissed the young woman who over the course of the afternoon I learnt was Ileria, a keen restauranteur like her parents who having learnt all she could from home was hoping soon to be London bound! I loitered in the kitchen to admire the work of the two tubby kitchen hands working methodically through great piles of peppers as they started prepping the evening service. Mama threw together a (lovely) pasta dish followed by an ice cream and fruit pudding accompanied by shots of a green liqueur which she pressed upon me clearly feeling I was in need of fortification. After this everyone retired for an afternoon snooze (myself included in a garden shelter) and then I was sent on my way with a Pannini for my supper! Not for the first time on the journey I wished I could pay back Ileria's family for their kindness with more than my contact details. I am ashamed to say I missed the fourth biggest surviving Roman amphitheatre in Italy in Alife but my way after such an extended lunch lay forward not back!

I was waved off with some concern about my night quarters which I minimised reckoning I would be able to find a place to pitch beside the Volturno but as the evening light started to fade a good campsite proved elusive once again in this intensively cultivated region. Coming upon a road-side bar I took a quick beer to emerge into the gloaming and the time of commitment. Round the next bend in the road I came across some sort of country celebration judging by the number of cars drawn up outside a collection of buildings. A kilometre later, where the road crossed a minor tributary, an agricultural track led down beside the stream and looked promising. Sure enough a couple of hundred metres along the track I hit upon a grassy unploughed area and my tent was up and panini out before darkness set in. Once again I blessed the lovely Ileria and family for their kindness to a stranger far from home. The stars were out that night as I lay on my poncho savouring the warm still night air. Occasional snatches of noise drifted over from the hamlet – was that music? Swiftly rejecting any idea of a night-time recce I got into my little tent and slept through until rosy fingered dawn.

After an early start I followed the Volturno south east through agricultural land on minor roads until the river abruptly turns south west to force a route to the sea near Naples. I was happy to be skirting to the north east of southern Italy's major connurbation. I had enjoyed exploring the faded baroque arcades of the city 20 years before on a flying visit but now was set on my progress across to Puglia which beckoned since my bar discussion the other evening. The first town of the day, Telese, was a little place built on a suspiciously grid like pattern which spoke of a Roman past. Sat having breakfast at the only café open at this early hour it seemed a sleepy little place so I was amazed to learn its eventful history. Taken by Hannibal in his epic march south then retaken by the Romans it was indeed laid out on their characteristic grid. It had been raised to the ground three times, by the Saracens in the 800's, the Normans in the 1000's and by an earthquake in the 1300's. Now it's main significance relates to the railway station at the end of the high street which was my next waypoint where I picked up the trainline to head past a local lake (not particularly inviting for swimming) following the train tracks out east parallel with the River Calor.

During this stretch a remarkable thing happened. My mobile phone rang and it was my wife Susannah at the other end. A letter had arrived at home marked NHS

Pensions and she thought I would want to know. I did indeed as anyone who has taken their pension will know the estimates always come hedged with uncertainties which only really fall away once crystalised and here was my moment of truth. Asking Sus for a moment to stop, I sat myself on a grassy verge with Hermes lying on the ground beside me and met my fate. All was satisfactory and having got off the bike a vagabond I remounted a pensioner (it was now official). How surreal was this - as I ran the thought repeatedly through my mind – as if trying it on for size! If the ride was some sort of rite of passage then here was the climactic moment of transition. But could that be....a phone call relaying numbers... when the external reality of the ride was what was filling my soul. I was on that soul ride still and adapting to my newfound status as a pensioner would have to wait. But I did stop at the next place, a tiny town called Ponte (built around a river crossing unsurprisingly) where I drank a coffee surrounded by men playing cards at 11:00am in the morning without a woman in sight. I had arrived in the Deep South!

Beyond Ponte my route left the river which complicated route finding as I headed towards the only city between Rome and Bari, Benevento. The earlier Eurovelo signage had by now petered out, presumably responsibility had been devolved to provincial levels and I had by now crossed into Benevento province. From my anthropology days I knew the Deep South (and indeed the whole Mediterranean coastal region including North Africa) was characterised by an 'honour and shame' culture. In such a cultural milieu the world of the vendetta thrives. On a family holiday in Sicily I had been enthralled by Peter Robb's Midnight in Sicily (Robb 2014) in which he weaves a contemporary history of the Mafia together with an intimate account of southern Italian food. I always recall the parallels drawn between the bloody annual tuna catch as floats of tuna were spotted, encircled and speared in a thrashing crimson turbulence known as the mattanza and the slaughter of families in the early 1980's Mafia power struggle which came to be known by the same term. This internal struggle had been triggered by the new riches associated with the global drug market. What had given the Mafia an edge over their competitors was their existing distribution network across the United States for ….olive oil.

Down in the south there's an intensity which can turn dark despite the brilliant Mediterranean light fuelling those olives to synthesise their oil. These ruminations were interrupted by route finding challenges as I battled my way into Benevento that day. According to the Eurovelo planners there should have been a route which weaved no doubt an attractive way into the city but I never found it. Instead I found myself riding on an empty dual carriageway which petered out on a hillside above the city where kerbs had been laid out in preparation for a development which had never happened. It all felt like the results of a scam to attract building subsidies to be syphoned off. I had seen similar in southern Sicily and assumed the Camorra, the Naples based version of the Mafia, had been weaving their webs. So resorting to 'visual navigation' I headed down a lane going in the right direction for the town below me and after a few twists and turns emerged in the centre near the railway station.

Set at the convergence of two rivers, the Sabato and Calore Irpino, Benevento was built on a ridge though the modern town sprawls down the sides of both riverine valleys presenting a challenge to the cyclist. However, on arrival it was a relatively straight forward mission to identify a trattoria and fuel up. I was by now getting the feel for Italian lunch habits and instinctively identified a good but not fancy neighbourhood place where I was served a delicious fixed price lunch menu of the day. The actual main dish has by the time of writing merged into the general memory of excellent Italian lunches. What remains fresh in the memory is the ambience as the place filled up with all manner of people. Couples, mothers and daughters, men meeting from their offices, single people in transit from the nearby station all enjoying a civilised home cooked lunch prepared and served by an exclusively female team. I suspect in many equivalent towns in modern Britain one might struggle to avoid the ubiquitous convenience food offering!

Reviewing the map I bought for the next section of my route at the railway station shop I figured I had time enough to explore Benevento's Roman remains. Its

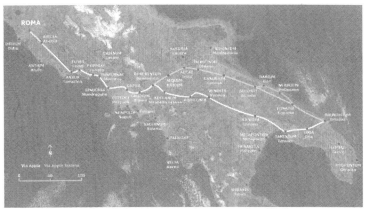

significance back in Roman times and still for me now was its position on the strategic road network which the Romans built to take them South. The first and most important strategic route to the south was the one I had left Rome by, the Appian Way, which I here rejoined after my pleasant detour to its north. But this reunion would be short lived as my route lay closer to its more northerly less hilly branch built by the Emperor Trajan (98-117) to trim the journey time by a day. Named the Via Appia Traiana this reached the coast near Bari and therefore served my purpose well. It was to mark this important extension of the road network that an arch was erected by Trajan (53-117 CE) which has stood the test of time so well that it not only occupies a traffic island at the heart of the city (thankfully now pedestrianised) but a friend seeing my blog shared that it had been on the cover of his undergraduate architecture textbook in the United States. Without knowing this provenance it was obviously exceptional even to the non specialist. The well preserved

287

inscriptions were easily decipherable and I was amused, in this world cup year, to read the celebration of Trajan's hard-won victory over the Germans. It seems that 'beating the Germans' is a common yardstick for strength across the ages in Europe, and it is no coincidence that Trajan's successful military campaigns left the Empire at its greatest extent in this period.

The theatre built by Hadrian (76-138 CE) was the best preserved Roman theatre I had come across and included some intriguing monumental mask sculptures in stone which were like nothing I had previously seen. I tried the local site attendants but they couldn't tell me anything of their significance. There was a haunting quality to them which made me think of John Fowles' Magus novel (Fowles 1968). Researching the Roman Theatre later it became clear that this was another medium by which Greek ideas entered the Roman culture. Hadrian earned himself the nickname 'Graeculus' for his fondness of all things Greek including theatre. Classic revivals were mounted but probably in a somewhat debased manner. References can be found to onstage copulation of actors and even bestiality. Mime was very popular, as were juggling and other circus skills. The impression is more cabaret than tragedy in line with the rather simplistic contrast drawn conventionally between the Romans and Greeks, mirroring that between the Spartans and the Athenians. Anyway masks were used aplenty and these stone images must have ornamented the theatre amidst all the other imperial iconography associated with theatres (Sturgeon 1977).

By now the afternoon was wearing on (and cooling down) and it was time to tear myself away from Benevento, a town which like so many I never would have thought of visiting prior to this journey but which had proved fascinating. The route on Eurovelo 5 necessitated finding a minor road that tracked the south bank of the Calor avoiding the A16 Autoroute which sweeps past Benevento on the same side of town. The key manoeuvre proved to be a traverse through an unlikely, rather down at heel, housing estate which at its heart had a municipal coin operated iced water machine. I joined the queue and got 3 litres for 30 cents. Topping up with carbs at a local convenience store I was good to head on following what was fast becoming my 'deep south' regime. A good morning shift, prolonged lunch break in the middle of the day, followed by a mid afternoon/evening shift. The light was getting magical as the sun lowered and the route stayed high for 20 kms with sweeping views down across the Calor and far away across rolling agricultural land.

Suddenly it plunged down towards the river in an exhilarating descent which led to a small hamlet beside the river where a sign promised welcome refreshment. On a pretty terrace an unusually snazzy café was serving rather superior snacks and wine to half a dozen clients including the patron's tennis professional son and girlfriend, a couple of local business men and two rather well made up middle-aged women enjoying an end of day drink. The patron was keen to see his son's English in operation and I obliged with a pleasurable discussion around cycling, tennis and the different pressures on the respective pro tours. He was clearly an ambitious and likeable lad though I couldn't help but think his dad's expectations felt way too high. But his mama was lovely – as I was learning so many Italian mamas are. So when the lowering light forced my departure I left supplied with a bottle of local red and a half pizza. Slipping into a large field sloping down to the river and pitching my tent next to a small area planted to vine I was just lounging beside the tent, enjoying my wine, allowing myself to count my blessings on this my first day as a pensioner when I heard a tractor complete with over-cab flood lights heading my way. Ironically I was just lying there reflecting to myself that this had been the smoothest pitch of camp since Rome. Fortunately, the nocturnal farmer turned into the neighbouring field but there worked methodically ploughing until past 11 at night under his lights. Never again will I accuse the southern Europeans of taking it easy. In this part of Italy the agricultural community in August were working like the clappers. Just as I was climbing into the tent a train rattled past down by the river where the mainline into Benevento must lie. I took to my tent counting my blessings after another eventful day.

Eventually things quietened down and after a reasonable night I was up at the crack of dawn, packed up and on the road in need of a coffee. As I had found right across Italy places for refreshment seemed to appear as if perfectly to order, this time in the form of a gas station with attached café/bar where I breakfasted with local farmers and truckers. Too early in the day for more than perfunctory nods and grunts I was soon off beginning a climb which I was glad I hadn't been aware was coming. The day turned out to be my second crossing of the Apennines. Fortunately this far south they are nothing like they were in Ligur('f...ing-hill)ia but it was still one of the more memorable morning climbs. Steep and moderate in length I pulled up at the next little place and looked around me. I was on the roof of this part of Italy at 500 metres with panoramic views below me to the North and across the high land to the south. I figured out I had just crossed the watershed between the Tyrrhenian Sea (as the Mediterranean to the west of Italy is known) and the Adriatic. Ahead lay Puglia, the road to Bari and my ferry to Greece. Feeling pretty good it was by now a social hour in the next café and the old men were keen to engage.

There were three of them, moustachioed with sticks I recall. 'Dall'Inghilterra' one old boy with broken English back translated to his coffee companions approvingly. "Where was I going?" "Bari", I replied. This was chewed over a little before the spokesman came back with advice, "keep away from Ariano

Irpino….its a stronghold of Tony Blair's friend Silvio Berlusconi!" This was not the first reference I had heard to our ex-Prime Minister's relationship with the ever-colourful ex-Prime Minister of Italy. I would describe myself as moderately politically engaged on the progressive left and once found myself participating in the 'great conversation' in a room with said Tony Blair. He was hugely impressive in his ability to listen to our many contributions detailing policy priorities as we saw them before delivering us a version of Labour Party policy which picked up and contextualised the widely varying points made at the gathering. All very impressive – but what on earth did he think he was doing hanging out with a dodgy property developer/media moghul who turned to politics to stay out of jail. Does high politics push you into the company you keep…no, as ever, we all make choices and I'm afraid the company that you keep does say something about you! Once I had got going again (off my high horse) the ridge I was following did lead towards Ariano Irpino but I took the old men's advice and bypassed it, not least because the town was perched a further 250m above my route. The minor road I had been following from Benevento merged with the main Napoli-Foggia road just below the town. As always on the main road I made good progress, head down so to speak, partly because of the excellent surface, partly because speeding traffic keeps you focussed on the task in hand and partly because I always want to get it over with to enable the more 'head up' cycling style minor roads afford. On this occasion it was only two or three kilometres before I was turning off on a very minor agricultural road which ran true east into Puglia. The country had changed since climbing up into this southern extension of the Appenines. The complex ridging of the western slopes had now been replaced by long sweeping shallow high altitude valley systems, much less intensively farmed. This had once been a route of transhumance, the so called *tratturi,* up which flocks of sheep and herds of cattle would be led north into the high Appenines pastures for grazing during the hot summer months. About the time I was travelling the flow would be in my direction south into lowland Puglia where the benign winter months could be passed. I had a sense of the drovers' life in this high, bright, windswept sort of country, notably less wooded than the hilly country I had been travelling through hitherto. What surprised me up here though was the replacement of this now vanished transhumance by a highly developed wind farm system. Big modern turbines dotted the bare landscape. I hugely enjoyed this big almost carless terrain encountering a single tractor all morning. The population density had plunged and it felt like I had these uplands to myself that morning. I was feeling exhilarated as I pushed on with a breeze blowing behind me gently rotating the massive turbine blades on the skyline. Eventually the next town came into view, Monteleone di Puglia, confirming I was now into my last Italian region. I had assumed up here I might find somewhere on the level but no, the Italian habit of building on hilltops, in this case on the only prominence for miles around, persisted. It lent the place a rather impressively medieval aspect, no opportunity for modern sprawl, simply a town on a hill surrounded by big open spaces with my lane heading directly for the foot of the hill. Up close it was actually higher and steeper that it had appeared from afar. So I took the chance of locking the bike with its panniers to a lamppost at the foot of the hill and walked up the stepped old mule path leading into the town.

All was quiet until I emerged into the Piazza where a market was just wrapping up. I found the fruit and veg stall which was probably the best I had ever seen. There were of course the brilliant reds of the peppers and chillis, the deeper red of the tomatoes but also the purple hues of aubergines and ripe figs, black shiny grapes and green rocket. Opting for some grapes and figs I started back across the square. Behind the stalls now being dismantled into big white vans there was a prominent memorial which caught my eye. Investigating further I read a notice crediting the support of a UNESCO peace project reminding the reader that 'since wars begin in the minds of men it is in the minds of men that the defences of peace must be constructed'. I found this unexpected appeal to our higher nature strangely moving. Why this emphasis on war and peace up here on this depopulated windswept plateau? My ride-by of Monte Cassino had been a stark reminder of the ravages of the Second World War on this part of the world. I sometimes think us British, whilst remembering the blitz, insufficiently reflect on the losses experienced by our European neighbours. The European Union was always in part a peace project making it all the more embarrassing that half of my fellow citizens want out. Throughout this journey I had experienced nothing but warmth and kindness with my nationality never held against me. Will this be the same for my kids I wonder?

But returning to the question facing me I wasn't convinced this place had been a battleground in the Second World War. Maybe the answer lay in the plaque below, on which inscribed in stone were over 60 names of men who had 'fallen' in Ethiopia. This immediately chimed with my own Ethiopian experiences. Whilst living there I had learned of the much celebrated defeat of an Italian army by an Ethiopian army led by Menelik II at the battle of Adwa in 1896, claimed as a very rare instance of African victory against a European army. Of course, as always, the truth is far more complicated than this heroic tale of national resistance claims. The Italians were playing catch up in the colonial 'Scramble for Africa' and were attempting to join up their existing colonies in Eritrea and Italian Somaliland with tacit British support whilst the Russians were supporting the Ethiopians. The net result was a better equipped Ethiopian army over a hundred thousand strong which fell on an under equipped Italian army of 18,000 raw recruits, presumably from poor southern Italian towns like this one. At the height of the battle the Ethiopian Oromo cavalry fell upon the scattered Italian Brigades slaughtering many. I could empathise with this loss of life as I too had experienced war in Ethiopia with the Oromo!

As a young doctor I worked with the Oromo Relief Association in south-west Ethiopia as the Oromo struggled against first the Menghistu Marxist regime which was opposed on all sides by various 'liberation' movements and latterly the Tigrayan Peoples' Revolutionary Force, who had triumphed in the liberation struggle taking the capital Addis Adaba and were then involved in clean-up operations against their erstwhile allies to consolidate power. I was living in a military camp under Oromo protection as we attempted to deliver basic healthcare to a million people in the newly liberated area. However on the day of EU supervised elections to determine the political make up of the newly liberated country the Tigrayans launched a pre-emptive strike against the Oromo. The first we knew was waking to the sound of AK47s and being told to run for our lives. Our three person 'Health Unlimited' group accompanied by our Oromo health colleagues headed out into the bush getting away from the fighting as quickly as our legs would carry us. As we headed up the hill we passed ironically a building denoted to be a voting booth complete with EU sponsored posters urging people to vote. But this political contest was destined to be resolved the old way – by force - just as Menelik would have done.

Over the next few days as we scurried away from the front line we encountered several ragged platoons of Oromo fighters headed for the front. I had found myself searching their faces, for what I don't know, but what I found was grim faced resolve as we exchanged the perennial greetings of the struggle, *jabadha* – be strong! When five days later we had walked deeper into the Oromo heartland at Dembi Dollo we re-met the Oromo leadership whose charismatic field commander reflected to me 'If only we had been colonised by you people rather than by those Amharas and now these Tigrayans'. This reflection on the complex politics of ethnicity in Africa struck me as interesting in its tacit acceptance of the inevitability of colonisation on the journey to statehood. The history of Africa is being re-written and the role of the Horn of Africa in its tortured relationship with Europe will surely figure. That night I heard 'incoming' artillery fire and was hugely relieved to discover the leadership had disappeared into the bush overnight to spare the locals, themselves and us a one-sided battle that could only end badly. I then got caught up in a farce as our host, a local teacher, persuaded my two companions including my then partner that the Oromo Liberation Front hadn't left at all but had fanned out around the town to defend us all. Toasts were drunk of the local honey beer to the Victory of the Oromo people but then seeing fleeing young men he finally came to his senses and organised a surprisingly efficient evacuation by back routes to a church run boarding school where we were hidden away in an accommodation block. A few days later when the town was considered secure by the occupying Tigrayan forces the little airport reopened and we were able to take a flight to Addis. I later learnt my report, denouncing the attack on the BBC World Service recorded on arrival in Addis was heard by our erstwhile comrades hiding in the bush. Totally bizarrely we were lunching beside the Thames less than a week later though it took several weeks for my panic attacks on the Tube to subside. Some folk seem to get a kick out of conflict zones but I knew I never wanted to get near something like that again if I could help it. So it was in a spirit of peaceful solidarity with the good people of this dramatically situated and likeable town that I reclaimed my bicycle and cycled on.

The terrain became hillier and the cycling more strenuous as the sun reached its zenith. On reaching the next town of Accadia I alighted at a water fountain to eat my fruit and drink my fill taking turns at the spout with a local who used it to wash down his lorry which didn't exactly encourage me to linger. The town was having its main road repaired and was all topsy turvy so I carried on and almost immediately the hilly plateau country gave way to steep sided wooded valleys down one of which my road fell precipitously. As the gradient eased enough to permit terracing I was suddenly amidst olives overlooking the Frugno flowing east into the Adriatic. I was in Puglia and it felt different. The country was rougher, stonier, the land less fertile and the heat had been turned up a notch. I had been going since dawn and I started to fret about my route. I needed to confirm a ferry from Bari as a bifurcation of the route was now approaching. If for any reason I had to switch to a Brindisi ferry then I needed to push on along the Eurovelo 5 route further south whilst if Bari, my preferred crossing was confirmed I would soon be leaving it to cut due east. Checking my phone charge it was empty as was my power bank. I connected to the USB feed on the bike powered by my front dynamo which gave a trickle of charge into the power bank and set off again. After the glorious morning ride it was now the early afternoon with the sun at its hottest and I was approaching empty. The minor road started to converge with a busy autoroute leading to the Adriatic coast. I could see where it came down a long incline on an embankment under which my lane went. After all the magnificent scenery I was approaching a rather ugly connurbation, Candela, next to the autoroute intersection. As my quiet agricultural road came up from the underpass below the town it went past a building which can only be described as a Moorish castle. It wasn't ancient, but it was in its way quite striking and more importantly it had some trees lining a driveway which provided shade. Pulling up knackered, I sat in the shade taking stock of my situation. I was out of water but there was now a little power in my mobile so I started to search for the Bari ferry website. A very user-unfriendly site gobbled up the little power it had without satisfactorily answering my concern. The site had a bicycle option but when I tried to confirm it for the day I wanted to cross 4 days hence (the night before I was due to rendezvous with Alex) it wouldn't let me. Suddenly the phone died on me, as it does when the power gets too low. I had hit empty – no water, no food and no power. But here I was on the edge of a town so help had to be at hand. Without thinking too much (I really wasn't capable of much thought at this stage) I walked over to the Moorish castle assuming it was some sort of public building and tried the door. It opened into a shabby corridor off which there was an open door. I knocked and went inside to find a woman sat at a computer on a desk. I asked with a mixture of pigeon Italian and gestures whether I could plug a power cable in for my phone. She seemed entirely at ease with being confronted by a dusty Mamil and gestured in a relaxed manner for me to help myself. Having plugged in I ventured an enquiry for water which was again met with a relaxed affirmative gesture indicating an office water fountain. Being offered a seat we now struck up conversation and I had soon told enough of my story to convince her that though vagabondo I was harmless! But what was striking about her was her accepting manner as if people walked in off the street needing assistance all the time. Well that was closer to the truth than I realised. It turned out that Tania was a social worker and this building had been converted into a refugee shelter currently harbouring 40 women and children, mainly from Nigeria. I had blundered into a migrant processing centre as the many thousands landing on the Italian coast these last summers are moved on inland. Of course given that I teach a University global health course I was interested to see things firsthand and Tania was extremely gracious with her time. Understandably none of the temporary residents wanted to talk but I got an impression of their situation which spoke volumes for the humanity of the southern Italians who were providing a comfortable and more importantly safe haven for these women and their babies. There was inevitably the air of a transit camp about the place but it was cool and well provided with facilities for sleeping, washing and cooking.

Tania ended up letting me use the office phone to book my ferry confirming verbally that bikes were welcomed on board which banished my slightly irrational fear of being stranded on a quayside with a bicycle. So I now had a ticket to ride, I had cooled down and rehydrated and it was time to thank Tania for her kindness and see where the road would take me that night. I indicated my route on to Tania checking which turn I should take but she had no idea...like so many people I had encountered she had surprisingly little topographic knowledge...she lived in the town, drove to the coast and had never gone the obscure way I indicated! Thanking her profusely I headed out into the heat, picked up Hermes and cycled back up the drive. I now could see there was a service station just a couple of hundred metres further along (previously invisible to my exhausted tunnel vision) where I could get some food. As I cycled up I realised just how much I needed sustenance when I got my feet in a muddle negotiating the service station entrance and toppled over clipped in. Unlike my previous fall in Paris where I was viewed with disdain, or in Tuscany when the ex-pat runner simply ran past I was now in southern Italy. An entire car-load of people rushed to my aid and I needed to fight them off! Far better this excess of concern than none! Two double coffees, a couple of sandwiches, bag of crisps and chocolate bar later I was feeling re-energised. It was surprisingly busy as the end of workday commuters and transit holiday makers had pulled off the autoroute to refuel (a little less dramatically than I). I shared a stand-up drinks table with a pair of elegantly dressed business women who were perfectly at ease exchanging pleasantries with me. There is something easily convivial in the Italian manner which I was learning to appreciate. But I knew I wanted to press on – Tania had been my saviour in Candela but it didn't feel like an overnight destination. More importantly I had come to appreciate in the deep south that the late afternoon was the best time of the day for riding as the sun descended, it cooled down and the golden hour of evening light arrived!

I had noticed a rather unpromising lane heading off in the right direction on my way up to the service station. The concrete had broken up and there was evidence of fly tipping which made it look like it was out of commission. But as soon as I had persevered 500 metres I could make out where it looped over the trunk road and headed east. This was my route on – but to what? The scenery had lost its wooded hilly aspect here as it approached a major river - the Ofanto - which drained the high country known as the Irpinia that I had crossed that morning. Although at this time of year the flow was sluggish this was clearly a major source of irrigation and the entire valley had been given over to high intensity horticultural production, including acres under greenhouses. And judging by every plant I got near and later the lorries that went past the whole valley was now a massive tomato farm. I didn't know so many tomatoes existed on this planet. Now the shadows were lengthening and the valley was strikingly deserted. Realising the river here was a significant barrier I took the first lane that crossed it to gain the south bank before dark. As I crossed the river in the gloaming a significant group of buildings came into view. It turned out to be the fortified farmstead (or *Massa*) of Parasacco. It dates only from the 1800s but speaks of a time before Italian unification when these parts were roamed not by cycling vagabondi but by proper brigands! Then this was still sheep country and these major farmsteads had grown up at the junctions of the Roman roads and the sheep tracks. This is where the *traturri* came down to for the winter. In the failing light it certainly looked atmospheric if rather forlorn in its abandoned state. I was not remotely tempted to wild camp near here. Especially since the wind of this morning had returned and strengthened which being a westerly meant it was a tailwind blowing me firmly towards my destination.

As soon as I remounted the lane joined the bigger access road for the horticultural agribusiness and I had to dodge two massive lorries driving in convoy laden with thousand upon thousand of tomatoes. By this time I had my lights on in ernest when out of the darkness came the grim sound of howling dogs. As I came round a corner three big guard dogs emerged from a gateway to confront me. Fortunately I didn't have time to think and my body went straight into flight mode. Given I was well over the 100 kms that day I was impressed just how quickly I could still peddle urged on by these hounds from hell literally snapping at my heels. I was so terrified I was urging Hermes on in all ernest! Once we had shaken off the dog pack I slowly got my pulse back under control when I became aware of flashing orange lights behind. As they came closer I realised they belonged to a convoy of three tractors. Rapidly computing they must be knocking off for the evening I decided to follow them, on the rational that where workers went at the end of their shift would be more hospitable than tomato valley and its guard dogs.

As we turned off on a side road I could see we were headed towards a church which was encouraging because where there is a church there may be a bar. This proved happily to be the case but as I rode up (now about 9 o'clock at night) what really flabbergasted me was to see three fully laden touring bikes parked outside the bar. It appeared to be at the cross-roads of a two street purpose built workers' village which had seen better days. But the café was clean and well stocked with some tables under a concrete arcade running the length of the street. Diagonally opposite was the church and at the end of the street a lorry park.

The clientele seemed to be in three clusters of a mixed bunch of locals, a huddle of drivers and three young bandana wearing hipsters whom I took (correctly) to be the cyclists. Taking a beer I unceremoniously sat myself down at the spare fourth chair with the hipsters and introduced myself. Eloi, Mont and Jaume explained they were three college friends from Barcelona who having toured Croatia had crossed the Adriatic by ferry to Bari. Faced with strong headwinds (the reverse of my tailwind of course) and a mechanical issue they had been offered a ride as far as Napoli on a tomato lorry! It turned out our café/bar was the distribution hub for tomatoes across southern Italy. A call here would have a lorry load of tomatoes heading your way within a few hours! After the efforts of the day and the escape from the dogs I was ready for some R & R with good company. And it must be said three idealistic young Catalan students proved to be excellent company!

I am a tailender of the Boomer generation - my father came back from the war, married his friend's sister and had three boys. My eldest brother 5 years older than me went hitchhiking in 1968 and came back with a bell round his neck and tales of riots in Paris. This contradictory dynamic between peace, love and revolution was to form the backdrop to my formative years. Dylan and the Beatles, the latter together through my childhood and separately through my adolescence, provided the sound track. As a university lecturer I have plenty of opportunity to observe the changing mores of the generations. Generation X, who followed, had missed this dynamic and struck me as being pretty comfortable with the status quo pursuing their entrepreneurial leanings. The Millennials to whom my new three friends belong are closer in spirit to us Boomers. These guys certainly had that sense of classless freedom to which many boomers aspire. Equally comfortable with watercolour painting and bike mechanics (Eloi and Jaume were friends from the same engineering course) we talked bikes, routes, people encountered and Catalan politics until the circle widened with the arrival of their tomato lorry driver, friends and the patron. We started toasts to Europe (I think I may have had something to do with that, ordering Prosecco all round as I made a pension announcement for some absurd reason...it was, in my defence, still less than 36 hours since I had become a pensioner and this was my first opportunity to share the passing of the milestone). I then broke out the St Semillion for the young Catalans which needed smoking before I got on a cross border ferry and things got a little more disjointed. At some point the decision was made to bed down for the night so we wheeled our bikes across to the small patch of grass in front of the church. In an impossibly cool manoeuvre Mont threw up a hammock whilst the boys snuggled down on blankets under the stars. I felt rather outward bound as I pitched my one-man tent. But we all slept very well and were rather groggy the following morning over coffee back at the café.

Taking the opportunity of a little downtime that morning to do some clothes washing and cycle maintenance under expert mechanical engineering supervision by lunchtime I was ready to make a move and we all enjoyed a final coffee. I was rather touched to be given a watercolour of Padova painted by Eloi and signed by all three with the dedication

'For the random meetings that will last forever, stay strong and if you can't....
just stop and have a beer'.

What sort of impression must I have made on them, those Catalan travellers encountered in the rather appropriately named tomato truck stop café of Villaggio Gaudiane? Joking aside this felt true inter-generational cycling camaraderie.

Having rolled up at night without a plan I had only learned the name of the place in the morning whilst studying the map weighing up my options for my remaining time in Italy. I now had three nights before I was due to take the ferry from Bari which was only 110 kilometres away. The question was where to spend the time. Unsure what lay ahead I decided, as usual, to let the journey dictate where I should stop rather than impose a solution based on prior research. The map indicated a lake within striking distance and I wondered whether that might provide lakeside options. Heading over there I rapidly realised it was a reservoir filling the base of a side valley to the Ofanto and way up on the far side lay a white apparition of a town which must be Minervino. I say apparition because the town buildings seemed all to have been painted white and it really was perched on a very steep valley side stretching all the way to the top which gave it a rather other worldly dimension unlike any other Italian hill town I had come across to date. The terracotta reds of the north and the classical stonework of the Centre had now morphed into the brilliant white of the deep south. I took all this in from the shade of roadside olive trees which also excited me. So much so that I decided to go no further and booked a rather nice sounding apartment, the only place advertising on Booking.com in Minervinho, as the prospect of resting up for the rest of the day was suddenly very appealing.

So off I set round the surprisingly large reservoir and began to climb up the other side. Well what had looked steep but short from far away was now in reality steep and quite long. I hadn't eaten anything since a croissant with my morning coffee and was starting to get that progressively disengaged woozy feeling that happens when I go hypoglycaemic. In pro cycling circles I gather this is referred to as 'the bonk'! Just at that moment my mobile phone went and it was Booking.com (Italy) to explain (in Italian) that the booking I had just made online should never have been made available and the owner now wanted this booking withdrawn. What about these two alternatives offered the Milan based caller at Melfi or Venosa. How far away were these places?....60 kms back the way I had come or 40 kms in the wrong direction. Seething I answered 'Grazzi Mille'....thanks a million....with heavy irony though I feared my pigeon Italian had failed to convey the depth of my emotions at that moment. I actually lay down on the pavement and shut my eyes briefly. Looking back this was a low point and measure of how exhausted I was. On returning to my senses I decided the way forward was to grasp the bull by the horns, march through the streets of Minervhino and find accommodation the old way by myself if Booking.com weren't up to the task! So refuelled by anger off I set up a series of switchback town streets unable to take the more direct pedestrian stairs as I was hauling Hermes fully laden beside me. The first lady I encountered helpfully contributed the Italian for room 'camera' which I'd forgotten in my manic mime of sleeping to accompany my request for help. No, she didn't know anyone who rented out rooms. Nor did the next person I confronted with my newly fluent 'camera per dormire?'. Just then I passed a sign advertising the 'Taverna Garibaldi con camere'. Locking the bike I climbed the stairs to the adjacent terrace where a rather elegant stone building advertised itself as the said Taverna. Mounting more stairs to go in I entered what was clearly a serious restaurant serving serious food to well heeled clients, the last of whom seemed to be in the act of settling up with a stocky man with a greying beard who was manning an elegant little wooden desk. Suddenly conscious of the fact that I was a Mamil vagabondi I approached the man and asked for 'camera per dormire'. Looking me over keenly he rapidly established that English was the optimum medium of communication and suggested I took a seat whilst he finished dealing with the business at hand. I sat nervously awaiting the outcome of what I assumed was a pause to deliberate. The more I took in the scene the more I wanted that room, and the promise of classy refuelling which came with it. I had been pushing myself since leaving Rome, had been riding hard for 5 days, under canvas for the last three nights and I was ready for some comfort. I reasoned that if he was full he would have sent me away directly. My reasoning was spot on, as once he had established that I didn't smell too bad (you will have noted I mentioned washing stuff that morning thank goodness) and despite hypomanic presentation ('room to sleep' shouted without so much as a 'buongiorno') appeared to be in possession of most of my senses he suggested I follow him out of the restaurant to inspect 'the room' . I nipped back down gesturing to the bike to collect the panniers partly to establish my traveller credentials (though I assume the outfit would have already done this) before following Rocco (as I would learn to call him) up another flight of stairs whereby we gained the next switchback of a street. Along the upper side was a stone built terrace of cottages and with a flourish he produced the key to one. Gesturing me in I entered a pleasant studio space with a mezzanine floor under a barrel vaulted roof housing a very comfortable looking double bed. Bliss; handing me the key he said simply dinner would be served at 7 pm and left me to it. I could hardly believe my luck – this was just what the doctor ordered.

After a shower and nap I set out to explore the town. It was Saturday evening, and the place to be as ever was on the piazza at the top of the town. There several café bars housed a variety of clientele and I found myself drawn to the alternative café where the guy had a major cabinet speaker belting out funky Italian pop grooves. This was clearly a hip take on the contemporary Italian scene but judging from the very mainstream young people lapping it up it wasn't bohemian fringe stuff. As the magic hour of the fading light took over centre stage I found myself hypnotised by the view west. There below me lay the plain of the endless tomatoes of Puglia backed by the higher ground I had traversed previously dotted with wind turbines. These turbines were now lit with flashing red lights presumably as a warning to low flying aircraft. The net effect was like something out of Close Encounters. I suddenly realised I was in danger of being late for dinner and enjoyed scurrying back down a pedestrian staircase only to realise I had taken the wrong one. Over the course of the next half an hour I became intimately familiar with the unusual layout of Minervino, the pedestrian stairways every 100 meters or so bisecting the switchback streets which wind up to the top.

Finding the correct stairway I turned up for dinner more suitably attired than at lunchtime. Rocco was there to greet me, introduce me to his aunt who was also dining with us tonight and proceed to serve me a fantastic four course dinner cooked by his wife and her assistant in the kitchen. The emphasis was of course on local produce which here meant pasta, tomatoes (of course), aubergines, peppers, olives, figs, hams, cheeses, sausages washed down with great local reds, suitably rich and full bodied as one might expect down in the deep south.

After sleeping like I hadn't slept since Piedmont, over breakfast Rocco explained his philosophy of using local produce seasonally in accord with everything I had come to appreciate about the Italian slow food movement. Sharing with him my mission to take my bike to my olives in Greece the conversation turned to olive husbandry and we considered the appalling tragedy that has befallen some areas of Puglia olive trees (thankfully not yet Rocco's area). This infestation by a new world bacterium, xylella fastidiosa, was first detected in Puglia in 2013. Previously unknown in Europe It has already spread according to the Royal Horticultural Society to ornamental plants in southern France (including Corsica), the Balearic Islands and southern Spain and most recently to the Porto region of Portugal'. It affects a wide variety of plants though olives, vines, coffee and lavender stand out on the lengthy list resulting in leaf scorch, dieback and plant death. These are signs of any significant stress so laboratory confirmation is apparently critical with destruction of all surrounding vegetation in a 100 meters radius the recommended control strategy. This of course is what is proving so painful in Puglia and according to some accounts is not necessarily being observed. Rocco heard my account of the organically farmed grove up on the slopes of the Taygetos and kindly expressed approval – as he put it if the trees are hardy and well adapted to their environment they are best prepared to fight disease. I fear whilst this applies to endemic bugs the arrival of new pests with globalisation provide fertile epidemic conditions whatever the local husbandry system.

Rocco was taking the family to the nearby seaside for a few days after the Sunday lunch service he explained which he encouraged me to attend as there would be no dinner service. I took myself off and found a quiet square from which to enjoy tai chi with a view from 'the balcony of Puglia' as I learnt Minervinho was known. I explored the neighbouring streets until it was time for another Pugliese feast. I retired sated to my cool stone barrel vaulted quarters where in unspeakable luxury I took to my bed for a Sunday afternoon siesta.

Having slept late into the afternoon I whiled away the evening strolling the town's upper streets observing Italian street life. Many of the townspeople retained a connection with the surrounding countryside and could be seen sitting in their arched stone entranceways peeling walnuts which were now in season. Life in Puglia it appeared rolled on much as it had done for centuries past. It had been a long time since I had passed such a relaxed Sunday.

The next morning I dropped off my key in Rocco's post box and cycled slowly up the switchbacks to the top of the hill. It looked like my route for the morning started near the large piazza at the top. I took a coffee watching stall holders set up for what was clearly going to be a busy Monday market. Shame to be missing it but I had a morning ride across the hills of the National Park dell'Alto Murgia. Quite how high 'alto' would remain to be seen. I was agreeably surprised to slip out of the square and basically contour as the road rolled due east.

This was more like the highlands of two days ago. Big open spaces, dry stone walls and a tailwind pushing me ever eastwards – a lovely way to start the day. The main objective of the morning started to feature on signs and eventually a massive beautiful octagonal stone bastion rose into view commanding the last ridge of the Alto Murgia...the Castel del Monte of Holy Roman Emperor Frederick IInd built in the 12th century. Walking the last few metres up towards the Castel suddenly the blue Adriatic Sea and the coastal plain dotted with olive trees opened up 500 metres below. As so often on this journey this chance encounter shed light on a whole period of European history of which I had very little knowledge. We last left the historical competition between the Holy Roman Emperor and the Papacy in the battle between Ghibelline Siena and Guelph Florence during which the intervention of heavy German cavalry fighting on the Sienese side proved decisive. Now I was to learn how this all came to pass from my visit to Frederick's Castel, a Southern Italian icon commemorated by the Italian state on its euro coinage. As I walked the perimeter of the Castel mound admiring the almost polished surface of the octagonal stone walls glinting in the brilliant light I noted the classical features of the ornate gateway and felt this to be a piece of the jigsaw linking ancient classical culture with medieval Europe. It turns out this was but one small piece of a fortification system built by an unusually enlightened medieval man – the Tower under which I had camped at San Miniato up in Tuscany was another.

Born in Puglia the son of an Emperor and grandson of no less a figure than Frederick Barbarossa, he inherited a rule extending from Sicily in the south to the north German coast, thanks ultimately to Charlemagne's eldest grandson some 500 years earlier. However he made full use of this silver spoon being said by his contemporaries to be a man of such extraordinary culture, energy, and ability as to be referred to as 'stupor mundi' (the wonder of the world). Later Nietzsche honoured him with the epithet 'the first European'. He was certainly a canny politician, managing to finesse Jerusalem by treaty having turned up both late and excommunicated for the sixth crusade. The cachet lent by his new found status as King of Jerusalem cemented his reputation in Europe and on his return he was able to consolidate power north of the Alps though continuing strife with the papacy would preoccupy him to the south for much of his remaining reign. However it was his awareness of the increasing threat to Europe posed by the Mongols who had come roaring down the silk road which really places him at centre stage for one of the most pivotal moments in European history. His refusal to face the highly effective army of the Mongols on the battlefield, adopting a siege mentality instead by shoring up fortifications and hoarding food, all helped to famously turn the Horde back at the gates of Vienna. Here at Castel Mundi one gets a sense of the man not just as a master strategist but as a far-sighted man of culture who saw himself, like Charlemagne, continuing imperial Roman rule. The unusual octagonal shape of this bastion with its echoes of Charlemagne's Palatine Chapel in Aachen and the Dome of the Rock in Jerusalem contributes to the sense of Frederick's keen awareness of the past and his role in its onward transmission. Speaker of six languages, the small exhibition in the castle that day was devoted to his published manuscript on hunting with birds. In this empirical study he contradicts explicitly some of Aristotle's observations on birds. Frederick, like Aristotle, applies observational scientific method to this study. Frederick is so familiar with Aristotle because he commissioned a fresh translation of his work from Arabic into Latin. Remarkably the man he employed for this task, Michael Scott, was a polyglot wandering scholar originally heralding from the Scottish Borders. Scott refined his Arabic in Toledo and joined Frederick's court in Sicily as science advisor and court astrologer where he would meet Fibonacci and share an interest in mathematics with the man credited with widespread adoption of the Hindu-Arabic numbering system we still use as opposed to the much less efficient Roman numerals used up till Frederick's day.

One could spend all day exploring the many strands of Frederick the man and his reign but the Adriatic was beckoning and the downhill did not disappoint. There was a messy bit finding a way across the coastal autoroute which led me past a scruffy lay-by with what appeared to be a prostitute sat outside her caravan hinting at the poverty to be found down here in the south. Amongst the endless olive trees I passed a sign on the approach to Corato as 'the capital of Puglia's olives' giving its name to the local cultivar, the Coratino. I was instantly reminded of Koroni, a town local to where I was headed in Greece and our cultivar the Koroneiki. Now I was down amidst the olives of southern Puglia this land reminded me strongly of the Mani, my Greek destination. There were dry stone shelters called *Trulli* with the same conical roof structure as I had found in the field shelter on the land I had bought in Mani. These are a technical solution to dry stone building without cement – the overlapping of courses of stonework so called corbelling resulting in the same attractive dome shapes as the Mycenaeans arrived at in their 'bee-hive tomb' funereal monuments. This building adaptation had been in use for 3,500 years in these parts!

I got into Ruvo di Puglia in good time to find myself a pleasant B & B before exploring a town making the most of the holiday season with a late summer music festival in the square outside the church. An orchestra had been assembled to play a mixed programme lent great seriousness by the maestro who conducted passionately a mixed bunch of musicians of no little skill. It made for a pleasant diversion in what by now had been a month long Italian traverse.

And so the final leg to Bari which began at a fountain where I was filling my water bottles when I was asked where I was going by an extrovert countryman waiting to do likewise. Explaining I was headed for Greece he commended my choice as it was 'less spoilt than here'. I was interested to hear this frank observation from a man who appeared deeply invested in rural tradition. The Puglia – Mani parallels were not limited to the stone and the olives.

The towns I traversed as I approached the coast were livelier and more prosperous than their inland equivalents with several busy cafés to choose from for my morning coffee stop. A little further along the road, around 5 kilometres back from the coast, a sign indicated the entrance to an ancient barrow which told how the tradition of stone building had been deeply ingrained over thousands of years. This chamber tomb turned out to be just one of a group known collectively as the Bari-Taranto dolmens dated by associated pottery jugs to the second millennium BCE. This was the time period when olive and vine cultivation was being added hereabouts to the more ancient farming complex of wheat, pulses, sheep and goats which dates back to the 5th millennium BCE in Puglia(Broodbank 2013). I would like to think those jugs were being used for oil but that's probably a stretch!

I finally reached the coast at Molfetta, where an ancient stonewalled church abuts a quay in a shimmering stone ensemble beside the southern harbour mole. Finding a handful of people swimming off the mole into the turquoise water on the open water side I joined them. It was the perfect arrival on the Adriatic after my morning's cycle and after towelling down I pushed my bike over to the nearby restaurant at which I was only the second occupied table and could have my pick of the fresh seafood on offer. I went for an octopus risotto cooked in thick black ink which was delicious washed down with a chilled white. I was going to miss this Italian food! Reembarking feeling well fed and relaxed I enjoyed an hours' coastal cycleway progress before the approach to Bari when it all started to go wrong.

For a start the coast was becoming increasingly tatty as the roadside development increased the closer one got to Bari. Then crucially the main SS16 autoroute swung around Bari airport to take up the narrow strip between it and the coast obliterating my pleasant minor coast road route. So there was nothing for it but to strike inland past the airport which then deposited me in a large industrial zone with signage designed only for lorries to get onto the autoroute. Having described three circles I was beginning to doubt my sanity when, faced yet again by an autoroute slip road, I found myself irately marching into a neighbouring McDonald's and rudely demanding of the manager directions to Bari on a bike. To his credit he didn't take offence at my challenging tone (I had personally identified him as the representative of mass consumer capitalism which had caused this mess) and calmly pointed out a service road which would lead me out the back of the services to where I was trying to reach. And sure enough it did – an unlikely escape through the Golden Arches!

Regaining my more usual calm composure I made my way straight down to the massive harbour gateway and headed for the 'superfast' ferry terminal for Patras. I was in very good time for that evening's sailing so I wasn't too flustered by the time lost on navigation. Hang on why was there a handwritten sign hanging on the door? In Greek, English and Italian it said 'Cancelled due to strikes!'. Aaarrrgh. Several others caught in the same predicament were exchanging news and it was immediately apparent this was due to a strike by Greek seamen in protest at draconian cuts taken as part of the continuing Greek economic woes. The ship was stranded in Patras and would only head for Bari once the strike was over the following day. Well at least it was only a 24 hour strike (so far). Absorbing all this I started to relay the news via text to my brother-in-law Alex whom I had planned to meet in Patras the following day. It looked like this would push things back but we had built in some slack so it wasn't a drama. By this time I had been befriended by two young English cyclists who had taken the eastern coastal route down through Italy so I was intrigued to exchange our stories. We repaired to a harbourside part of the old town where cheap student bars provided outside tables a plenty and got to exchange stories. They were modern young travellers who were blogging in a more purposive way than I to kind of launch themselves as a travel brand if I understood them correctly. One thing led to another and by the time they had led me halfway around Bari in search of an Irish bar recommended to them by some other young travellers I was beginning to doubt the wisdom of falling in with them. But it was all good fun and when they turned back into the harbour gates to find somewhere to bivouac I elected to have a final quieter nightcap at an outside café/bar serving the local harbourside late-night drinkers. This was certainly more colourful than the Irish bar and I ended up exchanging relationship advice with an unlikely looking cast of locals. I was however a bit thrown on returning to the harbourside gates to find them firmly locked against me. I had noticed a sward of beautifully kept lawn against the old town bastion to which I repaired and had my tent up ten minutes later to pass a surprisingly good night despite some street lighting.

Returning to the ferry terminal first thing I was relieved to have the confirmation that the strike had been lifted and our ship was steaming over to Bari as we spoke. But it would not depart until the usual time ie 10pm so I had 12 hours to enjoy in Bari. The previous evening I had seen enough to know I was going to enjoy the old town proper so I headed straight for the cathedral, at the heart of it, before being waylaid by anyone else.

I decided down in the heart of the sightseeing area my stuff would be safe enough chained up with Hermes right outside the cathedral. As with the bastion under which I had camped the cathedral is built from the most marvellous limestone which glints in the brilliant southern sunlight. The 12th century Romanesque church there today is the third on the site, and an inscription on a mosaic remnant of the original can be reliably dated by the name of Bishop Andrea to his period of office 758 – 761. This is an ancient city and that day in the cathedral crypt one got a sense of it. The atmosphere down there was more akin to the orthodox world I was headed for, with a strong perfume of incense and an atmosphere which felt mystical. This appeared to be borne out as I approached a prominent icon which was being venerated by the faithful. I learnt this to be an important oriental 8th century icon of the Madonna Odegitria, literally mother who points the way, a much copied cult expression of the Virgin Mary. People around me slipped forward to touch the frame of the icon. Things got even more weird at the Basilika di San Nicola. Likewise built in beautiful light coloured shimmering stone this is an important pilgrimage sight given that it houses the relics of Saint Nicolas. Apparently there was intense competition for these between Venice and Bari and the fact that the St Nicolas resides in Bari is testament to its influence in these early days. Again the faithful were pressing forward to get close to the relics. From my anthropology student days I recalled the mechanism of so-called sympathetic magic whereby through contact mystical power could be transmitted. Here I was in 21st century Europe with magical belief systems alive and well. Of course the genius of the Catholic Church is to absorb local cults into their Great Tradition. Perhaps the most striking examples of this I have come across is in Latin America where I have been invited to raise a glass to Pachamama, the Andean female spirit, cleverly disguised as the Virgin Mary. This looking towards a mother figure for nurture seems to be a central aspect of human nature. Springing from biological hard wiring it finds representation in the ubiquitous female cult figurines, known as Venus figurines, found throughout the upper palaeolithic across Eurasia. Indeed the oldest of these (found only ten years ago) had been carved out of mammoth ivory between 35 and 45,000 years ago. Incidentally calling these Venus figurines is a nice example of how we overuse classical mythology as a lens on the past, here projecting a Roman take on the theme back into the old Stone Age.

As a paediatrician I have spent much of my professional life observing the intense two way bond established between the primary carer and young infant. In a world where breastfeeding was universal that primary carer was female. In my doctoral studies describing the challenges faced by newborn infants who had suffered brain injury during birth in Kathmandu I became fascinated by the emerging science of neuroplasticity describing how the brain learns and adapts. Microradiographs of complex synaptic webs demonstrate beautifully the pluripotentiality with which we are born. Those connections which are used and encouraged strengthen and become habitual. Those that we don't use wither away and die through a rather chillingly named process of 'programmed cell death'. A nice example I have used to illustrate this to a generation of medical students is that of language. We are all born with the ability to speak any one of the approximately 6,000 surviving human languages as a native speaker. Beyond about the third year of life those 5,998/9 languages we weren't thoroughly exposed to will never be available to be mastered as a native speaker – if we come to them in later life and devote ourselves to learning one or two we will always speak them with a foreign accent. Those synaptic control mechanisms which allow for the marvellous palatal contortions so as to produce a Khoisan click consonant for example will simply not be there. Experience sculpts the neuroplastic brain by shaping its internal connectivity.

Escaping the claustrophobia of the crypt to wander through the streets of the old town crowded with both tourists and locals it felt like a living town. Down an alley I found an impressive historic building which turned out to be the restored convent of Santa

Scholastica now housing an excellent archaeological museum of local finds. What was particularly striking was a very early bowl dating back over 6000 years to the 5th Millenium BCE from the coastal strip near Bari which places it in the middle/late neolithic, when the farming complex of cereals and domesticated animals was just arriving in this part of the world. Given that current archaeological research places the 'invention' of this first farming complex at between 7000 and 6000 BCE in the Levant (modern day Israel/Syrian/Iraq borderlands) to the immediate east of the Mediterranean this begs the question how did the Neolithic revolution reach Puglia? If on foot a simple arithmetical exercise would suggest the approximate 2500 kms distance might take 2000 years if the process proceeded by a long day's walk (25 kilometres) every generation (reckoned at a duration of 20 years due to earlier childbirth). However it is now thought canoes, which had been in growing use amongst hunter-gatherers of the late neolithic to reach obsidian mines on certain islands in the Mediterranean were used by early farmers to short cut some legs along the north Mediterranean littoral. This was almost certainly the case in reverse of the route I was following (across the Strait of Otranto which separates the Adriatic from the Ionian stretches of the Mediterranean). As Broodbank suggests the progress of agriculture westwards likely proceeded in 'punctuated, leapfrogging jumps by small founder groups from one suitable patch directly to the next each creating a little enclave.... This proceeded at a kilometre or two a year (i.e. a day's walk per generation) except where maritime short cuts were used where navigable with available technology (Broodbank 2013).'

The late Neolithic bowl I saw that day in Bari is an example of Serro d'Alto ceramic ware, a high prestige pottery type which was fired from high quality clay at high temperatures suggestive of kiln technology. Whilst it's decoration looks back to the pre-pottery days of basketware its technology suggests a settled people with an emergent specialisation in pottery production. The people of this part of Puglia in the 5th millennium BCE were already well settled farmers and producing specialised trade goods.

So the day turned out to be a real bonus to enjoy the incredibly rich culture of Bari's old town. And speaking as a Liverpudlian I always think to sail in or out of a port allows one to enjoy it as it should be experienced. Returning down to the quayside there was the 'Superfast' ferry safely arrived no longer strike bound and steaming promisingly. With an absence of any drama this time round I was soon pushing my bike on board a major ferry for the second time on my journey. The departure at sunset into the Adriatic emphasised why it can feel more like a lake than an ocean with a complex shoreline and a narrow neck of only 70 kilometres between the spur on the heel of Italy and Albania. It was balmy on deck as we left the Adriatic portion of the Middle Sea (Mediterranean) to enter the

Ionian. I spent much of the evening enjoying the passing lights of Corfu to our East chatting with the many lorry drivers who seemed equally happy to take the air – notably a Greek driver doing a weekly German run who was amused at my faltering attempts to dust down my Greek. As I sketchily communicated my dream of taking my σύνταξη (pension) and retreating to a Greek village despite or perhaps because of his many trans-continental journeys he agreed there was no better place to retreat to in the third age than a coastal village in Greece. After a reasonable few hours on my sleeping bag I was awake to enjoy dawn as we steamed past the site of the sea battle of Actium, with a keen sense of history now that I had learnt just what a key staging post this had proved to be. The victory of Octavian against Mark Anthony that day decisively put Greek Apollo in the ascendancy over much longer-lived Egyptian gods. The Augustinian age that followed put Greek culture at the heart of the Middle Sea. It would be Holy Roman Emperors like Frederick IInd who transmitted this through an emergent Europe. And it would be successive waves of colonising European powers who would extend the cultural hegemony ever outward into a newly re-globalising world.

Chapter 9. Across the Land of Pelops

My arrival in Patras was all the more exciting as I looked down from the high sided ferry to see the tiny figure of Alex, my brother-in-law, standing beside a bike on the quay far below. After a brief but warm greeting we agreed that the need to make up for lost time was paramount. Since we were both packed and ready to roll there was nothing to delay our departure heading east along the coast road from the ferry terminal obviating the need for me to actually enter Patras proper at all.

Checking in with Alex as we rode he had passed a pleasant enough evening in my absence getting his stuff rigged up on the rental bike (delivered to Patras by our Kardamyli outdoors shop contact Ianni) before exploring the town and finding himself an evening meal. I confirmed my understanding that the most prominent sight in the city was the cathedral whose fame relates to its importance in the cult of St Andrew, known in the Greek Orthodox tradition as Πρωτόκλητος, the first called, in other words, Jesus's first disciple. His much-travelled skull was returned by the Pope to the bishop of Patras in 1964. Andrew is said to have been crucified in Patras by an irate Roman governor for not only curing his wife of some malady but then, fatally for him, converting her to Christianity. When Byzantium was the regional power St Andrew's relics were installed in Constantinople as the Patriarch of that city is considered the apostolic successor to

Andrew just as the pope is considered the apostolic successor to Peter, who just happens to have been Andrew's brother – both fishermen on the sea of Galilee. You may recall the fratricide at the heart of the Roman foundation myth seemingly replaced here by a bit of good old sibling rivalry. The skull was taken to Italy following the sacking of Constantinopole by the lads of the fourth crusade in 1204, although another version has it being taken to Italy in the face of Ottoman conquest in 1462. Either way its return to Patras is only made more fascinating by the fact that this gesture of fraternal goodwill was fiercely resisted by some in the Greek Orthodox Church who continue to consider it a sin to join in prayer with their catholic siblings. The Great Schism ain't over yet! Anyway, it seemed that apart from the odd piece of holy cranium I hadn't missed too much in Patras and Alex was happy to go with my plan which was basically to head towards the north east corner of the Peloponnese and find somewhere by the sea to sleep, preferably after food and drink!

Alex has spent 30 years in the military and this has lent him the excellent travel companion qualities of an ability to cope with just about anything allied with an easygoing ability to rub along with all manner of folk – even a brother-in-law who has spent the best part of two months being a vagabondi! So he appeared quite happy to pick up my rhythm on the ride and go with the flow. The coast road ambles eastward along a coastal plain which is pretty in parts without being especially dramatic. As expected the Patras coastal sprawl dragged on for a few kilometres then gave way to a world of agriculture and sleepy market towns. I had been trying to get a fix on the coastline both by studying maps and looking out from the starboard side of the ferry as we rounded into the Gulf of Corinth on my approach that morning to Patras. Neither had shed much light on what was clearly not a particularly dramatic or much populated stretch of coast. As we got deeper into Achaea, as this north east corner has been known since the days of antiquity, we got progressively more surrounded by horticultural polytunnels, presumably to retain moisture as there felt to be no lack of heat! Eventually we came to Nea Manolada, a scruffy settlement with a roadside kiosk where we bought drinks and snacks. I asked the lad serving at the kiosk for directions towards the sea and he gestured towards a track off the road we had been following which we duly headed down, without feeling the situation looked particularly promising. However, that had been the case so often on my journey at this hour of commitment a couple of hours before dark and it had almost always previously turned out alright. I was thinking to myself how unfortunate it would be if it didn't come good this time when I'm 'leading' two of us for a change.

We got a bit confused by a junction of tracks which didn't tally with our map and sought the advice of a passing young lad with excellent English who looked like he might be of Indian origin. Pushing on round the corner we hit another belt of flat agricultural land covered in polytunnels with gangs of Indian workers and started discussing this pattern of migrant labour doing agricultural work across the eurozone which clearly remained the case even here for its poorest member Greece! The paradox of populist resentment at these hard-working migrants 'taking our jobs' is of course a theme whipped up by nationalists in some countries. Here in Greece foreign workers are fully exploited with no protections, poor wages and in some cases virtual debt bondage. We had a short debate about the conditions these migrants endure - an opportunity to send home earnings to poor Indian families maybe but a degree of entrapment with minimal rights certainly. It would seem migrant labour satisfies no-one except the consumers like us all enjoying cheap imported food in our supermarkets. For the record the local crops were water-melon and strawberries. The degree of agricultural specialisation across the eurozone has also been an eyeopener - the consequent loss of diversity my friend Rocco in Puglia would argue making us ever more prone to pest invasions!

This train of thought suddenly ended as we entered a belt of umbrella pines announced to be the start of a coastal nature reserve....a welcome break to strawberry land and somewhat more promising. Heading down the main woodland drive we approached a ragged group of buildings grouped around an attractive if wind-swept bay. They might once upon a time have been some sort of fish processing works but now lay disused and derelict – a discordant note in an otherwise attractive scene. A single battered old car was drawn up on the neighbouring quay and two old men sat in their camp chairs with a cold box between them from which they were enjoying a meze of octopus washed down with ouzo. We eyed them thirstily and in my best Greek I announced we were very hot and looking for beer, was there a café-bar near here? The answer from the elder man, with a twinkle in his eye (and a sense of comic timing) was that if we returned to the last crossroads and took the other turn this would take us "to Katerina's (pause)... and she had beer, ouzo and everything". I could have kissed him (though his bushy grey moustache was a significant disincentive). We turned our bikes round and followed the directions hopefully. As we broke through the umbrella pine belt onto a more westerly facing stretch of unspoilt coastline there was a wooden kiosk complete with tables, chairs and sun umbrellas on a windy sandy shore. Katarina was as welcoming and well stocked as our elderly gentlemen friends had led us to expect. We were the only clients, but waiving away any sense of being kept behind by late arrivals Katarina proceeded to slake our thirst with beer as she knocked up souvlaki and chips with a Moschofilero, a particularly floral Greek grape variety local to the Peloponnese. We assumed we would be able to put tents up after she had gone home but were unclear as to the role of the only other person loitering around, a tall, young, good looking guy who definitely wasn't Greek but who clearly had some sort of proprietorial role. Once we had a chat all became clear. He was Youssef from Morocco appointed as security guard for this seasonal beach café for the summer – clearly the investment value of 20 tables and chairs (and presumably more significantly a fridge full of booze) had been considerable relatively speaking. As Katarina ensured we had enough for our needs, and was locking up she made a comment about snakes in the sand dunes which was meant kindly indicating that we didn't have to slink away to put the tents up.

The three of us spent a convivial evening under the stars even trying out a little Arabic with Youssef, learning that for a seasonal job from Casablanca it was rather too quiet a place to spend the summer. It must be lonely for a sociable Berber man on this windy coast perhaps all the more so for his seemingly endless mobile phone conversations. However for us, on our first night in Greece it couldn't have been bettered! Pitching our matching little one-man tents behind a sand dune to avoid the wind I explained to Alex that Greeks are fixated by snakes and therefore perennially overate the risk of contact. With built in ground sheets I didn't waste any thought on snakes and passed out satisfied that Alex and I had shared the joys of the life vagabondi and wondering what the equivalent term was in Greek (αλήτης -aleetees-I later learned).

.

We woke to a lovely morning with calm seas after the wind and waves of the previous day. By the time we had swum, dried off and packed up Katarina was back and serving breakfast. I have stayed in many hotels less attentive to our needs than the wonderful Katarina, she 'who has everything'. Bidding her a fond farewell we set off back through the umbrella pines and across the agricultural belt knowing we had a decent ride if we were going to get to my planned destination of Ancient Olympia in time to visit the site. Bizarrely in planning this section of the route months before I had identified a cycle tour guide called Marco who runs cycle trips to Olympia from the quay where the cruise liners tie up a little to the south of where we had spent the night. I had run past him online my route to check the back lanes I was proposing would be cyclable and he had been reassuring so I was confident it would be fine. We would be crossing Elis, a region of the Peloponnese still bearing the archaic name of the *polis* from ancient days which used to intrigue me in a childish way because of the riff on my surname. I had only learnt recently that the people of Elis were the officiants of the Olympic Games so it was no coincidence that we would be crossing the region to arrive at Olympia. Indeed given the gathering that used to come together for the festival today's route would be following in ancient footsteps across 'the lowlands' of Elis. We were skirting the mountainous centre of the Peloponnese for good reason! Several rivers drain the rocky centre to flow into the Ionian Sea. We would be heading inland to join the Pineios where it had been dammed to irrigate the plain of Elis and then crossing a watershed to reach the sacred Alfeios river on whose banks Olympia sits. Both rivers feature in the labours of Heracles whose penance was set for the all too modern crime of murder of his wife and two children. The King of Elis, Augeas kept 3,000 cattle in a stable which hadn't been washed out for 30 years. He sets Heracles the impossible task of performing this demeaning job in a single day in return for which Heracles would receive one tenth of the cattle. Heracles succeeds by rerouting both the Pineios and the Alfeios rivers through the stables. Afterwards Augeas renegues on the deal and Heracles kills him. Henceforward to cleanse the Augean stables means 'to clear away an accumulated mass of corruption, physical, moral, religious or legal' as Brewer puts it in his marvellous Dictionary of Phrase and Fable (Brewer 2013).

But before our own Herculean task of crossing the watershed between these rivers we had to negotiate our way across the densely farmed coastal belt. Having got ourselves confused in some back lanes we stopped at a school to ask directions. Two lovely young teachers (of English and PE respectively) insisted we took refreshments with them. There was a relaxed end of holiday atmosphere as the staff were preparing for the start of the new school year. Our new friends wanted to know from where we came and how we came to be in this (presumably little visited) place. On hearing the story they were suitably impressed by the exploits of the (white haired) ιατρός (doctor) and the (balding) καραβάνια (karavania literally 'old mess tin') as we were referred to when being introduced to the headmistress. I particularly enjoyed learning this new term of colloquial Greek from our delightful teachers – something with which to rib my companion. Tearing ourselves away we finally extracted ourselves from the polytunnel maze and struck inland for the basin of the River Pineios. Coming over our first short but steep climb of the day the dammed basin of turquoise water shimmered below us in the morning sun. It was a lovely swooping descent to reach the bank and follow a new road round its perimeter. Before getting Marco the cycle tour guide's reassuring email I had intensively researched this section to ensure I wouldn't be dragging Alex on a wild goose chase as I had struggled to identify a crossing point of the Pineios on Google Earth. I needn't have worried as the road actually ran along the dam wall and over the sluices controlling its onward flow (which is presumably why I missed it!). For a while we followed the Pineios through the lovely plain of Elis and I was hoping to find traces of archaeological remains en route but the main site lay some distance to the west of us and we had a watershed to cross. In retrospect some time spent leisurely exploring the site might have been better spent than struggling through increasingly hilly country as the sun rose towards its zenith.

Our country lane was in the process of being upgraded into a two lane road with attendant machinery and dust along its length. Added to which the old surface was by now in poor condition on what was quite a hilly route. All this took its toll especially on the less acclimatised old mess tin who got quieter as the afternoon wore on.

So we were pleased to come to an end of this section at a road junction with the main road up to Olympia. I was increasingly dismayed to pass the 'Olympia service station' and 'Olympia restaurants' and 'Olympia coach parks' all depressingly a reminder of how much it had changed since my last visit 30 years before when I was here with two medical student friends, Matt and Lyn, having just completed our five shared years of medical school together in Liverpool. I had arrived in Athens ahead of them as I intended to devote all of my precious month between finals and starting work as a junior medical houseman to the trip. So I headed for Delphi which remains a highlight amongst the great archaeological sites of the world in my opinion. Completing my swing around the Bay of Corinth with a night bivouacing on the old Frankish Citadel high above the modern and ancient city of Corinth I had headed to Nafplio where I was due to meet the others. Towards the end of our tour of the Peloponnese we came to Olympia. Matt and I did the classic Olympic sprint together in the stadium and for some reason after completing our visit to the site I took a long walk. I was transported into a more pastoral age encountering a shepherd with his flock amongst olives on the banks of the Alfeios. The whole experience had been magical.

These were the memories floating through my mind as we approached the site, this time I felt immensely proud being self powered, 32 years later. We cycled right up to the ticket office where we locked up and made our way into the sacred site. Olympia is above all else a cult centre to the father of the Olympian gods Zeus. To briefly give a sense of how the Greeks themselves saw Olympia here is the Greek poet Pindar (Fennell 1879) writing in one of the many odes written for individual victors, this one (Olympian 10) dedicated to a certain Hagesidamus for winning the Boys' Boxing in 476 BCE. Picking up the story from where we left off after Heracles killed the king of Elis...

'Heracles divided the gifts of war and sacrificed the finest of them, and how he established the four years' festival with the first Olympic games and its victories. Who won the first garland, with the skill of his hands or feet or chariot, setting the boast of victory in his mind and achieving it with his deeds? In the foot race the best at running the straight course with his feet was the son of Licymnius, Oeonus, who had come from Midea at the head of an army. In wrestling, Echemus won glory for Tegea. And the prize in boxing was won by Doryclus, who lived in the city of Tiryns. And in the four-horse chariot the victor was Samos of Mantinea, the son of Halirhothius. Phrastor hit the mark with the javelin. Niceus sent the stone flying from his circling arm beyond all the others, and his fellow soldiers raised a sudden burst of loud cheering. The lovely light of the moon's beautiful face lit up the evening and in the delightful festivities the whole precinct rang with a song in praise of victory. Even now we will follow the first beginnings, and as a namesake song of proud victory, we will shout of the thunder and the fire-wrought shaft of Zeus who rouses the thunder-clap, the burning bolt that suits omnipotence'.

Zeus's statue which stood here in the great Doric temple at the heart of the site, one of the seven wonders of the ancient world, took Phidias the greatest sculptor of the age, 13 years to create using gold panels and ivory plates to embellish the massive figure on a cedar wood throne. 13 metres high as we know from the physical ruins of the building in which it was housed, images have survived on coins made in Elis but the statue and indeed the whole complex was lost between 400 and 600 CE. As we have seen after winning power at the battle of Actium, Augustus embraced all things Greek. With the Empire expanding to absorb the Peloponnese as the Roman province of Achaea there was still great respect for the old cult centres. Thus, after sacking Corinth in 146 BCE, the Roman general Mummius had 21 gilded shields mounted on the walls of the Zeus Temple in a pointed statement of battle honours blatantly attempting to subvert the Olympian Gods to the Roman cause. However much later in the empire's development when it became expedient to suppress 'pagan' cults the temple was intentionally destroyed. Earthquakes, floods and silting of the valley in which it stands obliterated all local trace until the 18th century when it was identified and in the 19th century the first exploratory digs were led by French archaeologists. This process of rediscovery continues to the present day.

The Temple of Hera actually predates that of her brother/husband Zeus. It seems likely it was rededicated by the Elis polis from a prior local deity when they took control of the area and developed the games around 776 BCE, one of four such sites at which sacred peace treaties were observed for the duration of pan Hellenic games on a rotating four year cycle. The modern Olympic torch begins its journey here at Hera's temple. Hera and Zeus themselves were the result of an incestuous union between their mother Rhea and their father Chronos. Rhea, Chronos and their Titan brothers and sisters, resulted from the union of Gaia (earth) and Ouranos (sky). So in terms of family history we are right back to the beginning of how these people we call the Greeks saw themselves. If the Romans can be characterised as having fratricide at the heart of their origin myth the Greeks have incest and infanticide at the heart of theirs. Whilst we understandably focus on the higher conceptual outputs of Athens transmitted to us through the ages my reading of the Iliad in my tent at night had been a brutal reminder of the savagery described by Homer. But this story of Heracles reminds us that Homeric myth had no monopoly on gore in the tales Greeks told themselves about the world and their place in it.

The other important cult building at Olympia, the Pelopium, lies between that of Zeus and Hera. Dedicated to Pelops, a mythic hero king of the Peloponnese after whom the entire southern region of mainland Greece (and this chapter) is named, was the grandson of Zeus through his father Tantalus. When his father decided to cut Pelops up and make a stew of him for the gods his taboo act of infanticidal cannabilism was detected by Zeus and his punishment was to stand in a pool of water beneath a fruit tree with low branches. Whenever he reached for the fruit, the branches raised his intended meal from his grasp. Whenever he bent down to get a drink, the water receded before he could get any. Tantalising indeed. Meanwhile Pelops, once his shoulder (bitten and eaten by Persephone before the cannabalistic feast had been abandoned) was mended with an ivory prosthesis by Hephaestus, the mechanical wizard of Olympia, became a master charioteer famously winning the hand of his bride in a chariot race and in so doing receiving a curse from his vanquished competitor. This curse would play out in the greatest of Greek Tragedies, Aeschylus' Oresteia, in which over a series of three plays we witness with horror the murder of Agamemnon on his heroic return from Troy by his wife Clytemnestra and her lover and her subsequent murder by her son Orestes. No wonder libations to Pelops were considered the dark side performed in the ritual pit at night before sacrifices were made at the altar of Zeus in the light the following day in preparation for the games. We both ran the stadium though this time I added a tai chi session high on the spectators' bank overlooking the sacred temples. There right at the end of the visiting day with very few other sightseers about it was possible to get that sense of connection with the sacred past which make these ancient power places so special.

We had a conference over refreshments and decided that we had done enough for the day and heading to the town campsite which was run by a local family with a marvellous grandfather figure who clearly harked back to the days of French excavation as he launched into a French song for our benefit. We passed a surprisingly enjoyable evening meal at a family run restaurant in the overdeveloped, knick-knack festooned streets of the town. When all is said and done, it's all about 'heart' which the Greeks know better than most. Our hostess was a middle-aged woman whose daughter and friend were the front of house staff. The place was quiet, I think we were the only guests, not because of the quality of the cooking but as a by-product of over supply – whether Olympia even reaches 50% occupancy in the height of the season I would doubt - certainly by mid-September I would guesstimate their occupancy was more like 5%. Which could have meant a soulless evening in an empty tourist spot but far from it once we had eaten our fill our hostess, Angela, came out to sit with her daughter and friend and regale us with good advice for living a wholehearted life. By the time the 'old mess tin' had been inducted in the delights of Tsipouro, the powerful home distilled Greek spirit, we were all heart siblings at the shrine of the Olympians although unlike the Gods no incestuous unions were proposed nor thankfully imagined!

On our return to the campsite I fell into a late-night exchange with an ageing German who had come down from a remote ruined monastery he had found higher up the Alfaios. He was much versed in Pausanias, the ancient authority on mainland Greece who travelled extensively in the second century CE. I made a mental note to return to the area armed with a copy. The evening petered out amidst rather far-fetched speculative comparative features of Ancient Greek cults and shamanistic practices we had respectively experienced in contemporary far flung cultures. Definitely time for my waiting sleeping bag in my little tent sharing a terrace under the olives with the tent of a now stertorous 'old mess tin'!

We were up and off at first light as we had a decent ride ahead if we were going to attain the Arcadian Gate into Ancient Messene before nightfall as was my plan. We climbed up and out of the valley of the Alfaios to the south taking the route the Spartans would have followed when coming to the great Panhellenic gathering at Olympia. This led down to the coast road which I had decided was our best option towards Kiparissia and our turn off later into the hills for Messenia. I was reassured to find it relatively quiet at this time of the morning with a beautiful rolling surface and we were able to make fast progress. Taking our morning coffee break in the square of the small provincial market town of Zacharo I was pleased to join the local weekend crowd enjoying the end of school holiday sun. Looking ahead on the map for a likely spot for the day's swim we identified a possible candidate encouragingly called καλό νερό (good water). Well, it was justly named and just as importantly there was a fish taverna overlooking the beach which hit the spot. Indeed we lingered over our lunch a little as it was such a pleasant scene but all good things have an end and we got back on the bikes for what was going inevitably to be a main road shift as we took the east-west E55 road which cuts inland from this section of the coast. Quieter than parallel routes north and nouth this turned out to be a good choice with acceptably light traffic as we doggedly took it in turns to lead out along the white line that separates the main apron of blacktop from the somewhat ragged margins. By holding this line traffic can comfortably pass you whilst we also enjoyed the benefits of the fine road surface. Our way was gradually climbing leaving the verdant coastal stretch behind as we started to encounter wooded hills. We were now heading into Arcadia, which for the ancients was a wilderness where Pan resided amidst fertile woods and hills with grazing for flocks and Hermes could be encountered passing hither and thither attending to the business of the Gods. Maybe Hermes the bike had a sense of homecoming because we made good progress on the hard post lunch shift gaining the height we needed before attempting to cross into Messenia. After a couple of hot hours we had broken the back of it and took a chance on a minor turn off. According to a mixture of map reading and google mapping there appeared to be some agricultural roads to our south passing through a little place called Kastro which should lead to Ancient Messenia from the sorth which was our objective. We conferred at the first refreshment break we had seen all afternoon. It was a pig joint staffed by a rather sullen young man just firing up a side of pork with which to feed hungry weekend travellers later in the day and clearly not happy to be at work. We enquired as to the route to Kastro and interpreted his grunt to suggest that it was where we thought it to be, just beyond his family pork refuelling station. Heading off the main road we were delighted to encounter our old friend the Kalamata railway, last seen heading west from Patras. This narrow gauge (1 metre) railtrack ran over 300kms winding its way round the Peloponnese and had only closed when the crisis hit in 2011. This sighting suggested to us we were 'on the right track' and a conversation ensued about a project to turn it into a cycle way! As we were musing on the difficulties the Greek planning system might pose to agree such a radical change of use we hit a fork in the agricultural road.

We had just crossed an Arcadian river with good water flow and steep bushy sides. It was not obvious which path we should take as no such fork appeared on our map. At this moment in a typically Greek way a saloon car came bouncing down the right-hand track towards us. A middle aged moustachioed man with one arm resting on the car window whilst steering nonchalantly with the other shared the front seat with an attractive woman. There was something wonderfully Greek about their appearance, a couple of lovers out for a weekend drive without a care in the world coming down a steep rocky track that would make many people exercise extreme caution in a 4x4! Yes, they confirmed, this was the way to Kastro. Sure enough as we climbed up and away from the gurgling river below the castle rose into view. My later research identified it to be the Frankish castle of Mila attributed to Isabelle Villehardouin (1297-1301) who would have known it as Chateaunef built to control the route the old mess tin, Hermes and I were now traversing towards Messenia and the important fortress at Kalamata. At this stage of Peloponnesian history the Franks had established control over the Principality of Achaea, seized from the Byzantines following the fourth crusade. That was the one when they got side tracked from saving Jerusalem and sacked and pillaged Constantinopole instead (possibly taking Andrew's skull in the process) before returning to the southern Mediterranean and alighting on the Peloponnese. And touring football fans have a bad reputation! The next hundred or so years saw a power struggle over the Peloponnese between the Franks and the Byzantine 'Greeks.' During this period a major castle building programme left its enduring mark across the southern Peloponnese of which this was our first example. Ultimately the Byzantines were set to wrestle control and create the rather marvellously termed 'Despotate of Morea'. Meanwhile we had forced the route and emerged onto a high contouring road which looked to me like it would take us exactly where we wanted to be headed. With sweeping views south down to Kalamata and the coast, west down to Tripoli and orth into serious mountains that I had no regrets having skirted it felt like we were on the balcony of the Peloponnese. Enjoying this section hugely we paused for breath in the first village encountered after Kastro where to my delight an open café willingly provided me with a 5pm beer. I was wilting and had learned from experience this would fuel me for the last hour. Alex resisted the siren call and so I was not allowed to drag it out which was a good thing.

The final push would have been just that without the beer, with it I managed a steady climb for over an hour until just when I feared we were losing the light we came round the corner and there it was, the Arcadian Gate of ancient Messene, perfectly silhouetted against the indigo evening sky.

The Messenian Helots had suffered at the hands of the dominant Spartans for generation upon generation (Cartledge 2012). They had been absorbed into the Spartan city state as an agricultural underclass which freed Spartan citizens to form the only professional fighting force in ancient Greece. As Spartan influence grew with their military reputation (not least the doomed but glorious defence of the 'hot gates' at Thermopylae by the 300 under Leonidas against Xerxes Persian army numbering in the tens and possibly hundreds of thousands in 480BC) they came to dominate a Peloponnesian League. As the Persian threat waned and hostilities broke out in 432 BCE between alliances led by Sparta and Athens respectively the Messenian Helots had no choice but support Spartan dominance resulting in the near ruin of Athens. It was only in 371 BCE that the Spartans were finally defeated at the battle of Leuctra when for once their ambitions to control land north of the isthmus of Corinth led them to overextend and pay the price at the hands of a certain Epaminondas. After defeating the Spartan army this resolute leader at the head of an international army marched into the Peloponnese and quite deliberately supported three fortified city rebuilding programmes to neutralise Sparta's dominance once and for all. The well preserved ancient city we cycled into dates from this period (369 BCE) and the surviving impressive fortifications (9 kilometres of wall 7-9 metres in height) had proved a longlasting deterrent to Spartan ambition thereafter. The gate at which we now stood is one of only two entrances, still 2 storeys high leading into a circular control zone before a second gate bridged by a massive limestone lintel admits entrance to the city. To this day the public road (which we were following) leads straight through this gateway complex. Soaring above are the twin peaks of Mount Eva and Idon, which being relatively flat topped were themselves included in part of the urban development. Pausanias, of course, has much to say in favour of this well-designed city.

For now however our immediate aims were more prosaic – food, drink and shelter. As we freewheeled down from the gate into the lovely village of Mavromati which occupies the upper town and the all important Klepsydra spring, around which the modern village clusters and below which the ancient city sprawled, Alex pointed out a particularly convenient olive grove pitch for later. Armed with this insurance policy we could relax and eat and drink our fill at the village's excellent taverna. I found myself chatting to an interesting party of South African archaeologists at the next table who were involved in the ongoing dig of the enormous site. As the evening drew on the party referred to the recent discovery of a missing Isis shrine described by Pausanias. The large Aesculepius sanctuary on the site is one of its most striking features but Hellenistic importations of Egyptian gods are a reminder of just what a melting pot the eastern Mediterranean had become. It was now time for bed and our well rehearsed night pitch went smoothly enough in what seemed in the dark to be all olive grove. A few loud fruit falls in the night however alerted Alex to the fact his tent was under a fig tree.

We woke in the morning to sounds of agricultural workers heading past for work but they never saw us which somehow pleased us – the perfect wild camp should go undetected – and this was the last camp of my journey. It was going to be a big day – our wives awaited us in a favourite beachside place at Kardamyli down the coast to the south where they had arrived via a flight to Kalamata the previous day. There are three fingers protruding from the Peloponnese into the Mediterranean and we were bound for the middle one.

The Bay of Messenia lies between the westernmost finger and middle finger generally referred to as Mani. At the head of the bay sits Kalamata, a port city which lends its name to the big fleshy black olives which are grown on the lowest slopes around the bay. Down the spine of the middle finger runs the mighty Taygetos Mountain chain which divides Messenia from Laconia to the east so effectively that for much of its length there are only a few footpaths which cross its heights. To add to the geological challenge of the Mani the torrential downpours that strike its west facing mountains have carved a series of impressive gorges through the limestone karst. We would be trying to dodge the deepest of these (the Rema Mili gorge).

I orientated Alex to this topology as we looked south over the Bay of Messenia which was clearly visible from the ancient site. It was strange to think that Susannah was down there with Caroline, Alex's wife, no doubt still lying in! We were too early for any sign of life at Mavromati so we started our descent to the coastal plain and it was actually a good 15 kilometres before our little road took us past a place with evidence of a stove on the go! It was a lovely little pastoral café tended by one of those ageless little old ladies in black who seem to tenaciously survive and monitor the Greek charge for modernity. A couple of locals were also up with the lark and looked us over with mild curiosity but remained mute at this early hour. Fuelled up with Greek coffee and bread we rapidly emerged on the plain below and found ourselves following a lane alongside a massive irrigation channel. Kalamata is tobacco country but also produces a wide range of horticultural products and we saw evidence of much of them as well as rather splendid reed beds with grasses way higher than a man standing on his pedals! Stopping for a mid-morning refreshment break at a small agricultural town I suddenly remembered it was Sunday as the largely elderly faithful congregated outside church in their Sunday best at one of the two cafés on the square. The unfaithful seemed to have selected the opposing café, where we had also gravitated. The old lady running the place was cordial and told me where to find bakery goods which she was perfectly happy for us to eat at her café tables. This place was not much more than an hour's drive from where we stay and reminds what a cosmopolitan place Mani has become. In this little town, contrastingly, it felt like everyone knew everything about everyone and I was happy to push on for the big city of Kalamata. We didn't quite get the approach right emerging from our agricultural lanes right by a massive supermarket just up the main southern coast road from the airport. Kalamata airport is what UK regional airports were like in my childhood ...a human scaled terminus handling one planeload at a time for the daylight hours of spring to mid-uutumn closing all together by the all-important olive harvest season in November and December. It enjoyed a brief notoriety in the UK as the airport where brave and innocent Brit plane spotters were arrested for (foolishly) taking pictures of (military) aircraft. It is both a civil and military airport which is why, following the Greek crisis, when most things in Greece were put up for sale, it wasn't. Of an afternoon down on the Mani when I am up a ladder pruning an olive tree a distant hum heralds the arrival of the twice daily patrol by a pair of jet trainers who describe lazy circles in the sky before retreating to their Kalamata base. Unlike when being overflown on a quiet Welsh lane on my bicycle by the version flown these days by the RAF which sounds and feels like a profoundly disturbing visitation by Zeus (thunder and lightening bolts were his speciality) this feels much more benign – perhaps Hermes like?

Anyway we got into town relatively painlessly despite the main road because it was a Sunday and found a pleasant part of the old town in which to take refreshment. Kalamata suffered badly at the hands of an earthquake in 1986 which had only just happened when I first passed through as a callow medical student. The city was heavily damaged with tents lining the streets and we stayed only long enough to change buses from Sparta for the Mani. The subsequent rebuild means much of the city is a planned place of wide boulevards with an elegance which can catch one unawares when emerging from a Mani wild place. It is also the only city in southern Europe I have visited where the bicycle is factored into the city plan with traffic free cycle routes linking the centre with the long curving promenade on the seaside running for 3 to 4 kilometres between the port and the beginning of the Mani peninsula. I was determined to cycle this for the first time and it felt not dissimilar to some of my south coast run along NCN 2 after leaving Alex two months ago. Strange to think of our very different summers in the intervening couple of months. And now like streams finding their way to the sea we had coalesced and were headed to our final destination. However before that I wanted to introduce Alex to my (adoptive) home turf and had a great afternoon in store including lunch at one of my favourite beachside fish taverna halfway down the coast so there was no time to linger.

The promenade around the head of the Messenian Gulf leads to the only road leading south down the steep sided Mani peninsula. The Wall of Verga is passed on the left (or rather the sign for it – when I ventured up the vertiginous lane in search of said Wall I encountered only drystone walls of the regular variety – a mystery recently cracked in finding reference to their significance in an account of the war of independence against the Turks in 1821). Then the road divides as the coast road continues as far as Kitries whilst the main road climbs up from this point for some 500 vertical metres before plunging back down 400 of them to cross an enormous gorge (aforementioned Rema Mili) before climbing up once again. If, however, you take the coast road to Kitries it crosses the mouth of the gorge before coming to a dead end due to vertiginous sea cliffs. Therefore, I reasoned, by staying low as far as Kitries there should be only one 500 vertical metres of climbing as opposed to two. Besides which Kitries is the best swim/lunch stop I have ever found – and I have tried quite a few around the Mediterranean. The coast road driven many times was very different when cycled (for the first time) and what had always appeared a relatively flat route turned out be quite a lot more 'bumpy' than I had reckoned on. Each little bay is preceded and succeeded by a rocky headland which 'kept us honest'. The bays gradually got smaller and quieter but the headlands seemed to get higher and steeper as we worked our way down the peninsular and it was with a sense of relief that we came down into the delightful little pebble bay of Kitries where Giorgos and his family's fish taverna share the pebble beach with a swankier place I've (ridiculously) never tried. The water is a calm turquoise mirror where not infrequently I have been overflown by a kingfisher. We jumped in and enjoyed a couple of lazy laps around the bay before beer καλαμαριές (fresh squid) and Βαρβούνη, the little prized red mullet with a Greek salad and a shared portion of πατάτες τιγανητες (chips). Is there anything better on a hot summer's day in all the world?

But not for the first time all good things must come to an end and now we had to earn the lunch. Even in a car the road up from Kitries is a real pull so I warned Alex we were in for a 'mare. Within 200 metres of the restaurant the turn off heads straight up the hillside at a gradient which exceeds anything I had done en route from Bristol. If Mont Cenis in the alps was 9% this felt more like 12-13%. You know it's <u>steep</u> when you have to stand on your pedals even with a 'gentleman's cog' engaged. You know it's <u>really steep</u> when you also have to zig-zag up the road to take the edge off. And you know it's <u>impossibly steep</u> if you can't keep your front wheel in contact with the road! That climb was really steep! It also proved that despite being an old mess tin legs that once yomped across the Falklands still had it in them – by the top I was more done in than Alex! Still we had made it and were rewarded with the magnificent sea views from olive groves perched on limestone terraces that appeared to have been moulded into the contours of this magnificent scenery. We had some respite between Doli and Kampos where we rejoined the main road but then started the final climb up the shoulder of the Taygetos mountains to gain the pass and our entry point into ExoMani proper. Why I fell in love with this part of the world 30 odd years ago is this combination of mountains and sea. On that bus from eathquake riven Kalamata we were tipped out somewhere just below this pass as the snaking road had been broken by the 'quake and we had descended to Ritsa beach below by one of the many old mule paths (or *kalderimi* as I have subsequently learnt to call them). 30 years before it had been the gloaming, too dark to really get a feel for the country through which we were rapidly dropping or indeed the backdrop above. We found a simple taverna at the foot of the path, took a room and proceeded under the starry firmament over jugs of wine to discuss the meaning of the universe and the role, if any, of God. The following morning I swam out with a thick head and looked back and was awestruck – these mountains were beautiful and green! My father had taken us to Athens, Crete and Rhodes but I'd never seen anything like this. I was smitten!

This now forms but one stream of the flood of memories which flow through me whenever I swim at Ritsa but Alex and I were still way above enjoying the big mountain views from this, the balcony level of the three worlds of the Exomani. The seaside, beloved these days by visitors and dotted with holiday homes was traditionally a place for fishing and embarking and disembarking from the daily boat, which pre Second World War was the only means of reaching this isolated peninsula other than walking in on the kalderimi. The balcony level villages where the olives are master is home to a series of agricultural villages near one of which (Proastio) lies my olive grove and above lie the mountain villages, home to shepherds but also brigands in the old days! We paused at a vantage point where the volunteer Gaia organisation maintains a seasonal fire watch. I pointed out the intricate coastline, the lines of the gorges cutting like knives through the balcony terracing to emerge at their respective beaches, most pebbly - one sandy, the long thin throat of Trachilla 25 kms away signalling the end of this stretch of accessible coast and finally the mountainous way to the south and surprisingly distant Deep Mani lost in the heat haze beyond. And down below us the pan tiled unusual settlement of Kardamyli nestling beside a turquoise sea with its pretty little island and trademark Palmolive chimney reminding that this place was always connected albeit on its own terms like most remote places I have had the privilege of visiting. After pointing out our destination below, a cluster of holiday cottages run by Stavros behind Ritsa Beach, and warning wives of our impending arrival by text there was nothing for it but to swoop down the snake like coils of this fabulous descent, passing a climbing cyclist who hailed us en route and we later realised was Iannis (who had provided Alex's bike) and suddenly we were down and coming along the little lane behind the beach and there were Susannah and Caroline holding a mock finishing line which we crossed together and Susannah and I fell into each other's arms. We had arrived! Toasting arrival and reunion a little later on our balcony in the magic hour with the deepening orange hue of the escarpment above catching the sun just after it had sunk beneath the wine-dark sea there was a deep sense of a deed done, obstacles overcome, family reunited and an odyssey drawing to a close.

Chapter 10. To the Sacred Grove and the Future

But the beautiful beachside holiday accommodation where we had reunited was not quite the final destination. The next day before the sun was high Alex and I set off on the final leg – up to the 'sacred grove' as an anthropology friend had dubbed Pyromali, also referred to simply as the land. We rode back along Ritsa beachfront, the light blue water lapping on the smoothed white limestone cobbles glistening in the endless light as if it was the first morning not the last which in both senses, of course, it was. Past the taverna where Lynn, Matthew and I had bunked down 32 years before. Into Kardamyli along the main (only!) street past the old men's café, the card-school bar, the souvlaki take-away, the café, the post office where PO Box 1 still bears the name of Patrick Leigh-Fermor, as if, in a Homeric touch, the now dead hero is keeping an amused eye over his adopted home's continuing development! Then comes our friends' Frozen Yoghurt place where Tenya and Vassili whip up soothing post prandial delights taken in the back garden with a glass of wine over conversations ranging from the new Europe and Mr Varoufakis' European Realistic Disobedience Front through feminism in Greece to Mani olive pressing traditions. Past architect Eleni's ETSI office, the Demos where all applications must be processed and the book shop – awaiting sale and tragic evidence that not all is light, despite the endless sun, in Mani.

Then up the steep incline to the rocky bluff where Dioskouroi, the taverna, sits looking down over the harbour with its resident kareta kareta turtle and stone custom house sitting on the quayside down below. The Dioskouroi are better known as Castor and Pollux born following a confusing conception in these parts after Zeus in one of his many forms as a swan impregnated the beautiful Leda, Queen of Sparta shortly followed by her husband, the King of Sparta (blissfully unaware of the divine tryst). The ensuing pregnancy was said to have resulted in two eggs with two children in each, Castor and Pollux and Helen and Clytemnestra. Helen is the very same Helen who falls for Paris' charms and elopes to Troy whilst we have already met Clytemnestra at the heart of the Oresteia tragedy, doomed to murder her husband Agamemnon, supreme leader of the Greeks at Troy on his victorious return. It is easy to see why Freud had plenty of material to work on as he used Greek myths to shed light on our subconsciousness and in so doing helped to create our modern minds. Kardamyli's twin claim to mythic fame is a lovely barrel tomb below the stronghold of Old Kardamyli said to be the resting place of Castor and Pollux - hence the Taverna. But what really lends Kardamyli some distinction is a mention in the foundational Greek epic of Homer, the Iliad (Homer, Rieu et al. 2003). Early in book 9 with the Greeks driven back towards their ships under severe pressure from the Trojans, their warrior hero the semi-divine Achilles is sulking in his tent over Agamemnon's treatment in taking some of his spoils and in particular a woman with whom he had formed an affinity. In some desperation Agamemnon tells wise old Nestor what he is offering Achilles to rejoin the struggle and save the day for the Greeks...

'And if in due course we get back to Argos, the most fertile of all lands, he can become my son-in-law, and I will honour him as I do Orestes, my beloved son, who is being brought up there in the lap of luxury. I have three daughters in my strong palace, Chrysothemis, Laodice and Iphianassa. Of these he shall choose for his own whichever he likes best and take her back to Peleus' house, without the usual bride-gifts. Indeed, I will give him gifts, generous ones, more than anyone has ever given with his daughter. 'Not only that, but I will give him seven prosperous towns: **Cardamyle**, Enope and grassy Hire; holy Pherae and Antheia with its deep meadows; beautiful Aepeia and Pedasus rich in vines. They are all near the sea, in the farthest part of sandy Pylos. Their people are rich in flocks and cattle. They will honour him with their gifts as though he were a god and, being under his authority, give him rich dues.'

It was not to be – Achilles only returned to the fray when his companion Patroclus was killed and Kardamyli slipped back into obscurity until it entered the modern world in the 20th century as an olive oil supply and soap processing centre for the American Palmolive soap business.

On we cycled past the beautiful Kalamitsi bay where Paddy and Joan settled and received their guests and is being converted into a writer's retreat. Bruce Chatwin, a frequent visitor, and many other visiting travel writers would have approved. Just after the steep kalderimi up which Paddy and Bruce would climb we take the long double switchback on the bikes where the perspective down the coast gradually extends towards the Deep Mani, then reverses until finally on reaching the firewatch point becomes an aerial view down on Kardamyli town with its pantiles and chimney 300m below. But there the road cuts in heading straight for mighty Mount Ilias, high point at 2404m of the Taygetos before it levels out on reaching the shady fruit trees of the well-watered extended village of Proastio. Past the Byzantine church of Aghios Nikolaos, rough stone cottages and finely hewn town houses as we approach my friend Erhard's place for a welcome drink. But no tarrying, after exchanging the news (olive fly season looking bad this year), onwards up through the top end of the village, past the ruined tower house following the goat herd up to the upper road.

Swinging downhill we approach that marvel of 1930's engineering, a beautifully constructed single lane arched stone bridge spanning the Noupadi gorge glimpsed far below leading down to my favourite swimming place the sheltered cove at Phoneas. Once across a stiff climb back upto the endless olive terraces on the other side. Past the last straggle of houses with attached power cables leading down from two solar photovoltaic farms then we have left the grid behind as the narrow, newly laid road follows the old agricultural ways through the groves. At a sharp turn beside the oak tree the old Saidona dirt road leads off up the hill to the left in poor condition with an improbable 'STOP' sign marking its junction with the 'main road'. Then we turn off the Saidona 'road' and follow a tractor trail through the groves. Olives to left and right with bushy Holm oaks lining the trail. Where the land is untended prickly wild pear takes root lending this hillside it's name 'εχλαδοκαβος' the place of the wild pear. Too early for the raptors shrieking to each other overhead as they ride the afternoon updraughts. Up and around a steep turn of the trail as it climbs over a rocky spur onto a slightly higher level of the balcony terraces, known as 'πυρομαλι' (pyromali) referring we think back to a time when fire swept through here back in the day when old ladies now were little girls listening, in their turn, to old ladies' tales. Alex and I were now on the last leg, contouring round we could see the Cyprus trees guarding the entrance to the old cave perched above the land. There below is our own pair of Cyprus trees towering above the olives. Then suddenly we are beside the concrete skeleton which speaks of future plans and the old stone καταφύγιο (refuge) under the olive tree surrounded by the sheep fold, witness to a history extending back to the Bronze Age - we had truly arrived.

I checked on the trees as I do on arrival, observing their luxuriant summer growth seeking the tiny hard green fruits which mature into the oily olives we would be harvesting in 2 months' time. Seeing the piles of cuttings from my early season pruning back in February I shared with Alex my delight in the Greek verb to prune κλαδεύω which has given us the biological term clade, describing a branch on the tree of life, consisting of an ancestor and all that ancestor's progeny. In the hours I have perched on a ladder choosing which shoot will be given a chance to prosper and which will be pruned, over and over, I have had plenty of time to reflect on life's branch points and the choices we make every minute of every day which slowly sculpt our lives just as experience sculpts our neural connections. If journeys are a metaphor for life the route we take is also a series of interconnected branch points, akin to the waypoints I learnt to input into the Garmin, going all the way back to that first step out of one's door. As a paediatrician I have been handed many a newborn to help them breathe and watched the journey begin with wonder. But of course the journey actually begins with conception, a part of our story which is rarely straightforward as seems to be acknowledged in the Greek myths. But this would take us into our parents' tales which are not ours to tell.

So the experiences of the summer's ride on the roads to freedom haven't been random events, but the result of the multiplicity of decisions taken about which road to take, where to stop and who to talk with. And of course the history I have braided in with my own is similarly subjective, selected to illustrate the story, my story. This summer's journey had allowed me to explore one foundational strand which had indeed led all the way back here to this rocky hillside. Susannah and Caroline joined us under μαμά (mama) olive, our most beautiful tree sat within a drystone sheepfold itself moulded around the 'S' shaped bedrock of the terraced slope. Beside it sits the drystone shelter with a door you have to crawl through but which opens up into a corbelled dome structure you can stand up in. Here, during the growing season, previous generations would sleep by night surrounded by their flock whilst tending the olive grove in the day. Hence μαμά olive was especially well fertilised and grew to be the beauty in whose shade we now sat. Lunch was a loaf of bread, graviera cheese (made locally from sheep milk), olives and wine. Conversation petered out amidst the buzzing of the cicadas. Everybody relaxed back in the shade. There was a calm sense of satisfaction, of a journey completed as I lay there reunited with my wife, opposite my cycle companion brother-in-law and his wife as we all drifted off into the arms of Morpheus at journey's end, in the shade of the sacred grove above the wine dark sea.

Some months later I am back in Liverpool at my eldest daughter's graduation ceremony in St George's Hall, sitting on its eponymous plateau at the heart of the municipal esplanade it shares with the Liverpool Museum, the Walker Art Gallery, the Law Courts and Lime Street Station all the result of the mid-nineteenth century Liverpool Improvement Act. The great bronze doors bear the monogram SPQL for the Senate and People of Liverpool - a reference to the ancient Roman SPQR (senates populusque romanus). Entering through the north door one climbs up a grand stone staircase into the north hall with elegant Greek Doric colonnading and a copy of the Parthenon frieze in a Wedgewood bas-relief style with portrayals of galloping horses and heroic figures in white standing proud of a light blue background. In pride of place flanked by two caryatids (weight bearing columns fashioned to imitate the female figurative form also to be found on Athens' Acropolis) stands a statue of Henry Booth, engineer and promoter of the Manchester and Liverpool Railway, holding a scroll depicting the world's first locomotive, the Rocket on which he worked with the Stephensons. This is the Liverpool of my youth, proudly commemorating its imperial aspirations and global significance. Whilst awaiting the academic procession which would announce the ceremony proper my mind returns as it frequently does to my journey. Could I now explain why a railway engineer in the 1850s should be depicted quite so bizarrely, flanked by caryatids in a Greek Temple?

Reading Homer on the journey certainly helped to embed the ideas at the heart of the Greek myths in my mind and became embodied in Hermes the bike. There is Kardamyli being offered to Achilles (half man half god) back in the Bronze Age. In Olympia I encountered Zeus and Hercules beside the river Alfaios. As I sailed past Actium I had saluted Octavian/Augustus who would cloak himself in all things Greek and ensure that through Rome the ideas of Ancient Greece would find a wider audience. In the Italian peninsula I found plenty of evidence of the Byzantines, the eastern branch of the Roman Empire that persisted for a further thousand years and in communication with Muslim neighbours kept the Ancient Greek language alive and updated the texts. I had rediscovered Charlemagne and the subsequent Holy Roman empire and grappled with 2000 years of Catholicism to better understand their competing versions of the credo state across Europe. I had travelled the pilgrim route of the Via Francigena which allowed people and ideas to freely move across the Alps. I had been fascinated by the travels of the crusading Franks and the enterprise of the Tuscan bankers which lay commercial foundations that would eventually create markets that linked the states of Europe and beyond. The phenomenal wealth of the French Kings brought Italianate Renaissance masters to the north. With burgeoning wealth the aristocrats of an increasingly self-confident Great Britain started to travel in the other direction to partake of the grand tour bringing home physical specimens with which to beautify their newly built great houses. But it was in the city of my birth at the height of Empire that Liverpool cloaked itself in neoclassical trappings, just as Octavian had cloaked himself in Greek ideas, to legitimate the perceived destiny of the city to promote progress and reap its rewards! The trail had not gone cold - and amidst a rash of modern publications on Greek myths and epic spinoffs there appears to be on ongoing appetite for classical themes.

And what of this 60-year-old cyclist, the third age neophyte – what has the odyssey taught me? I have been reminded on a daily basis that the overcoming of obstacles is integral to life's journey. Just as I have learnt to sit back in the saddle and savour a climb despite the burn in the legs so I have been encouraged to embrace life's struggles...without which the life force evaporates, fading away to settle silently amongst the ghosts.

This life cycle and the ghosts re-encountered along the way have given me fresh insight on a life veering between the Apollonian rationalism of my father and the Dionysian emotionality of my mother. Riding, like Tai Chi, is a practice requiring balance. When I am in balance these warring aspects somehow find their equilibrium, the dialectic is resolved. I sip and savour all that life has to offer rather than gluttonously gulp it down as if there is no tomorrow. When every day brings new delights and fresh challenges then balancing the past and the future in the now is a joy. The third age promise is to let go of the drudgery - weigh the opportunity costs as time presses – but keep trying, at the same time, to live in the moment. Sure, it's a delicate balancing act – but like riding a bike, it is mastered by not thinking too hard about it – it's a flow thing.

I have certainly rediscovered my youthful taste for adventure. The increasing numbers of ghosts that accompany life's wandering have not been laid to rest, but as with Odysseus' visit to Hades, have been honoured and relationships redefined. They cannot be banished but live on, as they must, in our minds. As I will in the minds of those who once knew me. I have renewed an acquaintance with myself, learning anew to relish my strengths and forgive myself my trespasses. Because to trespass is to cross boundaries, to explore....to live. And now I am learning to relinquish the need to fill each unforgiving second and to allow myself to enjoy those reflections on life which I have been presumptuousness enough to record here.

Riding with Hermes in the magic hour, warm air rushing past, beads of sweat trickling down my forehead to be caught by a headband before they blur the Tuscan tinted lenses of my shatter-proof glasses through which I watch the passing scenes of life's rich tapestry. I'm steering, in control, well sort of, a flow of sensations and images swirling through a unique labyrinth of mental constructs, built of memories and the learning of others. But Hermes and I are in the now, freed of life's regrets cycling hopefully into a third age with more (slow) adventures to come.

Map of the route

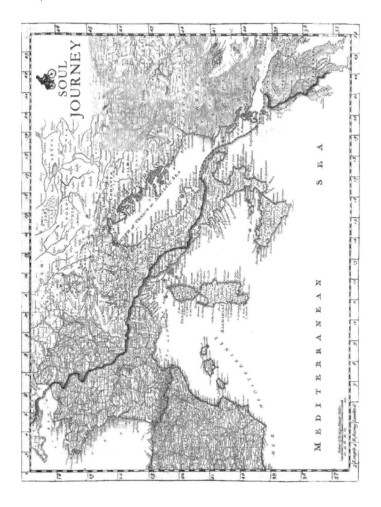

Route Distances and related practical data for third age riders

Way Points	Distance (kms)	Ascent (m)	Descent (m)	Days Riding
Bristol – Newhaven	287	962	985	4
Dieppe - Paris	222	914	889	4
Paris - Orleans	164	482	402	3
Orleans - Chapaize	373	1098	995	10
Chapaize - Lyon	121	423	468	2
Lyon-Turin	381	3002	2850	6
Turin- Moneglia,	235	1803	2030	3
Moneglia- Siena	233	2258	2215	4
Siena-Rome	230	2200	2200	4
Rome- Benevento	279	2514	2406	4
Benevento- Bari	228	2664	2818	5
Patras- Kardamyli	267	2396	2389	4
Bristol- Kardamyli	3020	20,716	20,647	53

Select Bibliography

Bakewell, S. (2011). How to Live: A Life of Montaigne in one question and twenty attempts at an answer, Random House.

Brewer, E. C. (2013). Brewer's Dictionary of Phrase and Fable 19th Edition, Quercus.

Broodbank, C. (2013). The Making of the Middle Sea: A History of the Mediterranean from the Beginning to the Emergence of the Classical World, Thames and Hudson Limited.

Cartledge, P. (2012). The Spartans: An Epic History, Pan Macmillan.

Davies, N. (2011). Vanished Kingdoms: The History of Half-Forgotten Europe, Penguin Books Limited.

Fennell, C. A. M. (1879). Pindar: the Olympian and Pythian odes, University Press.

Fowles, J. (1968). The Magus, Pan Books.

Frankopan, P. (2015). The Silk Roads: A New History of the World, Bloomsbury Publishing.

Harris, R. (2016). The Cicero Trilogy, Random House.

Homer, E. V. Rieu, P. V. Jones and D. C. H. Rieu (2003). The Iliad, Penguin Books Limited.

Kaeuper, R. (2015). Bankers to the Crown: The Riccardi of Lucca and Edward I, Princeton University Press.

Macfarlane, R. (2009). Mountains Of The Mind: A History Of A Fascination, Granta Publications.

Padgett, J. F. (2012). Corporate Merchant banks in Tuscany The Emergence of Organizations and Markets. J. F. Padgett and W. W. Powell, Princeton University Press.

Robb, P. (2014). Midnight In Sicily: On Art, Feed, History, Travel and la Cosa Nostra, Farrar, Straus and Giroux.

Sturgeon, M. C. (1977). Sculpture: The Reliefs from the Theater, American School of Classical Studies at Athens.

Printed in Great Britain
by Amazon